THE ROCKETS' RED GLARE

JOHNS HOPKINS BOOKS

ON THE WAR OF 1812

Donald R. Hickey

Series Editor

THE ROCKETS' RED GLARE

AN ILLUSTRATED HISTORY OF THE WAR OF 1812

DONALD R. HICKEY AND CONNIE D. CLARK

The Johns Hopkins University Press ★ Baltimore

This book has been brought to publication with the generous assistance of the J. G. Goellner Endowment of the Johns Hopkins University Press.

The Johns Hopkins University Press
2715 North Charles Street
Baltimore, Maryland 21218-4363
www.press.jhu.edu

Designed by Amy Ruth Buchanan
Maps by Lucidity Information Design / Robert Cronan

Library of Congress Cataloging-in-Publication Data
Hickey, Donald R., 1944–
The rockets' red glare : an illustrated history of the War of 1812 / Donald R. Hickey and Connie D. Clark.
p. cm.
Includes bibliographical references and index.
ISBN-13: 978-1-4214-0155-3 (hardcover : acid-free paper)
ISBN-10: 1-4214-0155-x (hardcover : acid-free paper)
1. United States—History—War of 1812. 2. United States—History—War of 1812—Pictorial works.
I. Clark, Connie D., 1957– II. Title.
E354.H525 2011
973.5'2—dc22   2010050261

A catalog record for this book is available from the British Library.

Special discounts are available for bulk purchases of this book. For more information, please contact Special Sales at 410-516-6936 or specialsales@press.jhu.edu.

CONTENTS

PREFACE vii

PROLOGUE   The Suspense Was Hell 1

CHAPTER ONE   Endless War in the Atlantic World (1793–1812) 9

CHAPTER TWO   Canada, Canada, Canada (1812) 27

CHAPTER THREE   Don't Give Up the Ship (1813) 67

CHAPTER FOUR   Don't Give Up the Soil (1814) 119

CHAPTER FIVE   A Lasting Peace (1815) 163

EPILOGUE   Legacies 185

CHRONOLOGY 195
NOTES 209
SUGGESTIONS FOR FURTHER READING 219
INDEX 221

Color illustrations follow page 118

In preparing this work, we have incurred many debts. We would like to thank Donald E. Graves and the late Robert Malcomson for reading portions of the manuscript and saving us from a number of errors. We would also like to thank Julian Gwyn and Commander Tyrone Martin, USN (ret.), for assistance on the naval war, Christopher George for answering our questions on the war in the Chesapeake, and Tom Kanon for information on the Duck River Massacre. Finally, we are indebted to Jeff Flannery and Tom Jabine of the Library of Congress for guiding us to some useful materials.

Selecting appropriate illustrations proved to be a daunting task, and we had a lot of help. Peter Rindlisbacher generously gave us access to many of the splendid images that he has created of the naval war of 1812. Robin Brass Studio was equally generous in sharing images. Brian Dunnigan and Clayton Lewis took time from their busy schedules to help us pick out items from the vast and magnificent collections of the William L. Clements Library at the University of Michigan. Scott Sheads of Fort McHenry National Monument and Shrine pointed us to a great many images, including some in the Fort's possession. Spencer Tucker and Kevin Crisman kindly shared items in their personal collections. Jerry Roberts, Executive Director of the Connecticut River Museum, brought to our attention his efforts to preserve the history of the British raid on Pettipaug and supplied us with images from a striking panoramic painting of the raid. Finally, we are indebted to Teresa Mitchell of the Great Lakes Seaway Trail for providing us with an illustration of the Battle of Sandy Creek and the carrying of the naval cable to Sackets Harbor.

Faye Kert educated us on British licenses and showed us what they looked like. Gabriele Thomas supplied us with a panoramic view of the Battle of Crysler's Farm from Upper Canada Village, and Irene Axelrod provided a copy of a privateering commission from the Peabody Essex Museum. Linda Bolla of the Erie Maritime Museum helped us procure an image of a certificate of citizenship, Jenny Ferretti helped us get two illustrations from the Maryland Historical Society, and Jennifer Nararre did the same for an illustration from the Historic New Orleans Collection. Clark Evans and Margaret Kieckhefer of the Library of Congress assisted us in locating and securing an image of the only known book to survive from the original congressional library. Finally, Rick Finch, the site manager at Fort Meigs, alerted us to illustrations that we might be interested in.

Throughout the course of our work on this project, the staff at the U.S. Conn Library at Wayne State College has patiently responded to our many requests for help. We are especially indebted to Terri Headley, who secured countless volumes, some quite rare, through the interlibrary loan service that she manages so efficiently. Edmund Elfers, the director of the Wayne State College Office of Teaching and Learning Technologies, took time from a busy schedule to touch up many of our illustrations, as did artist Lynn Bowder, who worked her own magic on the images.

Our experience with this book has confirmed our belief that the scholarly community, and particularly the 1812 community, has a cooperative rather than a competitive ethos. We have benefited greatly from this spirit, and our book is much better for it. Our thanks to all who helped us along the way.

THE ROCKETS' RED GLARE

★★★

PROLOGUE

★★★

The Suspense Was Hell

On June 1, 1812, President James Madison sent a war message to Congress. The soft-spoken, bookish, and diminutive Madison (he was only 5 feet 4 inches tall) was not a very imposing figure. Washington Irving described him in 1812 as "but a withered little Apple-john," and a British visitor the following year reportedly claimed that he looked like "a schoolmaster dressed up for a funeral."[1] These cuts were unkind but not inaccurate.

Madison himself probably never imagined that he would be a war president. After all, as Thomas Jefferson's secretary of state from 1801 to 1809, he had spent much of his time composing scholarly treatises expounding on the nation's rights and crafting long diplomatic notes upholding those rights. Moreover, as the chief architect of the restrictive system—the attempt to force Great Britain and France to show greater respect for America's neutral rights by withholding trade—he believed that he had found an alternative to war. The idea was to bring the two great European powers to their knees—and thus to terms—by targeting their commerce. In principle, this was a noble idea that appealed to all those who recoiled at the horrors of war. In practice, however, it did not work.

Withholding trade hurt Britain and France, but the impact was far less than Madison and other proponents of commercial sanctions had expected. It was certainly not enough to induce the two great powers, who were locked in a high-stakes war, to give up policies deemed essential to their war effort merely to satisfy America. Peace with the United States might be desirable, but not if it meant sacrificing crucial advantages in Europe. And the restrictive system actually backfired on the United States, destroying American prosperity and cutting

James Madison (1751–1836) was a shy and scholarly man who served as the nation's wartime president. Known as "the Last of the Founders," he outlived most of those who had played a central role in launching the new nation in the late eighteenth century. (J. A. Spencer, *History of the United States*)

sharply into federal revenue. Although some Republicans never lost faith in economic coercion, by the end of 1811 a growing number had concluded that the nation needed to consider stronger measures, especially against its most implacable foe, Great Britain. Madison himself seemed to agree. Hence, he summoned the first session of the Twelfth Congress to the nation's capital for an early meeting in November 1811.

The Nation's Capital

Washington in 1811 was still a frontier city, only recently carved out of pastureland and wilderness. Contrary to popular belief, it was not built on a swamp, but some of its low-lying areas drained slowly, and this only got worse as the city grew. Although it boasted of close to 9,000 people (17% of whom were slaves) and was the fourteenth largest city in the United States, it lacked the amenities and diversions of the larger and older cities, like Philadelphia, New York, Boston, and Charleston. Prices were high, the available housing primitive, and basic services inadequate. Cabinet officials and clerks alike had to scramble to find decent lodging, and members of Congress typically stayed in boarding houses. There were no street lights, and the roads were unimproved. In the rainy season the city became a sea of mud, and in the dry season dust and dirt were everywhere. Congress refused to appropriate money to improve the city, and there was periodic talk of moving the capital back to Philadelphia, which had been "the seat of empire" before it was moved to Washington in 1800.

Permanent residents and government officials in Washington fashioned a social life by exchanging visits. They also sponsored gala dinner parties and balls, which allowed congressmen from around the country to mingle with locals as well as visiting dignitaries and army and navy officers. Dolley Madison, who invented the role of the First Lady, did her part by making the White House the center of the social scene. Nevertheless, the cultural landscape of the city remained bleak. Few congressmen welcomed their sojourn in the nation's capital, and they probably would have welcomed it far less in 1811 had they known that they would face

Dolley Madison (1768–1849) sometimes served as Thomas Jefferson's unofficial White House hostess and then transformed the Executive Mansion into the social center of Washington during her husband's presidency. Not only did she single-handedly invent the First Lady's role, but she also saved White House treasures when the British threatened the city in the summer of 1814. (Based on a portrait by Gilbert Stuart. Library of Congress)

Henry Clay (1777–1852) was at the dawn of a long and distinguished career in 1812. As a rising star in Congress, he helped push the nation into war, and then as a member of the peace delegation two years later, he helped forge what proved to be a lasting peace. (Library of Congress)

the coldest December in memory (the Potomac froze in a night) or that the forthcoming session would last eight months instead of the usual three to five.

The Road to War

The Twelfth Congress included the usual factions of Republicans and Federalists. It also included close to a dozen Republican members dubbed "War Hawks" because they were known to favor war. Heading this group was Henry Clay, only 34 years old but already a power in Kentucky politics. Although never before a member of the House, "Harry of the West" was elected to the largely ceremonial position of speaker. By packing key committees and controlling debate and by effectively using secret sessions and interpreting the rules, Clay molded the speakership into a position of power, and he used this power to keep the war movement on track.

In his opening message to Congress, Madison accused the British of "hostile inflexibility" and recommended that the nation be put "into an armor and an attitude demanded by the crisis."[2] Congress responded with an ambitious program of war preparations and then waited anxiously to see if the U.S. Sloop *Hornet* (20 guns), which was expected to return from Europe in the spring, brought any news of British concessions. The long-awaited ship finally docked in New York's harbor on May 19, and the dispatches it carried were rushed to Washington. But the news from Europe was doubly deflating. Not only did the British show no sign of modifying policies that were inimical to American rights, but there was evidence that France, which in 1810 had solemnly promised to treat Americans better, continued to seize and condemn American merchant ships.

The administration had promised to move toward war if the British did not change their policies, and Madison now had to make good on that promise. His war message, however, was a typical Madisonian document. While laying out the case for military action to uphold the nation's rights, Madison, ever respectful of the prerogatives of Congress, merely asked "whether the United States shall continue passive under these progressive usurpations, and their accumulating wrongs." This, the president concluded, was "a solemn question which the Constitution wisely confides to the Legislative Department of the Government."[3]

In order to conceal the government's hand and avoid public clamor over the issue, Madison's war message was secret, and both houses of Congress remained behind closed doors to consider their response. The House acted quickly, first adopting a committee report supporting a declaration of war, and then voting 79-49 to approve a war bill. It took the House only four days to complete its action. Although voting against the war bill, the Federalists decided to remain silent to protest the House's secrecy, and the Republicans responded in kind. The bill thus sailed through, unimpeded by any long-winded speeches from either side of the aisle.

In the Senate, opponents of the bill, Federalists and Republicans alike, did not hesitate to air their views or to seek a change in the bill's essential character. At one point the Senate even voted to transform what was supposed to be full-scale war against Great Britain into a maritime contest limited to the high seas—waged by warships and privateers—against both Britain and France. But the vote was close, and the Senate later reversed itself, restoring the original bill. In the end, the Senate voted 19-13 in favor of the declaration of war, with all the Federalists again in opposition. It took members of the Senate two full weeks to reach a decision. In the meantime, everyone else remained in the dark. This prompted Jonathan Roberts, a Republican congressman from Pennsylvania who had voted for war in the House, to exclaim: "The suspense we are in is worse than hell—!!!"[4]

Aftermath

Although it was widely suspected that Congress was considering strong measures, not many people expected a declaration of war. It was not until Madison signed the war bill into law on June 18 and then issued a proclamation the following day announcing that a state of war existed that Americans learned that the die had been cast. Such was the state of communication and transportation, however, that word spread slowly and unpredictably. It took a week for the news to reach Sackets Harbor in upstate New York and the city of Quebec in what was then Lower Canada; two weeks to reach an American army marching north through Frenchtown, Michigan; three weeks to reach the port of New Orleans on the lower Mississippi and St. Joseph Island at the northern end of Lake Huron; and a month to reach Mackinac Island in northern Lake Michigan and remote Thunder Bay on the north shore of Lake Superior. The news did not reach London until July 30, fully six weeks after the decision for war was made.

If the pace of communication was slow, so, too, was the pace of military operations. The first fighting, a brief skirmish on the Canard River on the British side

BY THE PRESIDENT
OF THE
United States of America,
A PROCLAMATION:

WHEREAS the Congress of the United States, by virtue of the Constituted Authority vested in them, have declared by their act, bearing date the eighteenth day of the present month, that WAR exists between the United Kingdom of Great Britain and Ireland, and the dependencies thereof, and the United States of America and their territories; Now, therefore, I, JAMES MADISON, President of the United States of America, do hereby proclaim the same to all whom it may concern: and I do specially enjoin on all persons holding offices, civil or military, under the authority of the United States, that they be vigilant and zealous, & discharging the duties respectively incident thereto: And I do moreover exhort all the good people of the United States, as they love their country; as they value the precious heritage derived from the virtue and valor of their fathers; as they feel the wrongs which have forced on them the last resort of injured nations; and as they consult the best means, under the blessing of Divine Providence, of abridging its calamities; that they exert themselves in preserving order, in promoting concord, in maintaining the authority and the efficacy of the laws, and in supporting and invigorating all the measures which may be adopted by the Constituted Authorities, for obtaining a speedy, a just, and an honorable peace.

IN TESTIMONY WHEREOF I have hereunto set my hand, and caused the seal of the United States to be affixed to these presents.

(SEAL.)

DONE at the City of Washington, the nineteenth day of June, one thousand eight hundred and twelve, and of the Independence of the United States the thirty-sixth.

(Signed)   JAMES MADISON.

By the President,
(Signed)   JAMES MONROE, Secretary of State.

News of war spread first by word of mouth, then by broadsides (like this one), and then by newspapers. Many of the broadsides and newspapers reproduced President Madison's proclamation announcing that a state of war existed. (Library of Congress)

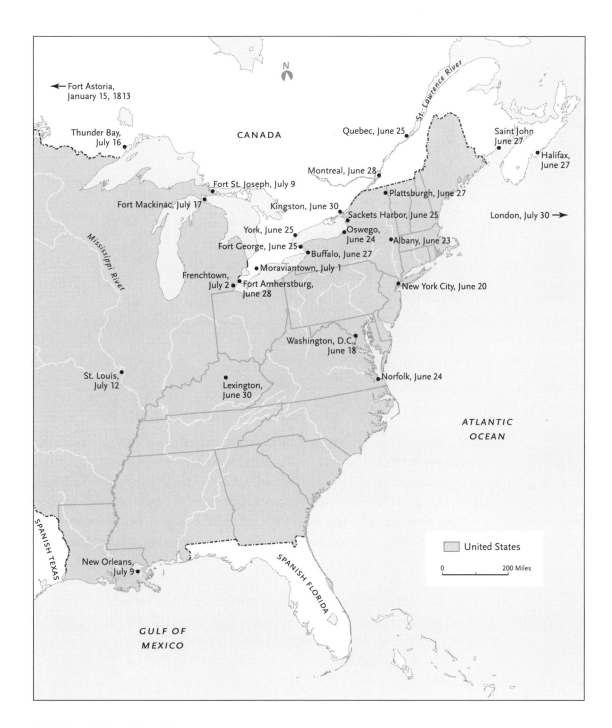

The News of War, 1812–1813

The news of war spread at an uneven pace across the United States and Canada. The news did not reach London until July 30, 1812, and Fort Astoria in the Pacific Northwest did not hear of it until January 15, 1813.

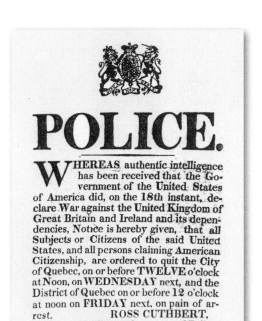

of the Detroit River in western Upper Canada, did not occur until July 16, almost a month after the declaration of war. The following day, the British compelled the surrender of Fort Mackinac, and a month later Detroit capitulated. However, it was not until October 13, almost four months after the declaration of war, that the first major battle, at Queenston Heights on the Niagara frontier, took place. Not only were the military campaigns slow to get under way, but for Americans the news from the northern frontier was uniformly bad. Despite all the heady talk about how easy it would be to conquer Canada and thus force the British to terms, the American military establishment, which had suffered more than a decade of underfunding and neglect, was not up to the task. For Americans, the early campaigns offered a hard lesson: It was one thing to declare war but quite another to wage it successfully.

CHAPTER ONE

Endless War in the Atlantic World 1793–1812

Although American grievances against Great Britain were serious enough to justify war, the British felt no corresponding enmity toward the United States. The British people might find Americans crude, money-grubbing, and contemptuous, but their Tory government in 1812 had no real quarrel with the young republic and certainly no desire for war. British policy making and strategic thinking during the War of 1812 were dominated by three men: the prime minister, Lord Liverpool; the foreign secretary, Lord Castlereagh; and the Duke of Wellington, who commanded British troops in the Spanish Peninsula and offered advice to the government on military affairs. Also influential in shaping overseas policy were two other cabinet officials: Lord Bathurst, who was secretary of state for war and the colonies; and Viscount Melville, First Lord of the Admiralty. These officials had little time to devote to America because all eyes were riveted on Europe, where the French menace had dominated British policy making for two decades.

By 1812, Great Britain and France had been at war off and on for more than a century. In what is sometimes called the Second Hundred Years War, this contest had begun in 1689 and would not end until Napoleon was defeated for the last time at Waterloo in 1815. The Anglo-French contest followed a pattern. Great Britain, with extensive financial resources and command of the seas, lined up allies on the Continent to prevent a more populous and more powerful France from extending its influence and dominion across Europe. Since both nations had overseas empires, their endless quarrel extended across the Atlantic and eventually to other parts of the world. Increasingly, the British and French found themselves engaged in a world war.

Lord Liverpool (1770–1828) became prime minister of Great Britain in May 1812 shortly after his predecessor, Spencer Perceval, was assassinated. He provided steady leadership during the War of 1812. Although he refused to surrender Britain's maritime rights in 1812, he also declined to press Britain's advantage in 1814 and settled instead for a peace that both sides could live with. (Portrait by Sir Thomas Lawrence. Wikimedia Commons)

The French Revolution

The character of the Anglo-French contest changed dramatically after 1789. On July 14 of that year, the French Revolution erupted when a Parisian mob, in search of arms and ammunition, stormed the Bastille, a medieval fortress that symbolized royal authority. At first it looked like the revolutionary upheaval would produce a constitutional monarchy grounded on parliamentary democracy, similar to the British model. But France had no democratic or parliamentary tradition, and once the dogs of civil disorder were unleashed they ran wild. France came under the control of ever more radical groups until the Jacobins seized power in 1793. Establishing a highly centralized republic, they beheaded the king and queen and initiated the Reign of Terror against their domestic foes. In 1795 a new government, the Directory, launched a counterrevolution, and this group was, in turn, succeeded by Napoleon's Consulate in 1799. In the space of a decade, France had limited and then discarded its monarchy, experimented with a republic, embraced the Directory, and then succumbed to the iron grip of a military dictator. In the process, the Old Regime had been shattered and along with it most of the underpinnings of France's traditional society.

A general European war had erupted in 1792 as France sought to extend its influence and spread its revolutionary ideals. France's enemies were equally determined to crush the revolution and prevent French dominion over Europe. The following year, Great Britain entered the fray on the side of France's foes, and for more than two decades thereafter the two powers clashed in Europe, the New World, and elsewhere around the globe. The stakes in the latest phase of the Second Hundred Years War were much higher than before. What once had been dynastic warfare waged for power and prestige was now an ideological contest that threatened the independence and essential character of the loser. In addition, new tactics, new technology, and new ways of organizing and financing armies changed the way that wars were fought. Whoever prevailed in the French Revolutionary Wars (1793–1801) and the Napoleonic Wars (1803–1815) would be master of Europe and in a unique position to shape developments around the globe. With so much at stake, little wonder that the two belligerents ran roughshod over the rights of lesser powers that got in their way.

Once part of the British Empire, America had long been accustomed to waging war against France and Spain and their Indian allies. The pattern continued in the American Revolution, although onetime enemies were now co-belligerents or allies. The American Revolution, in other words, was another phase of the Second Hundred Years War, with the British waging war against not only their former colonies but also their traditional enemies on the Continent. Once this war ended and independence was secured, Americans hoped to steer clear of Europe's conflicts. But this was no easy task. The worldwide contest waged by Great Britain and France between 1793 and 1815 cast a long shadow across the Atlantic, and neither belligerent showed much interest in accommodating the young republic, even if the alternative was war.

With its vital interests and basic rights threatened, the United States was repeatedly in danger of being drawn into the European conflict, and as a result foreign policy issues dominated public discourse. The central problem that American policy makers faced in this era was this: How could a second-rate power like the United States protect its rights and promote its interests in the midst of a world war? Federalists and Jeffersonian Republicans alike had to grapple with this vexing problem.

The Federalist Hegemony

With George Washington serving two terms as president (1789–1797) and John Adams one (1797–1801), the Federalists controlled the nation's destiny in the 1790s. They pursued a policy of military and financial preparedness at home and a pro-British neutrality abroad. The sheet anchor of their foreign policy was the Jay Treaty (1794), an Anglo-American agreement that resolved many outstanding differences, defined neutral rights, and established the terms of trade between the two English-speaking nations. Under this agreement, American commerce, and thus the entire American economy, flourished. From 1794 to 1801, U.S. exports soared from $33 million to $94 million and U.S. imports from $35 million to $111 million.[1] Whatever other problems the European conflict created for the new nation, Americans found that, as long as the British navy gave them some latitude, they could make a handsome profit by supplying markets disrupted by war.

The U.S. Frigate *Constellation* battered the French frigate
L'Insurgente into submission in 1799 during the undeclared
naval war with France. The captured vessel's career as a trophy
ship was short-lived, however, for it was lost at sea with all
hands in a storm in the West Indies in 1800. (Painting by
E. Savage. Dudley W. Knox, *Naval Documents Related to the
Quasi-War between the United States and France*)

The Quasi-War

Deeply resentful of the Anglo-American rapprochement, the French Directory responded by severing diplomatic relations with the United States and unleashing a war on American trade. France's aim was not simply to enrich itself at America's expense but to bully the United States into paying tribute and repudiating the Jay Treaty. This was typical French treatment of small countries on the Continent. But Americans had two advantages that those hapless nations lacked: 3,000 miles of water separated them from France, and the British navy controlled the seas. This made it difficult, if not impossible, for France to directly menace the young and still fragile republic.

Instead of caving in to the Directory's demands, the United States authorized its infant navy to attack armed French ships and permitted its merchant vessels to arm for defense. The result was an undeclared naval contest known as the Quasi-War (1798–1801). Operating mainly in the Caribbean, where most of the French depredations had occurred, the U.S. Navy performed admirably, capturing three French warships and virtually destroying a fourth, while losing only one of its own. The navy also captured 82 French privateers and recaptured 70 American merchant vessels. At the same time, armed American merchantmen captured, defeated, or scared off numerous French privateers bent on plunder. As a result of this campaign, American insurance rates for merchant ships trading in the West Indies fell from a peak of 25–30 percent in the spring of 1798 to 10 percent at the end of 1799.[2] By this time Napoleon had come to power. Convinced that the American war was a distraction from more important European concerns, he called off the attack on American trade and authorized negotiations that ended the conflict.

The Republican Ascendancy

By the time the Quasi-War was over, the Jeffersonian Republicans were in power. With Thomas Jefferson and James Madison each serving two terms as president (1801–1809 and 1809–1817, respectively), the Republicans retained their grip on the federal government throughout this period. Jefferson initiated a policy of retrenchment, cutting taxes and defense spending and seeking to retire the national debt as quickly as possible. Initially, these policies appeared to do no harm because Britain and France signed the preliminaries of the Peace of Amiens in 1801, which put an end to the French Revolutionary Wars. Observers on both sides of the Atlantic, however, realized that nothing had been settled and that the peace was

Thomas Jefferson (1743–1826) may have been a great statesman, but his second term as president was marred by missteps. The loss of the Monroe-Pinkney Treaty increased the likelihood of war, while the embargo undermined the nation's ability to wage war. (J. A. Spencer, *History of the United States*)

little more than a temporary truce. This proved to be the case when 18 months later war erupted again. This series of wars, known as the Napoleonic Wars, put the United States and Great Britain on a collision course that ultimately led to the War of 1812.

The Napoleonic Wars entered a new stage with two battles in 1805. On October 21 Admiral Horatio Nelson defeated a combined Franco-Spanish fleet in the Battle of Trafalgar off the coast of Spain. This left the Royal Navy the undisputed Mistress of the Seas. Six weeks later, on December 2, Napoleon won a spectacular victory over Russia and Austria at Austerlitz in what is now the Czech Republic. France was now the unchallenged master of the Continent. Because both battles ended so decisively, the two great antagonists were left without any effective way of striking one another. It was like a contest between a tiger and a shark. Each was supreme in its element but incapable of delivering a knockout blow to the other. This was an ominous development for the United States because it suggested a prolonged war in which neutral rights might well be sacrificed in the pursuit of victory.

British Maritime Practices

Increasingly, the United States found itself at odds with Great Britain over maritime issues, many of which had first surfaced in the 1790s. First and foremost was the knotty issue of impressment. The American merchant fleet had expanded rapidly after 1793 to carry on the nation's growing trade. This, in turn, created an acute shortage of experienced seamen, a shortage that was met by employing British tars. But the Royal Navy was on a war footing and needed all the seamen it could get. Hence, British warships reserved the right to stop American merchant vessels on the high seas in order to remove British subjects. These seamen were "impressed" or conscripted into the service of the king. This practice sometimes left American merchant vessels dangerously shorthanded. Worse yet, by accident or design, many American citizens—probably around 6,000 between 1803 and 1812—were caught in the British dragnet. There was little the U.S. government could do to protect American tars other than issue certificates of citizenship, popularly known as "protections," that were supposed to offer immunity from impressment. U.S. officials issued over 100,000 of these documents, mostly through the customs offices in port cities, but through theft, fraud, or purchase, many ended up in the hands of British seamen. For as little as a dollar, it was said, a British tar in an American port city could instantly become an American citizen.

The impressment of seamen from American merchantmen touched a deep chord in the United States. Although the Royal Navy targeted British subjects, far too many American citizens were caught in the dragnet. This practice eroded American sovereignty and made a mockery of individual rights. (From a drawing by Stanley M. Arthurs. Alfred Thayer Mahan, *Sea Power and Its Relations to the War of 1812*)

As a result, Royal Navy search parties that boarded American merchantmen often gave little credence to the documents.

The British did not normally claim the right to impress from neutral warships, which were considered an extension of a nation's territory, but occasionally overzealous British naval officers did so. This was the genesis of the notorious *Chesapeake* affair in June 1807. When Captain James Barron, commander of the *Chesapeake* (40 guns), refused to allow Captain Salusbury Pryce Humphreys of H.M. Ship *Leopard* (52 guns) to dispatch a search party to reclaim British deserters, the British opened fire, killing four Americans and wounding 15 others. The *Chesapeake* affair ignited a war scare in the United States and remained an open sore in Anglo-American relations until a negotiated settlement was reached in late 1811.

By this time the United States had gained a measure of revenge in the *Little Belt* affair. After the attack on the *Chesapeake*, a military court suspended the ill-fated commander of the American ship for five years, and the Navy Department ordered all U.S. warships to resist any further insults to the flag. In May 1811, when the U.S. Frigate *President* (54 guns), Captain John Rodgers commanding, encountered H.M. Sloop *Little Belt* (20 guns), commanded by Captain Arthur Bingham off the coast of North Carolina, the two ships were unable to identify each other and thus exchanged fire. The British sloop sustained ten killed and 22 wounded, while the American ship had only one casualty. The *Little Belt* had gotten the worse of the exchange, but because officers on both ships claimed the other had fired first, the British decided not to press for an apology or reparations.

The British infringed on America's neutral rights in other ways. British warships sometimes violated American waters, chasing French privateers or stopping American merchantmen within the three-mile limit. The British also had a more expansive definition of contraband than the United States. Hence, food, naval stores, or even money might be confiscated when found on American ships headed for enemy ports. Nor did the British always comply with the accepted rules of international law in proclaiming and enforcing naval blockades. The Brit-

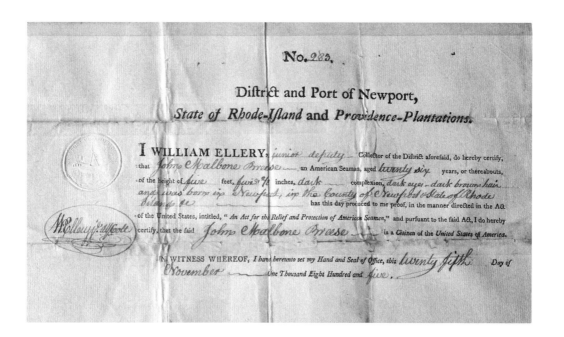

No. 283.

District and Port of Newport,
State of Rhode-Island and Providence-Plantations.

I WILLIAM ELLERY, *junior deputy* Collector of the District aforesaid, do hereby certify, that *John Malbone Breese* an American Seaman, aged *twenty six* years, or thereabouts, of the height of *five* feet, *five 3/4* inches, *dark* complexion, *dark eyes - dark brown hair* and *was born in Newport, in the County of Newport State of Rhode Island &c* has this day produced to me proof, in the manner directed in the Act of the United States, intitled, "*An Act for the Relief and Protection of American Seamen,*" and pursuant to the said Act, I do hereby certify, that the said *John Malbone Breese* is a Citizen of the United States of America.

IN WITNESS WHEREOF, I have hereunto set my Hand and Seal of Office, this *twenty fifth* Day of *November* One Thousand Eight Hundred and *five*.

A certificate of citizenship issued to John Malbone Breese (1778–1831) in Newport, Rhode Island, in 1805. Some "protections" mentioned an unusual characteristic, such as a limp, scar, or tattoo, but most (like this one) listed only height, complexion, hair color, and eye color. Such a description undoubtedly would have fit some British tars. (Courtesy of The State Museum of Pennsylvania, Pennsylvania Historical and Museum Commission)

This illustration shows the British removing seamen from the U.S. Frigate *Chesapeake* in 1807. Three of the four seamen (including Daniel Martin, a black man) were actually American citizens who had deserted from British warships after being impressed into service. (Engraving by E. Clement. William Cullen Bryant and Sidney Howard Gay, *A Popular History of the United States*)

ish also upheld the Rule of 1756, which prohibited neutral merchants from engaging in any branch of trade in time of war that was closed to them in time of peace. This dubious doctrine had no standing under international law but was devised to ensure that the trade of Britain's enemies would not be carried on by neutral ships after the Royal Navy had driven enemy merchantmen from the high seas.

The Monroe-Pinkney Treaty

British maritime practices offered a significant challenge to the United States, and there was considerable debate over how to respond. One alternative was to seek an accommodation with Great Britain on the best terms available. The Federalists championed this approach. Even before the British threat had fully matured, there was an opportunity to reforge the Anglo-American accord of the 1790s that had effectively ended when the Jay Treaty clauses governing trade and neutral rights had expired in 1803. On December 31, 1806, James Monroe and William Pinkney negotiated a new treaty with Great Britain. Designed to be a successor to the Jay Treaty, the Monroe-Pinkney agreement was actually more favorable to the United States. But because the British were unwilling to end impressment, Jefferson refused to submit the agreement to the Senate. The treaty was therefore lost. This was the last opportunity that the United States had to mend its relationship with Britain and take a road that might have led to peace and prosperity. Instead, it took a different path, one that led to economic sanctions and war.

The War on Neutral Trade

American relations with Britain and France deteriorated further after 1806 when the two European powers stepped up their war on neutral trade. France took the lead in 1806–07, when it issued the Berlin and Milan decrees, barring all British ships and goods from entering ports under French control. Known as the Continental System, this scheme was designed to bring the British to their knees by crippling their economy. The British retaliated with the Orders-in-Council (1807–09), a series of executive decrees that first restricted and then prohibited (via naval blockade) any trade with those ports from which their own ships and goods were excluded.

Both sides in this trade war winked at commerce that they considered beneficial even if it violated their decrees. In fact, the British made a mockery of the Orders-in-Council by issuing an average of 10,000 licenses a year that permitted trade with the blockaded ports. Both sides conceded that their actions violated

James Monroe (1758–1831) held several diplomatic posts before joining President Madison's cabinet on the eve of war. During the conflict he helped frame American policy as secretary of state and secretary of war. Although he was competent, his decisions were sometimes clouded by his presidential ambitions. (Based on a portrait by Gilbert Stuart. Library of Congress)

William Pinkney (1764–1822) was an accomplished Federalist lawyer in Baltimore before drifting into the Republican camp during Jefferson's second term. As Madison's attorney general during the war, he drafted the declaration of war and provided legal counsel on public issues. (Engraving based on an original by Alonzo Chappel. Library of Congress)

international law but insisted that they were justified by the law of retaliation. This was small comfort to American merchants who found that they were caught in the middle and effectively barred from trading with the Continent.

Fortunately, there were ways around the countervailing restrictions. Napoleon did not control all of Europe; ports in the Baltic and the Spanish Peninsula continued to welcome American ships. Although the former became overstocked with American goods, the latter remained a good market, especially after the arrival of British troops in 1808. In addition, some merchants were able to trade with the Continent by acquiring the much-coveted British licenses, which were openly bought and sold in British port cities. Others prevailed by carrying dual papers or by bribing customs officials in ports under French control. For the shrewd and the lucky, it was still possible to make a profit trading with Europe. But the losses were nonetheless heavy. Between 1807 and 1812, Great Britain, France, and their allies seized some 900 American merchant vessels for violating their restrictions on trade.

The Restrictive System

The United States responded to this assault on its commerce with its own economic sanctions—the restrictive system. In late 1806 Congress enacted a limited non-importation act aimed at Britain and then in late 1807 added a general embargo that prohibited American ships and goods from leaving port. When these measures proved futile, they were replaced in 1809 by a non-intercourse act that opened trade with the rest of the world but continued to prohibit all commerce with Britain and France and their colonies. When this measure also failed, it, too, was repealed, and there followed a period of free trade.

In the bill repealing the non-intercourse act, Congress promised to reimpose non-importation against either European belligerent if the other rescinded its restrictions on neutral trade. Sensing an opportunity to hoodwink the United States and further embroil the young republic with Great Britain, Napoleon in August 1810 instructed his foreign minister, the Duc de Cadore, to inform John Armstrong, the American minister in Paris, that the Continental decrees would be suspended. Cadore dutifully sent Armstrong a letter with the news. Napoleon had no intention of making good on this promise, and French officials remained under orders to seize American ships violating the Continental System. Nevertheless, the Madison administration chose to take the Cadore letter at face value, and in early 1811 Congress passed a new non-importation act that barred all British ships and goods from American ports.

This Federalist cartoon shows how the embargo (often portrayed as a snapping turtle) prevented an American merchant, who was trading under a British license, from exporting his premium-grade tobacco. Federalists worked the phrase "O-grab-me"—which was "embargo" spelled backwards—into their cartoons to highlight its coercive character and punishing effects. (Benson J. Lossing, *Pictorial Field-Book of the War of 1812)*

In the end, the restrictive system was a failure, winning no concessions from either Great Britain or France. In truth, it did far more harm to the United States than to its intended victims. American trade, particularly during the embargo, slumped badly. U.S. exports, which had peaked at $108 million in 1807, plummeted to $22 million the following year. In the same period, imports fell from $139 million to $57 million. The restrictive system had a similar impact on federal revenue, which fell from a peak of $17 million in 1808 to $8 million in 1809. Even though the embargo was replaced with less onerous restrictions, American trade and revenue never recovered. In 1811, the last year before the War of 1812, American exports and imports stood at $61 million and $53 million, respectively, and government revenue at $14 million.[3] However noble it may have been in conception, the restrictive system in practice was not simply a failure, but one that cost the new nation dearly.

War Preparations

With the failure of the restrictive system, Republicans had to decide what to do next. The war in Europe seemed endless, which meant there was unlikely to be any letup in the infringements on American rights. Most Republicans saw only three options: war, restrictions, or submission. Federalists saw a fourth—accommoda-

U.S. Trade and Federal Receipts and Expenditures, 1790–1815
(millions of U.S. dollars)

Year	Exports	Imports	Receipts	Expenditures
1790	20	23	2*	—
1791	19	29	2*	3
1792	21	32	4	6
1793	26	31	5	4
1794	33	35	5	6
1795	48	70	6	7
1796	67	81	8	6
1797	57	75	9	6
1798	62	69	8	8
1799	79	79	8	9
1800	71	91	11	11
1801	94	111	13	9
1802	72	76	15	8
1803	56	65	11	8
1804	78	85	12	9
1805	96	121	14	9
1806	102	129	16	9
1807	108	139	16	8
1808	22	57	17	9
1809	52	59	8	10
1810	67	85	9	8
1811	61	53	14	8
1812	39	77	10	20
1813	28	22	14	32
1814	7	13	11	35
1815	53	113	16	33

Source: Adapted from Curtis P. Nettels, *The Emergence of a National Economy*, 1789–1815
Note: All figures are rounded to the nearest million.
*estimated

tion, in line with the Jay and Monroe-Pinkney treaties—but to Republicans this was the same as submission. Although some Republicans wanted to stick with trade restrictions, a growing number favored war. That is why President Madison summoned Congress to an early meeting in late 1811, and why the War Hawks forced through a program of war preparations in the months that followed. But the debate over that program revealed deep fissures within the Republican party, not only over how best to fight and finance a war with Great Britain but also over the wisdom of war itself.

Congress was divided over the kind of land forces needed for the war. In the end, the regular army was expanded from 10,000 to 35,000 men, although this remained largely a paper force. The ranks of the old army were barely half full when Congress convened, and the pay ($5 for privates) and the enlistment bounty ($16) were so low that recruitment was slow. Although Congress now raised the bounty to $31 and 160 acres of land, this did not lead to a flood of new enlistments, and by June 1812 there were only about 12,000 regulars in uniform.

Most of the regulars had little training and no experience. They were also poorly led. Many of the officers in the old army were political appointees who did not understand their business. This so thoroughly demoralized the rank-in-file that Republican Nathaniel Macon suggested in 1810 that the army be disbanded. The men hated their officers so much, he said, that they could not be counted on to obey them in time of crisis.[4]

No less damning, the commanding general in the service was Brigadier General James Wilkinson, who was widely suspected—correctly, as it turned out—of being a Spanish spy. Wilkinson had an appetite for intrigue and booty and seemed to have little regard for anything other than his own interest. Congressman John Randolph of Roanoke, whose views were far from unique, claimed that the self-serving general was the only man he knew "who was from the bark to the very core a villain."[5] In 1809 Wilkinson lost 1,000 men—half of his command—to disease and desertion when he established camp in the swamps of Terre aux Boeufs so that he could enjoy the pleasures of New Orleans. This was the largest peacetime disaster to befall the army in the early national period.

The administration appointed a cadre of general officers to the expanded army in 1812, but most were Revolutionary War veterans who had lost their taste for combat and were unable to inspire their men or provide effective leadership. The nicknames that the soldiers pinned on their commanding officers told the story: "the Old Lady" for Brigadier General William Hull, "Van Bladder" or "Alexander the Great" for Brigadier General Alexander Smyth, and "Granny" for Major General Henry Dearborn. All the generals were called "Big Bugs."

Albert Gallatin (1761–1849), a Swiss-born immigrant to Pennsylvania, was one of the few House Republicans in the 1790s who understood Alexander Hamilton's financial reports. Jefferson rewarded him by naming him secretary of the treasury, a position he held for 13 years, longer than anyone else in American history. By 1813 Gallatin had grown weary of trying to squeeze money from a tax-shy and openly hostile Congress and thus welcomed an escape to Europe as part of the peace delegation. (Portrait by Thomas Worthington Whittredge. National Portrait Gallery, Smithsonian Institution)

Congress also authorized 50,000 one-year U.S. Volunteers and required the states to hold 100,000 militia in readiness for service. But only six Volunteer units were raised, and some of these proved so unruly that they could not be depended on. Even less could be expected from militia units, most of which were poorly equipped, poorly trained, and poorly led. Citizen soldiers were not very dependable in the best of circumstances, and except in the West they were wholly unsuited for the kind of offensive operations planned for Canada.

Congress put the nation's warships into service but, after a spirited debate, refused to expand the navy, which dismayed Federalists and commercial Republicans alike. Even more divisive was the issue of how to finance the coming war. Secretary of the Treasury Albert Gallatin presented a plan to pay for the regular operations of the government with tax revenue and most of the war costs with loans. For the plan to work, he said, Congress needed to double the customs duties on shipping and trade and enact the same excise taxes that Federalists had adopted in the 1790s. Fearing that taxes might make the war and their party unpopular, Republicans in Congress would not agree to any new duties until after war had been declared and positively recoiled at the prospect of excise taxes, which they believed had been responsible for the Federalists' defeat in the election of 1800. One Republican congressman thought Gallatin was trying "to chill the war spirit," and another accused him of conspiring with the British minister to avert war.[6] The administration had to exert considerable pressure behind the scenes to get Congress to sign off on Gallatin's plan. In the end, all the administration got was a series of resolutions that promised to enact the new taxes after war had been declared.

The Henry Affair

As Congress was putting the finishing touches on its war program, the nation was rocked by news that the administration had uncovered treason in Federalist New England. Several years before, during a particularly tense period in Anglo-American relations, Sir James Craig, the governor-general of Canada, had dispatched an Irishman named John Henry to New England to report on the state of affairs there. When the simpleminded Henry did not receive what he considered adequate compensation for his spy mission, a roguish Frenchman who styled himself the Count Edward de Crillon persuaded Henry to offer his papers for sale to the United States. The administration agreed to pay its entire secret contingency fund, $50,000, to get the documents. Henry then decamped for Europe, although not before Crillon had swindled him out of most of the money.

The administration hoped to expose both the perfidy of the British and the disloyalty of New England Federalists, but the papers did neither. Henry's information-gathering trip had been too routine to seriously implicate the British government, and he reported little more than that most people he met were opposed to the administration and to war with Britain. There was no smoking gun suggesting treason, nor did Henry identify by name anyone who might be disloyal. By tracing the treasury warrants, Federalists discovered that the papers had been purchased, rather than freely given (as Henry's cover letter had implied), and that the price was so steep it would have covered the cost of building a small warship. Not surprisingly, they were outraged. What was supposed to unify the nation for war looked to Federalists like a costly and mean political trick designed to discredit them.

The Decision for War

By the time the dust from the Henry affair had settled, Congress had completed its preparations for war. All in all, the war program promised much but delivered little, at least in the near term. Moreover, there had been so much huffing and puffing about war ever since the *Chesapeake* affair in 1807 that many Americans remained unsure about their government's intentions. Federalists were particularly skeptical. In fact, in 1809 Josiah Quincy of Massachusetts had injudiciously claimed in the House of Representatives that the Republican majority "could not be kicked into war."[7] With sentiments like these afloat, little wonder that many people in both camps were surprised by the declaration of war when it actually came.

There was no denying that the decision for war carried considerable risk. Great Britain might be engaged in a global conflict with her arch foe, Napoleonic France, but she was still one of the two most powerful nations in the world, and her command of the seas was undisputed. The United States, by contrast, was a second-rate power ill-prepared for war, and, judging from the vote in Congress, a great many people, perhaps a third or more of the population, opposed the decision to take the plunge.

I Josiah the first do by this my Royal Proclamation announce myself *King* of *New England, Nova Scotia* and *Passamaquoddy.* ——— *Grand Master* of the noble order of the *Two Cod Fishes.* ———

JOSIAH the FIRST

Josiah Quincy of Massachusetts (1772–1864) was an outspoken Federalist leader in Congress. Although an opponent of war with Great Britain, he made a speech on behalf of naval expansion in 1812 that some Federalists considered the finest ever delivered in Congress. Republican critics, convinced that he wished to head an independent confederation of New England states, pilloried him as "King Josiah the First." (Watercolor etching by William Charles. Library of Congress)

How could the new nation hope to win such an unequal contest? Some Republicans thought that the declaration of war by itself might induce the British to surrender to American demands. In this sense, the war was a kind of bluff. And if this hope were not realized, it was widely believed that taking Canada would be easy. The United States had a population of 7.7 million, while Canada had only 500,000, and this included many people of French descent as well as many recent American immigrants who had moved to Canada to take advantage of generous land policies. The loyalty of both groups was suspect. Some Americans thought that an American army might even be welcomed by the inhabitants. This explains why Jefferson thought that the conquest of most of Canada would be "a mere matter of marching" and why Henry Clay suggested that the Kentucky militia alone could do the job.[8] Events, however, would soon prove how wrong both men were.

CHAPTER TWO

Canada, Canada, Canada 1812

One of the oddest and most feared members of the War Congress was John Randolph of Roanoke, a Virginian who had once served as the Republican floor manager in the House but was now the most visible member of a small opposition sect, known as the Old Republicans, who believed that Jefferson and Madison had betrayed Republican principles by embracing a loose construction of the Constitution and strong central government. Randolph had never matured physically, and so he retained his boyish looks and a high-pitched voice into adulthood. Those who took him too lightly, however, soon discovered that he had a quick temper and sharp tongue, and that he gave no quarter in debate and had little fear of the dueling ground. In a speech delivered on December 16, 1811, Randolph uttered words that were to reverberate through history. "Agrarian cupidity," he insisted, "not maritime right, urges the war. Ever since the report of the Committee on Foreign Relations [recommending war preparations] came into the House, we have heard but one word—like the whip-poor-will, but one eternal monotonous tone—Canada! Canada! Canada!"[1]

Canada versus Neutral Rights

Randolph's rant was picked up by historians in the early twentieth century who argued that the desire for Canada was a major, if not the principal, reason that the United States went to war in 1812. What had traditionally been portrayed as a war to vindicate neutral rights on the high seas was now seen as a war of territorial aggression. This interpretation dovetailed nicely with the larger history of

John Randolph of Roanoke (1773–1833) was an Old Republican from Virginia who broke with the regular Republicans during Jefferson's presidency because he thought they had abandoned small government and states' rights. A fierce opponent of the war, he regularly voted with the Federalists. (Portrait by Gilbert Stuart. Library of Congress)

American expansion. It also made the war easier to understand because, while few people could explain the finer points of neutral rights, everyone could understand a land grab.

The administration contributed to the confusion because it never explained what it planned to do with Canada once it had been conquered. Presumably, it would be held for ransom on the maritime issues, and if the British refused to make concessions, then it would be annexed. But American leaders never actually said this, probably because they wanted to keep their options open. Perhaps, too, they realized that once Canada was in American hands, it might be difficult to relinquish. The American people were therefore left without any clear understanding of what the administration planned to do with Canada once it was conquered.

This ambiguity, however, does not prove that Randolph was right. As attractive as his theory might be, it is not supported by the evidence. In their newspapers, books, and pamphlets as well as in Congress, Americans in 1811–12 debated whether to go to war against Great Britain, and the focus was always on the maritime issues, particularly the Orders-in-Council and impressment. Even in the West, where annexationist sentiment ran deep, the war talk centered on neutral rights. Whenever Canada was mentioned, it was usually as a likely target for American military operations, not as an end in itself. As western War Hawk Henry Clay put it in late 1813: "Canada was not the end but the means, the object of the War being the redress of [maritime] injuries, and Canada being the instrument by which that redress was to be obtained."[2] In the language of the day, war was undertaken against Great Britain in 1812, not to acquire territory, but to vindicate "free trade and sailors' rights."

As it happened, of the two leading causes of the war—the Orders-in-Council and impressments—one disappeared at almost the same time that the United States declared war. On June 16—two days before the declaration of war—Lord Castlereagh announced in Parliament that the British would suspend the Orders-in-Council if the United States dropped the last of its own restrictive measures, the non-importation act of 1811. A week later, without waiting for any American action, the British government scrapped the entire system of blockades and licenses. Several Republican leaders (including President Madison) later said that this probably would have averted war if they had known about it, but it took eight weeks for the news to reach Washington. By then, the United States was committed to war and would not agree to peace unless the British also gave up impressment, which they refused to do. The war therefore lasted for another two and a half years.

The Battle of Tippecanoe

The United States was eager to target Canada in 1812 not simply because it was here that Great Britain was most vulnerable, but also because an Indian war had erupted that many Americans, especially in the West, blamed on British officials in Canada. This war had been some time in coming. Indians had periodically raided isolated American settlements, often using guns supplied by the British. Although Americans were convinced that the British encouraged these raids, this was far from the case. The British walked a fine line. On the one hand, they welcomed Indian allies, whom they called "Nitchies"—a corruption of the Chippewa word for "friend" or "comrade"—and they were happy to supply their needs because in the wilderness their legendary fighting prowess and scouting abilities could tip the balance in any war with the United States. On the other hand, the British had no desire to engage in an American war provoked by their native allies, and thus they discouraged them from attacking American settlements. In truth, however, many Indians in the Northwest were unaware of or ignored British wishes. Americans did not understand the nuances of British policy, nor did they realize how little real control the British exercised over many natives in the region.

The Indian war in the Old Northwest finally erupted at Tippecanoe in Indiana Territory on November 7, 1811. The war was provoked by William Henry Harrison, who had become governor of the territory in 1800 at the age of 27. Beginning in 1803, Harrison had imposed a series of dubious treaties on the Indians, culminating in 1809 with the Treaty of Fort Wayne, which deprived the natives of more than 2.5 million acres of land.

Spearheading opposition to the latest treaty were two Shawnee brothers, Tenskwatawa (better known as the Prophet) and Tecumseh. The Prophet had built a pan-Indian religious movement by preaching rejection of white ways and resistance to American expansion, while Tecumseh had superimposed a political and military alliance on his brother's spiritual movement. The Prophet was probably the more significant figure because he had marshaled the support of

William Henry Harrison (1773–1841) precipitated an Indian war with the land cession treaties he imposed on Native Americans in the Old Northwest. His victories at Tippecanoe in 1811 and the Thames in 1813 helped propel him into the presidency in 1841, although he died after only a month in office. (Alexander C. Casselman, *Richardson's War of 1812*)

Indians from a multitude of tribes from across the region. Tecumseh, however, had a more commanding presence and made a greater impression on whites. Harrison found the respect that Tecumseh received from other natives "really astonishing" and concluded that he was "one of those uncommon geniuses, which spring up occasionally to produce revolutions and overturn the established order of things."[3] To forestall American expansion, Tecumseh argued that Indian lands were held in common and thus none could be sold without the consent of all.

In 1808 the Prophet and Tecumseh had established a village for their followers on the west bank of the Wabash River just below the mouth of the Tippecanoe River in present-day Indiana. Whites dubbed this settlement "Prophet's Town." In the fall of 1811, Harrison decided to break up the settlement in the hope of striking a blow at the Indian resistance movement. Departing from Vincennes on September 26 with about 1,000 regulars and volunteer militia, Harrison began the 150-mile march to Prophet's Town. He spent most of October building a forward base, named Fort Harrison, at Terre Haute. By November 6, he was within a mile of the Indian village. Although Tecumseh was away on a mission to the South seeking allies, the Prophet and most of his followers were in the village. A small band of Indians visited Harrison and offered to hold negotiations the next day to discuss their differences. Harrison agreed and made camp for the night but ordered his men to sleep with their muskets and in battle formation.

Before dawn the next morning, some 500 Indians, mostly Kickapoos, Winnebagoes, and Potawatomis, attacked. Fierce fighting ensued until the Indians were driven off after daylight. Harrison's forces suffered heavy casualties, 62 killed and 126 wounded, partly because he had not fortified his camp and partly because to ward off the cold and rain in the night he had permitted large fires that had illuminated his men. Indian casualties are unknown, but were probably around 50 killed and 75 wounded. The native casualties were remarkably low for a force attacking a larger army in this era. The next day Harrison marched his men into Prophet's Town, which was deserted, and ordered the town burned and the food supplies there taken or destroyed. Some of his men also reportedly dug up Indian graves and scattered the remains.

Harrison called the outcome of the battle "a complete and decisive victory," and

30 years later it helped make him president.[4] But this assessment was an exaggeration. The only reason that Americans could claim even a close victory was that they had held their ground and driven off the Indians and then had destroyed Prophet's Town and the Indians' food supplies. Although friendly Indians insisted that the Prophet's power was broken and the resistance movement greatly weakened, this too was an exaggeration. The Prophet remained a force to be reckoned with, and he soon returned to the village with his followers. "The Prophet and his people do not appear as a vanquished enemy," commented British Indian agent Matthew Elliott. "They re-occupy their former ground."[5]

The Battle of Tippecanoe was the opening round in the Indian war in the Old Northwest that blended into the War of 1812. Indian raids in the region increased dramatically after Tippecanoe, forcing many isolated settlers to abandon their farms. The battle drove many natives deeper into the arms of Great Britain and served to further convince Americans that the British were behind the raids. "*The war on the Wabash is purely BRITISH*," said the Lexington (Kentucky) *Reporter,* "The SCALPING KNIFE and TOMAHAWK of *British savages is now again devastating our frontiers.*"[6] Unfortunately for American prospects in the War of 1812, the outbreak of the Indian war also shifted the focus of U.S. military operations further west.

Tenskwatawa (1775–1836), better known as the Prophet, was a Shawnee leader whose life was transformed by a vision he had in 1805. He responded by launching a religious movement to resist white ways. Although his influence diminished after his defeat at Tippecanoe, he remained a force to be reckoned with. Many years after the War of 1812, he returned from Canada to the United States and in 1827–28 helped relocate Shawnees west of the Mississippi River to what is now Kansas City, Kansas. By this time, however, the influence he once enjoyed among his people had all but vanished. (Benson J. Lossing, *Pictorial Field-Book of the War of 1812*)

American and British Strategy in 1812

Canada in 1812 consisted of six British colonies: Upper Canada (which today is Ontario), Lower Canada (now Quebec), New Brunswick, Nova Scotia, Prince Edward Island, and Cape Breton Island. (Newfoundland had a separate status.) Although the surface area of these colonies was immense, the small population was mostly spread along the St. Lawrence River and the northern shores of the Great Lakes. As a result, Canada was often compared to a tree. The principal sea lanes that connected the Gulf of St. Lawrence to the mother country were the taproots; the St. Lawrence River was the trunk; and the Great Lakes and their connecting waterways were the branches.

The Canadian tree could be felled by cutting the taproots, but that was impossible as long as the British controlled the seas. The next best option was to attack

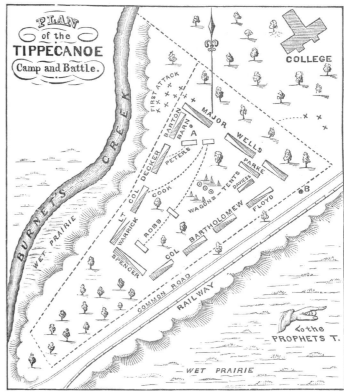

This sketch of the Tippecanoe battlefield, drawn in the 1860s, is reasonably accurate but includes a college and railway from a later era. (Benson J. Lossing, *Pictorial Field-Book of the War of 1812*)

Although William Henry Harrison tried to portray Tippecanoe as an unalloyed victory, he sustained far heavier casualties than the attacking Indians, and he was later accused of mismanaging the campaign. Friends of Major Joseph H. Daveiss (1774–1811), who perished in the battle, were particularly bitter because the Kentuckian had called for launching a preemptive attack the day before, which undoubtedly would have reduced American casualties. (Engraving from a book by Augustus L. Mason. Library of Congress)

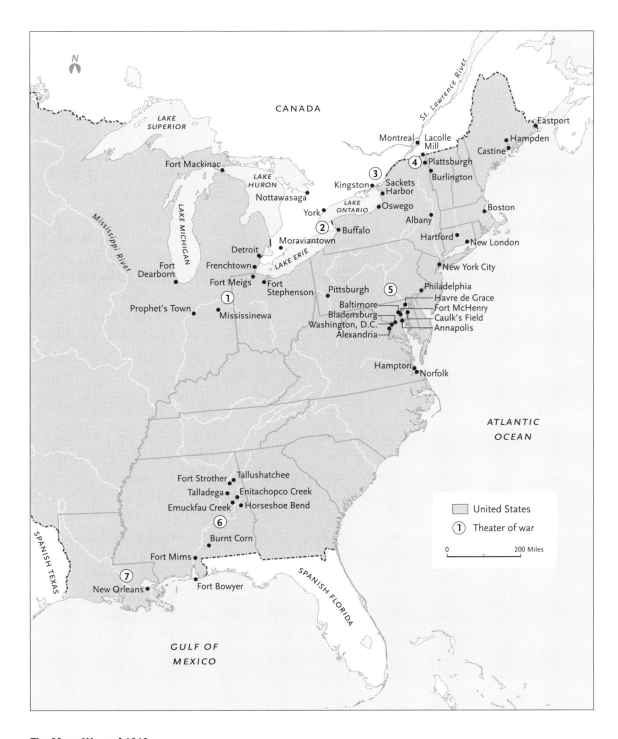

The Many Wars of 1812

Seven theaters of war ringed the United States: (1) the Old Northwest; (2) the Niagara Front;
(3) the St. Lawrence River; (4) the Lake Champlain–Richelieu River Corridor; (5) the Chesapeake
Bay; (6) the Old Southwest; and (7) the Gulf Coast. An eighth theater comprised actions on the
high seas, mostly in the Atlantic (see map on page 54).

the trunk. Cutting off traffic on the St. Lawrence would cause everything further west to wither and die. To accomplish this, the United States needed to take Montreal and Quebec, although this would still leave maritime Canada in British hands. The worst option was to concentrate on the West. The United States might conquer the forts and thus control settlements in western Canada, but these were of only marginal importance. Such a strategy would leave the bulk of Canada in the hands of Great Britain, with little incentive to make concessions on the maritime issues.

The United States had no war planning agency or board in 1812, and American leaders had done little thinking about how best to target Canada. Nor had they studied the successful British campaign against French Canada in the Seven Years War. American strategy therefore had to be developed on the fly, and the men responsible were ill equipped for the task. President Madison had no combat experience and thus lacked the military savvy and vision needed to forge a successful strategy. Nor could he get much help from his cabinet. The secretary of state, James Monroe, had seen considerable combat in the American Revolution, but he was so consumed by two overarching ambitions—to secure a major field command and to outmaneuver any potential rivals for the presidency—that his vision was clouded. The other cabinet secretaries were worse. Secretary of War William Eustis was overwhelmed by the daunting administrative duties of his office. He gave little direction to commanders in the field and busied himself with trivial tasks, such as "reading advertisements of Petty retailing merchants to find where he may Purchase 100 shoes or 200 hats."[7] He is "a dead weight in our hands," concluded a Pennsylvania congressman. "His unfitness is apparent to every body but himself."[8] Secretary of the Navy Paul Hamilton was no better. An alcoholic who was sometimes drunk by noon, he understood the value of a navy but not how to use it. A North Carolina congressman thought that Hamilton was "about as fit for his place as the Indian prophet would be for Emperor of Europe."[9]

The United States in June 1812 had about 12,000 regulars, and these troops could be supplemented with some U.S. Volunteers and volunteer militia for offensive operations, but just about everyone who wore a uniform was inexperienced. American leaders understood the logic of concentrating their forces against Montreal and Quebec, but in the end the focus of their operations was further west. One reason was that they expected little support from New England, which was the natural staging ground for an assault on Quebec. Federalists controlled New England and were unlikely to provide manpower or logistical support for an invasion of Canada. People in the West, by contrast, enthusiastically supported the war, and while most American militia refused to serve outside the country, western militia had no such reservations and thus could be counted on to participate in an invasion of Canada. The Indian war in the West gave the administration another reason to dispatch troops to the region. An American victory in the West could deliver a blow to both the British and their Indian allies and thus enhance the security of Americans living in the region.

The administration adopted a plan for a three-pronged invasion of Canada. One army would invade across the Detroit River at the western end of Lake Erie. A second army would invade across the Niagara River at the eastern end of Lake Erie. And a third army would follow the traditional invasion route along Lake Champlain and the Richelieu River and then travel overland or follow the St. Lawrence River to Montreal.

With their attention focused on Europe, British leaders had not done much thinking about waging war in America either, but their strategy was defensive and therefore much simpler. Since they could not afford to divert military or naval assets needed in Europe, their plan was to fight a holding action in North America. In June 1812 there were close to 10,000 British regulars in Canada. Most were veteran soldiers, and their officers were generally able and experienced. The British hoped that these troops, aided by Indian allies and locally raised regulars and supported by militia, would be able to preserve most of Canada from the American onslaught. Quebec—"the Gibraltar of America"—was the key. Perched high upon a bluff with ready access to the sea via the St. Lawrence River, Quebec was considered the front door to Canada, and all else would be sacrificed to hold it. The Royal Navy was expected to play a role in the defense of Canada, too. Besides keeping the supply lines to the mother country open, the navy could target American trade and establish at least a limited blockade of the United States. The plan, in short, was to fight war on the cheap in America without draining precious resources from the more critical war against Napoleonic France.

The man charged with carrying out British strategy was 45-year-old Sir George Prevost, the governor-general of Canada who was both civilian and military leader of British North America. After an impressive career in the West Indies, Prevost had been appointed lieutenant governor of Nova Scotia in 1808. Three years later, he assumed the top position in Canada. His predecessor, Sir James Craig, had feuded with the French inhabitants of Lower Canada, and Sir George, who spoke French and had successfully governed a captured French colony in the Caribbean, did a good job of conciliating this group. He also continued the policy initiated by his predecessors of gradually improving the defenses of Canada, particularly the city of Quebec, whose retention he considered indispensable to a successful defense of his domain. "I have considered the preservation of Quebec," he said

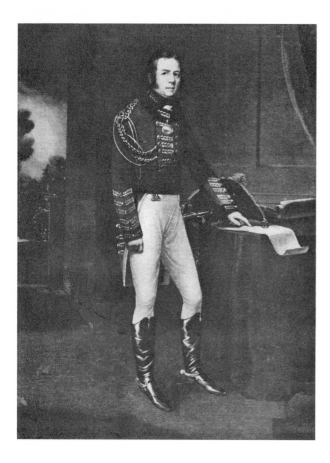

Sir George Prevost (1767–1816) served as governor-general of Canada during the war. Although the architect of a successful defense policy in the first two years of the contest, he was attacked by his enemies for timidity on the battlefield. Recalled to Great Britain under a cloud at the end of the conflict, he died before facing a court martial that might have vindicated him. (Portrait by S. W. Reynolds. William Wood, *Select British Documents of the Canadian War of 1812*)

on the eve of war, "as the first object, and to which all others must be subordinate."[10]

The Fall of Mackinac, Detroit, and Chicago

By the time the United States had declared war on Britain in June 1812, a campaign in the West was already under way. The man in charge was Brigadier General William Hull, a 59-year-old veteran of the Revolutionary War who was governor of the Michigan Territory. Hull had recently suffered a stroke and was ill suited physically and emotionally for a major combat command, but the administration could find no one better. Partly to overawe the Indians in the region and partly in anticipation of war with Great Britain, Hull was ordered in the spring of 1812 to march an army to Detroit. Assembling a mixed force of regulars and volunteer militia in Urbana, Ohio, the brigadier departed with the main body for Detroit on June 15. It was a slow and laborious march. Hull's heavily encumbered army opened a road and built blockhouses along the way, but in northwest Ohio it had to cross the Black Swamp, a marshy wetland 40 miles wide teaming with malaria-carrying mosquitoes.

Hull's force, which was called the "North Western Army," reached the Maumee River on June 30. Here the brigadier chartered the *Cuyahoga* and a smaller vessel to carry his baggage to Detroit and thus lighten the army's load. Shortly after the vessels had departed, Hull received word that war had been declared. When the *Cuyahoga* sailed into the Detroit River on July 2, it was seized by the British, who had learned of the declaration of war four days before. Hull lost not only irreplaceable medical supplies but also a chest carrying his papers, which provided the British with a great deal of information on the approaching army.

Hull arrived at Fort Detroit three days later with about 2,000 men. Across the river at Fort Amherstburg the British, then under the command of Lieutenant Colonel Thomas B. St. George, could muster only about 1,600 regulars, militia, and Indians. The British, however, had a huge logistical advantage: a small squadron of armed ships gave them control of not only the Detroit River but also Lake Erie.

On July 12, Hull moved the bulk of his army across the Detroit River and seized Sandwich (modern-day Windsor). Besides sending out reconnaissance and foraging parties, Hull issued a proclamation promising to free Canadians from tyranny and protect their persons and property. The proclamation also warned against employing Indians as allies. "*No white man*," Hull said, "*found fighting by the Side of an Indian will be taken prisoner. Instant destruction will be his Lot.*"[11] Many Canadian militia deserted and some of Britain's Indian allies left, both promising signs for Hull. The first skirmish of the war took place on July 16, when Colonel Lewis Cass of the Ohio militia seized control of a key bridge over the Canard River. However, Cass abandoned his position when Hull proved reluctant to support him. Moreover, Hull refused to assault Fort Amherstburg until his siege guns had proper carriages, which would take several weeks to construct.

While Hull dallied, his position deteriorated. On July 28 he learned that 11 days earlier the U.S. fort on Mackinac Island between Lake Huron and Lake Michigan had fallen. The American garrison under Lieutenant Porter Hanks, only 57 strong, had surrendered to a mixed British force of 625 Indians, fur traders, and regulars under the command of Captain Charles Roberts, an experienced British army officer who had sailed to Mackinac Island from his base on St. Joseph Island in Lake Huron. The loss of Fort Mackinac stunned Hull, who feared that it "opened the Northern hive of Indians, and they were swarming down in every direction."[12]

Brigadier General William Hull (1753–1825) surrendered his entire army at Detroit in 1812, forever tainting his reputation. Although each of the decisions he made might have been justified, their cumulative effect was disastrous, and for this there was no defense. (Alexander C. Casselman, *Richardson's War of 1812*)

Americans (particularly in the West) liked to fire "buck and ball," that is, a combination of two or three buckshot with a musket ball. This increased the chance of hitting a target, but reduced the range and lethality of the shot. This X-ray of a loaded Springfield musket, recovered from the Château-guay River more than a century and a half after the war, shows three buckshot nestled next to a musket ball. (Courtesy of Parks Canada)

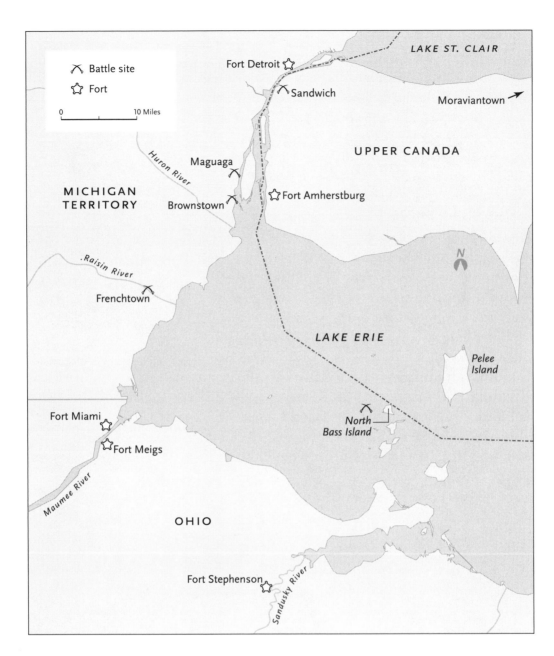

Battle site
Fort

0   10 Miles

LAKE ST. CLAIR

Fort Detroit
Sandwich

Moraviantown

UPPER CANADA

Maguaga

Huron River

MICHIGAN
TERRITORY

Brownstown

Fort Amherstburg

Raisin River

Frenchtown

LAKE ERIE

N

Pelee
Island

Fort Miami

*North
Bass Island*

Fort Meigs

Maumee River

OHIO

Fort Stephenson

Sandusky River

The Detroit Frontier, 1812–1813

Fort Mackinac dominated Mackinac Island, which was located between Lake Michigan and Lake Huron. Whoever controlled this island was likely to control the trade of the upper lakes and command the allegiance of the Indians who lived nearby. The British captured Mackinac in the summer of 1812 and held it for the rest of the war. (Benson J. Lossing, *Pictorial Field-Book of the War of 1812*)

More bad news followed. Hull was increasingly concerned about his supply lines to Ohio, which were menaced by Indians. On August 4, Hull dispatched 150 men under Major Thomas Van Horne to meet a supply train known to be on the way. The following day Tecumseh and a small band of Indians ambushed Van Horne at Brownstown (present-day Gibraltar, Michigan) and forced him to return to Detroit. A mail bag the Indians captured showed the British how much Hull's inaction had demoralized his army. That demoralization increased on August 7, when Hull ordered most of his army on the Canadian side of the river to return to Detroit. Four days later, he ordered the remainder of his force at Sandwich to return as well. With the American troops gone, the British now had free rein on their side of the river and could use their naval force to mount an amphibious operation against Detroit.

Hull again sought to open his supply lines by sending 600 men under Lieutenant Colonel James Miller, but on August 9 this force was ambushed at Maguaga

Major General Isaac Brock (1769–1812), the hero of Detroit, lost his life two months later in the defense of Queenston Heights. A gifted leader who inspired his own men as well as his Indian allies and made good use of intelligence to wage psychological warfare, Brock far outclassed his American counterparts. His loss was severely felt by the British. (Library and Archives of Canada)

(present-day Trenton, Michigan) by an Anglo-Indian army more than 400 strong under the command of Captain Adam Muir and Tecumseh. Although the Americans prevailed, Miller chose not to push on but instead stayed put until Hull ordered him back to Detroit. Hull made a final effort to open his supply lines by sending 400 picked men under colonels Cass and Duncan McArthur. This force made it further than the other two but not far enough to meet the American supply train, which was waiting on the River Raisin. Hull was now in such a panic that he ordered these men to return, but having lost all confidence in their commander, they chose to remain in the wilderness. By this time Hull had become so distracted that his militia officers considered removing him from command, but they could not get Lieutenant Colonel Miller, the ranking regular army officer after Hull, to take his place.

Meanwhile, Major General Isaac Brock, the 42-year-old civilian and military leader of Upper Canada, had amassed some 300 British reinforcements at Long Point and from there had sailed across Lake Erie to Fort Amherstburg. Brock was a commander of exceptional merit who inspired confidence in all who knew him. After arriving at Fort Amherstburg on August 13, Brock conferred with Tecumseh, the only time these two legendary figures would meet. Within 15 months, both would be dead on Canadian battlefields and both would be elevated to the pantheon of Canada's war heroes.

While the arrival of Indians was swelling the size of Brock's army, the desertion of militia was shrinking Hull's. Convinced from the captured mail bag that the American army was ripe for surrender or defeat, Brock took the offensive. To foster fear in the enemy, Brock dressed some of his militia in regular army jackets, and Tecumseh repeatedly paraded the same natives where Americans could see them. Then, on August 15, Brock sent Hull a note under a flag of truce demanding surrender. "It is far from my intention," Brock intoned, "to join in a war of extermination, but you must be aware that the numerous body of Indians who have attached themselves to my troops will be beyond controul the moment the contest commences."[13] Initially Hull refused this demand, and the two sides exchanged artillery fire. But Hull was simply buying time, and on August 16 he agreed to surrender his entire army, including those troops still in the wilderness with Cass and McArthur. His aim was to avoid an Indian massacre of not only the garrison troops but also the many women and children (which included members of his own family) who were sheltered in the fort. This stunning development changed the course of the war in the Old Northwest. The British were now in the ascendant, and many Indians, understandably preferring a winner, flocked to their standard. Brock had not only saved western Canada, but for more than a year thereafter the British occupied Detroit and controlled the Michigan Territory.

Hull's surrender thoroughly discredited him, and he became the scapegoat for the failure of the entire campaign in the Old Northwest. When the British later paroled him to the United States (which meant that he remained a prisoner of war and was honor bound not to fight again until properly exchanged), an American military court convicted him of cowardice and neglect of duty. Although the trial could hardly be called fair, the court nonetheless sentenced Hull to death but recommended that the president commute the sentence because of the brigadier's Revolutionary War service. President Madison complied with this recommendation, and Hull spent the rest of his days trying to defend his actions at Detroit, which was no easy task.

The day before the fall of Detroit, the United States suffered another disaster, the Fort Dearborn Massacre. Several days before surrendering, General Hull had ordered the small American garrison to abandon this isolated outpost (located in the heart of present-day Chicago), and the local commander, Captain Nathan Heald, had reluctantly complied. On August 15, 1812, he marched out of the fort with 65 regulars and militia and perhaps two dozen civilians. Although ostensibly under the protection of some Miami Indians, some 500 Potawatomis fell on the whites not far from the fort, killing some of them after terms of surrender had been arranged. One American, William Wells, came to a particularly grisly end. The Indians cut off his head and then carved out his heart and ate it raw. To the Indians, eating Wells's heart was probably both a mark of respect and matter of justice. Wells had been kidnapped and raised by Miami Indians and as a youth had shown considerable prowess on the battlefield. But after returning to white society, he had become an Indian agent and had cheated the natives out of part of their government annuities.

The Battle of Frenchtown and the River Raisin Massacre

The administration was determined to reassert American power in the Old Northwest before the year was out. As a replacement for Hull, popular sentiment in the West favored William Henry Harrison, the hero of Tippecanoe, and Kentucky

named him a major general in the state militia. The administration reluctantly bowed to local sentiment and put Harrison in charge of all American forces in the region. Harrison spent the fall building his army and stockpiling supplies, dealing with command disputes and discipline problems, and fighting deteriorating weather. He also had to contend with hostile Indians. In September, small American forces under Captain James Rhea and Captain Zachary Taylor (the future president), fended off Indian assaults on Fort Wayne and Fort Harrison, respectively, and in December American troops defeated the Miamis and burned their villages on the Mississinewa River.

The onset of winter exacerbated American supply problems, depressed troop morale, and increased the sick list. By the end of the year, Harrison was inclined to spend the rest of the winter on the Maumee Rapids and delay his offensive until the spring. He ordered Brigadier General James Winchester to the Rapids with an advance, but following his own counsels, Winchester decided to push on to Frenchtown (now Monroe, Michigan) on the River Raisin with about 1,000 men to help American settlers there who had pleaded for protection.

On January 22, 1813, an Anglo-Indian force 1,150 strong under the command of Colonel Henry Procter attacked Winchester. In the bloody Battle of Frenchtown, also known as the Battle of the River Raisin, Winchester was captured and persuaded to surrender what remained of his army. He later reported 400 men killed or missing and another 550 captured. The British and their Indian allies, by contrast, lost only about 200 men, and the victory attracted still more Indians to the British cause. Procter, fearing that the main American force might be nearby, hastily withdrew with most of his prisoners to Fort Amherstburg, leaving the wounded Americans to the mercy of the Indians, who killed about 30 of them the next day. This was known in the United States as the "River Raisin Massacre," and thereafter "Remember the Raisin!" was a battle cry heard throughout the West. Any revenge, however, would have to wait, for the campaign of 1812 in the West was now effectively over, and the British remained in firm control of much of the region.

The Battle of Queenston Heights

The United States fared no better on the Niagara front. In command of the American campaign here was Major General Stephen Van Rensselaer of the New York militia. Known as "the last of the patroons," this prominent 47-year-old New York Federalist was expected to hold command temporarily until a suitable regular army officer could take over, but he was never superseded. Van Rensselaer had no combat experience but had the good sense to rely heavily on his kinsman, 38-year-old Lieutenant Colonel Solomon Van Rensselaer, who had fought in the Indian wars of the 1790s and had served for many years as adjutant general of the New York militia. The younger Van Rensselaer had won his spurs at the Battle of Fallen Timbers in 1794, when he had sustained a chest wound that nearly killed him.

By October 1812, the senior Van Rensselaer had under his command a sizeable army, about 6,400 men—2,400 regulars and 4,000 militia and U.S. Volunteers. But he faced two critical problems: his citizen soldiers were obstreperous and unreliable, and some 1,600 regulars, who had only recently reached the camp near Buffalo, were under the immediate command of Brigadier General Alexander Smyth, who showed little interest in cooperation. Although Smyth was outranked by the New York militia officer and was expected to serve under his command, he declined to meet with Van Rensselaer to discuss operations.

On the opposite shore of the Niagara River the British were commanded by Major General Brock, who had taken advantage of his control of Lake Erie to return east shortly after the surrender of Detroit. Brock had only 2,000 troops—1,200 regulars and 800 militia—but he could also count on the services of 300 Grand River Iroquois under the leadership of John Norton, a 42-year-old

Colonel Henry Procter (1787–1859) led the British to a major victory over Brigadier General James Winchester (1756–1826) in the Battle of Frenchtown in January 1813. But Procter's victory was marred by heavy British casualties and an Indian massacre of American prisoners of war the day after the battle. (Benson J. Lossing, *Pictorial Field-Book of the War of 1812*)

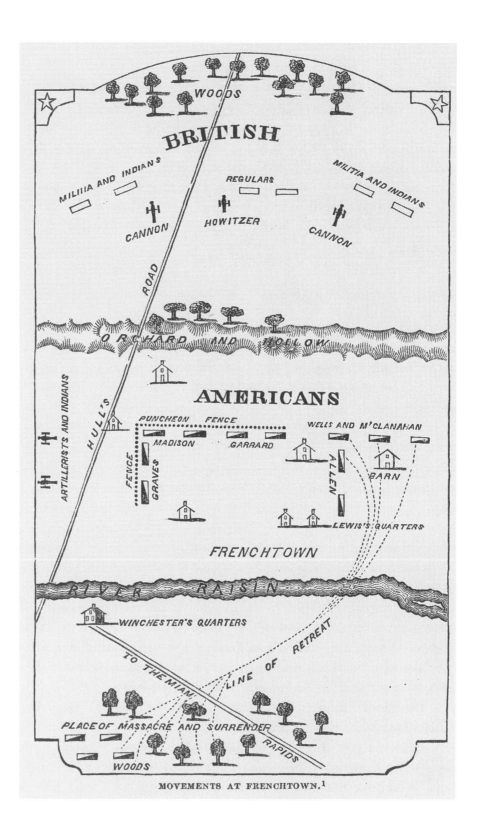

MOVEMENTS AT FRENCHTOWN.[1]

A VIEW of WINCHESTER in NORTH AMERICA DEDICATED to M.ʳ PRESIDENT MAD I SON!!

Extract from the Morn.ᵍ Chronicle Ap.ˡ 23.ᵈ 1813 | It appears from One of the Halifax Papers, it was the famous Wyandot Chief ROUNDHEAD, who took Gen.ˡ Winchester Prisoner: The Indian according to his notion of the Laws of Nations, & Courtesy due to Prisoners of War, stripped the American Commander of his Fine Coat, Waistcoat & Shirt, & then Bedaubed his Skin with Paint: In this ludicrous state having dressed himself in his Regimentals, he presented him to Col.ˡ Procter: who with difficulty Succeeded in getting the Discomfited Gen.ˡ his Coat, Sword & back

Pub.ᵈ by S. Knight Sweetings Alley CornHill London May 3.ᵈ 1813.

Scottish-Cherokee, who would take part in almost every major campaign on the Niagara front during the war. Just as Tecumseh's Indians had played a crucial role in securing western Canada for the British, Norton's Indians would prove equally important on the Niagara frontier.

This frontier was more densely populated and more heavily fortified than the Detroit River front. It also posed more geographic challenges to maneuvering armies. The 35-mile Niagara River, which connected Lake Erie to Lake Ontario, was traversed by a ridge—the Niagara Escarpment—through which flowed the spectacular and already famous Niagara Falls. Portages had been developed on both sides of the river to allow traders and travelers to get around the falls. Anchoring the British defenses on the west bank were two posts: Fort Erie at the southern end opposite Buffalo and Fort George at the northern end where the river drains into Lake Ontario. On the American side, there were also two posts, Fort Schlosser just south of Niagara Falls at the upper end of the portage road,

This cartoon, published in London in 1813, shows the aftermath of the Anglo-Indian victory at Frenchtown, when the Wyandot leader Roundhead stripped Brigadier General James Winchester of his clothing and sword, painted him, and then presented him to an embarrassed Colonel Henry Procter. (Library of Congress)

(*left*) Major General Stephen Van Rensselaer (1764–1839) was a New York militia officer without combat experience who was in charge of the American campaign on the Niagara front in 1812. The American invasion ended in defeat when New York militia would not cross the river to reinforce the first wave of invaders. (Engraving by G. Parker from a miniature by C. Fraser. Library of Congress)

(*right*) Solomon Van Rensselaer (1774–1852) led the attack on Queenston Heights in 1812 but was quickly knocked out of action with multiple wounds. (Benson J. Lossing, *Pictorial Field-Book of the War of 1812*)

and Fort Niagara across the river from Fort George. In fact, the two forts at the mouth of the Niagara were so close that they could exchange artillery fire.

The Van Rensselaers hatched a plan to launch an attack against Queenston that would draw off the regulars at Fort George and thus enable Smyth to take the British post with an amphibious assault launched from Fort Niagara. But Smyth refused to attend the council of officers summoned to discuss the plan, and that meant that the Van Rensselaers were on their own. They decided to attack Queenston anyway, in part because the New York militia threatened to go home if the men did not see some action soon.

The main attack was planned for October 11 but had to be postponed because in the midst of a rainstorm a junior militia officer disappeared in a boat that reportedly carried oars for all the assault vessels. Smyth had responded to Van Rensselaer's orders to advance but returned his rain-drenched column to camp when he learned that the attempt had been cancelled. Finally, before daybreak on October 13, Lieutenant Colonel Van Rensselaer led the first wave—300 regulars—across the river. They were quickly spotted by British sentries and came under small arms and artillery fire. An intense firefight ensued. Van Rensselaer was wounded five times (but survived to the age of 77), and six of the other ten officers with him were either killed or wounded. The British also took heavy casualties. Although additional waves of Americans reached the Canadian side, they were pinned down on the shore. Before being evacuated Solomon Van Rensselaer had put Captain John E. Wool in charge of a mission to proceed upriver and ascend a locally known but arduous path to heights above Queenston. Ignoring his own wounds, Wool led his men up the path and was able to take control of the heights because British sentries had been carelessly removed. Wool's men then seized one of the two British artillery batteries that had been harassing them.

Thereafter, reinforcements poured in on both sides, and there was a spirited battle over control of the heights. In one early counterattack, the British suffered an irreplaceable loss when Major General Brock, who always led his men from the front, was killed. Brock's aide, Lieutenant Colonel John Macdonell of the Upper Canada militia, was also killed that day. By 10:00 a.m. the fighting had subsided with the Americans, who were now under the command of 26-year-old Winfield Scott, in firm control of the heights. Some of the American soldiers now slipped into Queenston and looted the town.

In the early afternoon, Scott's men came under renewed attack, first from 100 of Norton's Indians and a British artillery battery and then from 900 British regulars and militia under the command of Major General Roger Sheaffe. Although Sheaffe botched the deployment of his men, his noncommissioned officers got them properly arranged so that they could attack. In the face of this attack, Scott's men performed reasonably well, but a combination of enemy fire and lack of adequate tools prevented them from establishing field fortifications to secure their position, and a growing number of desertions thinned their ranks.

Scott, whose force soon dwindled to less than 500 men, was supposed to be reinforced by additional men from the American side, but New York militiamen, many of whom were "violent democrats" who had earlier clamored for action, now refused to cross the river despite the pleas of their senior officers. "To my utter astonishment," Major General Van Rensselaer reported, "I found that at the very moment when complete victory was in our hands, the Ardor of the unengaged Troops had entirely subsided. . . . I rode in all directions, urged men by every Consideration to pass over, but in vain."[14] The citizen soldiers stood on their constitutional right to decline service outside the country, but most were simply frightened by the war whoops coming from the British side of the river and the

John Norton (1770–1830?), a Scottish-Cherokee who became a Mohawk leader, fought on Britain's side during the war. Known as "the Snipe," he kept the Grand River Iroquois loyal to Britain and saw action in almost every major battle on the bloody Niagara frontier. (Portrait by Mary Ann Knight. Library and Archives of Canada)

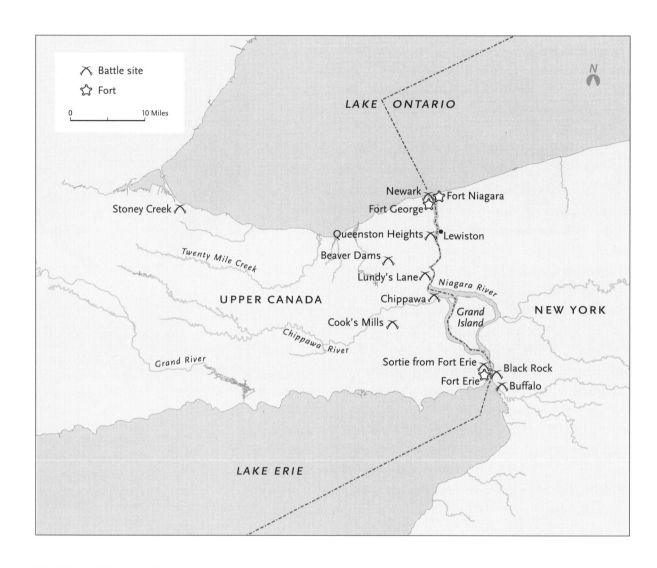

The Niagara Frontier, 1812–1814

This view of Queenston Heights shows the difficult cliffs that the American invaders had to scale to establish a defensible position. (Benson J. Lossing, *Pictorial Field-Book of the War of 1812*)

Though inaccurate in many details, this picture shows Major General Brock's death in the style of romantic battlefield deaths popularized by Benjamin West in the eighteenth century. (Painting by John D. Kelly. Library and Archives of Canada)

Major General Roger Hale Sheaffe (1763–1851) took command at Queenston in 1812 after Major General Brock's death and, despite some missteps, was credited with the British victory. But he was never popular with his men, and after his failed defense of York in 1813 he was reassigned to a non-combat zone. (Alexander C. Casselman, *Richardson's War of 1812*)

sad fate of the dead and wounded who were brought back to the American side. Van Rensselaer himself contributed to the defeatist mood by mismanaging the operation. The lack of adequate planning and proper logistical support hampered the operation from the beginning.

Overwhelmed by the Anglo-Indian attack, many Americans panicked and slipped over the edge of Queenston Heights as they looked in vain for some kind of path that would take them out of harm's way. Those who made it to the bottom took refuge in the caves or among the rocks on the shore or tried to swim back to the American side. Soon the shore was jammed with Americans, who made easy targets for British and Indian sharpshooters. Surrendering on the smoked-filled battlefield above was no easy task. After several unsuccessful attempts, Scott finally grabbed a white handkerchief and waved it during a melee that almost cost him his life. Escaping injury, Scott got to several British officers, who acknowledged his surrender and ordered an end to the fighting. In the daylong Battle of Queenston Heights, the British and their Indian allies had lost 150 killed, wounded, or captured, while American casualties were about 250. Although some Americans managed to escape across the river, 925 surrendered into British hands.

Several days later, Major General Van Rensselaer resigned, and Brigadier General Smyth succeeded to the command. Smyth spent more than a month preparing for a fresh assault on British positions. In the meantime, after a month-long armistice, Fort George and Fort Niagara exchanged artillery fire, and Smyth issued pompous proclamations that earned the contempt of his soldiers. Finally, in late November, Smyth sent two small assault parties across the river to secure a bridge and silence a battery, but instead of following up with his main group, he called off the operation, pleading an insufficient number of boats. Winter was now setting in, and the militia in Smyth's camp were becoming unruly. Unhappy with the brigadier's bombastic and dilatory leadership, some militiamen reportedly took potshots at his tent. After fighting a bloodless duel with Peter B. Porter, a New York congressman and brigadier general in the militia, Smyth departed for his home in Virginia. Several months later, without the formality of a court

martial, his name was struck from the rolls of the army during a reorganization. With the end of this campaign, the United States had lost its second army and suffered its second major disaster on the Canadian frontier.

The Battle of Lacolle Mill

The third and final American campaign of 1812 was launched from Plattsburgh, New York, north along Lake Champlain and the Richelieu River toward Montreal. This should have been the principal campaign of 1812 or at the very least an effective diversion that drew British troops away from the Detroit and Niagara fronts, but in point of fact it was too little and too late and accomplished nothing of value. The man in charge was 61-year-old Major General Henry Dearborn, who had an impressive combat record from the American Revolution that included participation in the assault on Canada in 1775. More recently, he had served as Jefferson's secretary of war. He was the customs collector at Boston in the spring of 1812 when President Madison chose him to be the senior of two major generals in the army and ordered him to New York to oversee operations in this theater. Al-

An idealized picture showing Fanny Doyle at Fort Niagara loading hot shot from a furnace into a garrison gun. The artillery was actually fired from the roof of the old French castle inside the fort to get enough elevation to hit Fort George. Note the incoming fire—an explosive shell—in the background. (Drawing by T. Walker. Library and Archives of Canada)

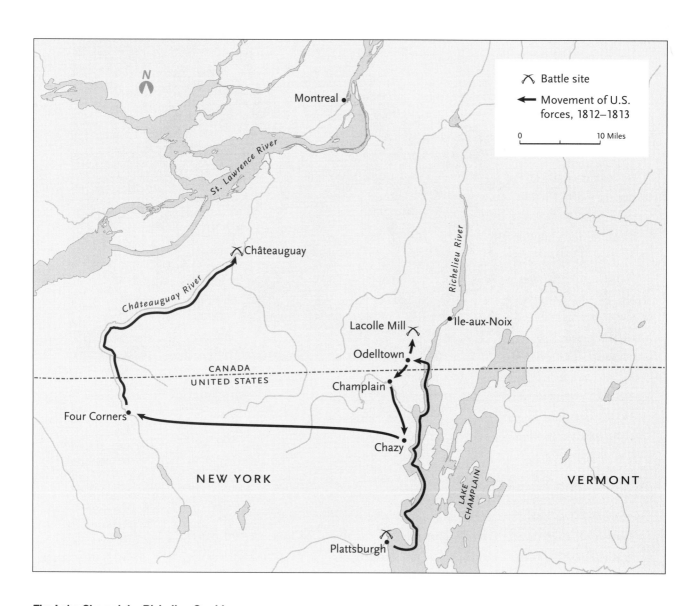

The Lake Champlain–Richelieu Corridor

though Dearborn accepted the appointment, he soon proved that he had lost his taste for battle. Instead of campaigning, he preferred to devote himself to building and administering his army and constructing defensive fortifications. In May 1812, Dearborn left his headquarters in Albany to go to Boston to promote enlistments and examine coastal fortifications. He failed to achieve much but nonetheless lingered in Boston until July. Given the state of Anglo-American relations and the prospects for war, this was unconscionable.

Although Dearborn returned to Albany in July, he felt no urgency and showed no enthusiasm for active campaigning. His army, about 3,500 regulars and 2,500 militia, did not leave Plattsburgh until mid-November, and Dearborn himself took command only after Brigadier General Joseph Bloomfield became too ill to conduct the operation. Dearborn's army marched north to the international frontier, where it encountered British outposts and Indians. Another 5,000 British regulars and militia under the command of Major General Francis de Rottenburg were in winter quarters in Montreal.

Major General Henry Dearborn (1751–1829) was in charge of the eastern theater of operations that embraced the St. Lawrence River and Lake Champlain-Richelieu River corridor. His reluctant and halfhearted invasion of Canada in 1812 demonstrated his unfitness for a combat command. He was not removed, however, until more disasters followed on his watch in 1813. (Engraving by Charles de Saint-Mémin. Library of Congress)

While Dearborn stayed put, Colonel Zebulon Pike, a 33-year-old officer who had made a reputation for himself as an army explorer, took 500 men to try to cut off Britain's Indian allies. When Pike could not find the native camp in the wilderness, he continued on to the Lacolle River, where he attacked a blockhouse known as Lacolle Mill. Pike's force drove off a small band of French Canadian militia and Indians but was then fired on by advancing American militia. Considerable friendly fire was exchanged, producing a dozen casualties, before the American officers realized what was happening and ordered a cease-fire. Although dogged by some Indians and French Canadian militia under the command of Lieutenant Colonel Charles de Salaberry, Pike returned to the main American camp to report that the occupation of Lacolle Mill would be easy.

But by now Dearborn realized that most of his militia would not cross the border. He used this as an excuse to call off the entire campaign and went into winter quarters at Plattsburgh. He offered to resign, but the administration declined to accept his offer. Congressman Charles J. Ingersoll of Pennsylvania later described the campaign, which was little more than a feeble demonstration, as a "miscarriage, without even [the] heroism of a disaster."[15] It marked a dismal but perhaps fitting end to America's ill-planned and unsuccessful invasion of Canada in 1812.

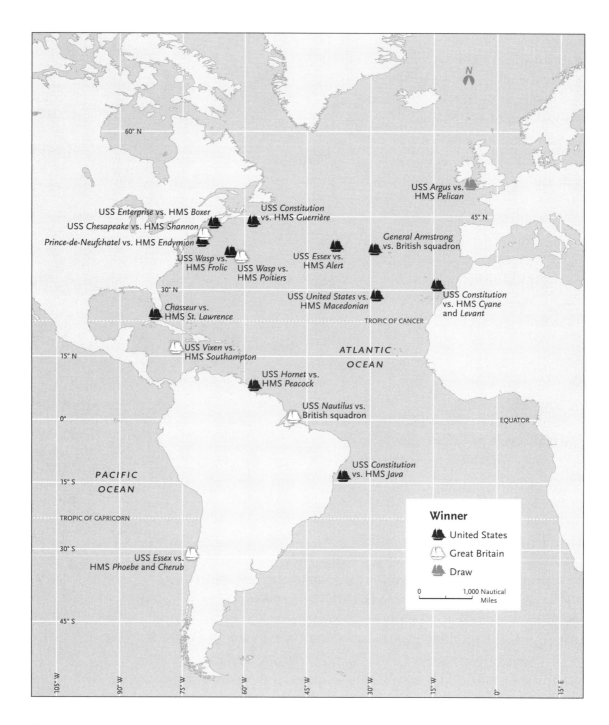

The War at Sea

Most of the engagements between warships or between warships and privateers occurred in the Atlantic. Although the United States enjoyed an initial rush of success, the British ruled the high seas throughout the war.

 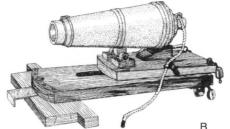 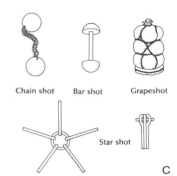

A   B

Chain shot   Bar shot   Grapeshot

Star shot

C

The War at Sea

If the war in Canada failed to live up to American expectations, the war at sea in 1812 went much better even though the U.S. Navy was clearly overmatched. At the beginning of 1812, the British navy boasted 527 commissioned ships, including 115 ships-of-the-line (the battleships of the day) and 126 frigates (comparable to modern cruisers).[16] With only seven frigates and ten smaller vessels, the U.S. Navy seemed unlikely to influence the course of the war at sea, but a number of circumstances in 1812 enabled it to do just that.

The British could ill afford to divert warships from European waters, not only because the Continent was the central theater in the Napoleonic Wars, but also because Napoleon was using the resources at his command to rebuild his fleet. Any reduction in Britain's naval presence in these waters could well prove disastrous. The rest of the Royal Navy was scattered all over the world, performing blockade and convoy duty, transporting and supplying British troops, tracking enemy cruisers and chasing enemy merchantmen, and carrying out a host of other duties. The rule of thumb in the Age of Sail was that it required three ships to maintain a continuous presence in a distant theater: one ship in the theater, a second on the way to relieve the first, and a third undergoing repairs so that in time it could relieve the second. This stretched the Royal Navy to the limit.

The British had four squadrons in the New World in 1812, one in Halifax (25 ships, including one 64-gun ship and five frigates), one at Newfoundland (which included one 50-gun ship and three frigates), and two in the West Indies (which between them had two ships-of-the-line and seven frigates). But the top priority of the Newfoundland ships was to protect the island and the fishing business, and those in the Caribbean were needed to defend Britain's huge trade with the West Indies. Only the Halifax squadron was available for immediate service in American waters, although it still had to be mindful of its other duties. The British had four naval yards in the New World, but a shortage of skilled workers and

Naval battles were usually decided by long guns (A), which had considerable range, and carronades (B), which had less range but greater firepower. Long guns fired a variety of projectiles (C). Round shot was most common, but other shot (shown here) was also used. Chain shot, bar shot, and star shot were all designed to disable a ship by destroying its masts, sails, and rigging. Grapeshot was commonly used to target people. (Guns drawn by Kevin Crisman. Courtesy of the artist. Projectiles drawn by William J. Clipson. Courtesy of Spencer Tucker)

essential materials slowed repair work, and major overhauls could only be done at the already overtaxed dockyards in the mother country. Moreover, a longstanding manpower shortage meant that virtually all British ships were shorthanded, and in the interest of preserving gunpowder the Admiralty after Trafalgar had prohibited gunnery practice with live ammunition, which undermined the readiness of Royal Navy crews.

By contrast, the U.S. Navy was in good fighting trim despite a decade of neglect by the government. Several warships could put to sea immediately, and the rest would be ready for service by the end of the year. American officers were every bit as good as those in the Royal Navy, and their ships usually had a full complement of men, most of whom were better trained in the use of small arms and large guns than their British counterparts. In addition, the heavy American frigates—the *Constitution, President,* and *United States*—were the most powerful ships of their class in the world. Rated to carry 44 guns (rather than the usual 36), they typically carried over 50, and this complement included not only powerful 24-pounder long guns but carronades that were extremely destructive at close range. In weight of broadside, they had the firepower of a British 50- or 60-gun ship. This made them super-frigates, capable of outfighting any other frigates in the world and outrunning anything larger.

The United States had another advantage in the war at sea. Because the young republic had declared war, its warships could act immediately while British warships remained in port or in the dark. Although the news of war reached Halifax in nine days, it took four weeks to reach Bermuda, five weeks to reach the naval station at Jamaica, and six weeks to reach the Admiralty in London.

The Cruise of the 'President'

While American leaders were still debating how best to use the navy, two squadrons put to sea, one headed by Captain John Rodgers in the U.S. Frigate *President* (54 guns) and the other headed by Captain Stephen Decatur in the U.S. Frigate *United States* (56 guns). Both were charged with protecting returning American merchant vessels, but Rodgers, who left port before receiving these orders, went in search of a rich convoy that had departed from Jamaica for the mother country in May and was expected to sail parallel to the American coast before veering northeast when it reached 40 degrees latitude (due east of New Jersey).

On June 23 Rodgers spotted and chased the British frigate *Belvidera* (42 guns), Captain Richard Byron commanding, and this led to the first military action of the war. The two ships exchanged fire during the chase, and both sustained casual-

ties. Rodgers himself was injured when the gun he was sighting exploded, killing or wounding 16 members of the *President's* crew. The British crew quickly and expertly repaired the damage that American fire did to the *Belvidera*, and Byron lightened his load by dumping equipment, boats, and water. The *President* was the faster ship and might still have caught the *Belvidera*, but the exploding gun caused momentary confusion, and Rodgers lost valuable time by twice yawing his ship to deliver ineffectual broadsides. As a result, the *Belvidera* managed to slip away in the night and make it to Halifax. The British won this engagement, not only because the *Belvidera* escaped capture and sustained fewer casualties (seven vs. 22 for the *President*) but also because the action diverted the American squadron from its pursuit of the Jamaica convoy.

Rodger's squadron captured few prizes during its cruise in the summer of 1812, but that cruise was nonetheless of enormous strategic significance. When Vice Admiral Herbert Sawyer, commander of Britain's Halifax squadron, learned from the *Belvidera* that the nations were at war, he considered detaching his ships for service along the American coast to intercept returning American merchantmen. But the *Belvidera* also brought news that there was a squadron of American warships cruising the Atlantic, and Sawyer feared that his ships might be defeated in detail if he spread them out along the coast. Hence, he kept his squadron intact, and with Captain Philip Broke of the frigate *Shannon* (52 guns) in command, he ordered the squadron to make a sweep through American waters in the summer of 1812. The squadron failed to capture many prizes. "We have been so completely occupied looking for Commodore Rodgers's squadron," one British naval officer complained, "that we have taken very few prizes."[17] This meant that hundreds of American merchantmen reached port safely. A local newspaper reported that 266 merchant vessels arrived in New York Harbor alone between April 6 and August 22, 1812. This surge in trade replenished the nation's stockpile of imported goods, boosted the customs revenue, and provided a large pool of seamen for the warships and privateers that were fitting out. Small as it was, the U.S. Navy actually prevented the British from blockading the American coast in the early months of the war.

The Cruises of the 'Constitution'

Few Americans appreciated the service performed by Rodgers's squadron in the summer of 1812 because their attention was on the feats of individual warships. The U.S. Frigate *Constitution* (55 guns), commanded by Captain Isaac Hull (the nephew and adopted son of the disgraced general, William Hull), was spotted by the Halifax squadron on July 16 and made sail to get away. Normally, the *Constitution* could have outdistanced her pursuers, but the wind died down. To keep the British at bay, Hull mounted guns on his stern and undertook a series of laborious maneuvers to propel his ship forward. First, he used his boats to tow the ship. Then, discovering he was in shallow water, he sent his boats ahead to drop anchor, his men then drawing in the rope to pull the ship forward (a maneuver known as "kedging"). The wind periodically picked up, and Hull took full advantage of it, on one occasion wetting his sails to better hold the breeze. In the course of the chase, Hull demonstrated remarkable seamanship, but the British matched each of his maneuvers to keep pace. Finally, after the wind picked up again, the *Constitution* got away and made it safely to Boston. The 57-hour chase became the talk of the nation, and even Hull's British pursuers conceded that his performance was "elegant."[18]

Hull's chase was but a prelude to more glorious service by the *Constitution*. Remaining in port only long enough to resupply his ship, Hull quickly set sail again. On August 19, about 750 miles east of Boston, the *Constitution* (55 guns) encountered the British frigate *Guerrière* (49 guns),

Captain Isaac Hull (1773–1843), commanding officer aboard the U.S. Frigate *Constitution*, electrified American opinion with success at sea. First, he managed to escape a British squadron, and then he defeated the British frigate *Guerrière*. Having experienced enough of the horrors of war, Hull sat out the rest of the conflict as head of the Portsmouth Navy Yard. (Library of Congress)

Africa   CONSTITUTION   Shannon   Æolus   Guerriere   Belvidera

Constitution's Escape from the British Squadron after a chase of sixty hours

Captain James R. Dacres commanding. *Constitution's* weight of broadside was much heavier than *Guerrière's*, and after some maneuvering the American ship delivered a broadside of double-shotted fire at 100 yards. Some 700 pounds of metal hit the British ship, forcing it to "reel and tremble as though she had received the shock of an earthquake."[19] The two ships continued to exchange fire and twice collided and then separated. The overmatched *Guerrière* lost her masts and sustained significant damage to her hull. Many of her crew members were also knocked out of action. Two hours into the battle, with his ship immobilized and in ruins, Dacres was forced to surrender. Unable to save the *Guerrière,* Hull sent her to the bottom the next day.

The victory over the *Guerrière* was particularly gratifying because the ship had been one of the most aggressive and obnoxious British warships patrolling the American coast before the war. Moreover, its officers were spoiling for a fight, eager to avenge the *President's* attack on the *Little Belt* the year before. In fact, the words "*Guerrière*" and "*Not the Little Belt*" were painted on its sails. Besides being the first American frigate victory of the war, the battle attained legendary status in the United States for another reason. When an American seaman noticed that during the engagement British round shot bounced off the American ship's thick hull, he commented: "Huzza! Her sides are made of iron!"[20] Thus was born the nickname "Ironsides," which almost instantly became "Old Ironsides."

When the wind failed, the *Constitution*'s boats tried to haul the big ship out of range of a pursuing British squadron. (Engraving by William Hoogland. Library of Congress)

The *Constitution* defeated the *Guerrière* in the first of three U.S. victories against overmatched British frigates. This engagement earned the American ship the nickname "Old Ironsides." (Engraving by Alonzo Chappel. Library of Congress)

Nor was "Old Ironsides" done. On December 29, while cruising off the coast of Brazil, the American ship, now carrying 54 guns and under the command of Commodore William Bainbridge, met another British frigate, the *Java* (49 guns), Captain Henry Lambert commanding. The American ship again relied on superior firepower and marksmanship to destroy the British ship. Completely dismasted, the *Java* was unable to move and thus had to surrender. Bainbridge removed the surviving crew members and passengers and sank the British ship. Both commanders sustained wounds. Lambert's were mortal, and he died five days later.

Other Naval Engagements

While the *Constitution* was winning its laurels, another heavy American frigate, the *United States* (56 guns) was proving itself. Commanded by Captain Stephen Decatur, the American ship on October 25 met the British frigate *Macedonian* (49 guns), Captain John S. Carden commanding, 600 miles west of the Canary Islands. Although the American ship was known as "the Wagon" because it was a poor sailer, Decatur took advantage of the ship's great firepower to stand off and batter the *Macedonian* into submission. Decatur managed to salvage his prize and shepherd it safely into an American port. For many years thereafter, the U.S. Navy kept the *Macedonian* on the rolls as a trophy ship, a visible reminder that a British frigate had once struck its colors to an American frigate.

Several other naval engagements early in the war also went America's way. On October 18, 1812, the U.S. Sloop *Wasp* (18 guns) defeated the British sloop *Frolic* (22 guns) off the coast of Virginia, and on February 24, 1813, the U.S. Sloop *Hornet* (20 guns) defeated the British sloop *Peacock* (20 guns) off the coast of British Guiana. The small American frigate *Essex* (which was overloaded with 46 guns) defeated the British brig *Alert* (18 guns?) and captured a troop transport carrying 160 soldiers from Barbados to Canada. Although the Royal Navy captured the *Wasp*, the *Nautilus* (14 guns), and the *Vixen* (14 guns), the balance in the campaign of 1812 at sea was clearly in America's favor.

The Constitution won its second great victory over the British frigate *Java*. (Engraving by J. Coquerel. Library of Congress)

Impact of American Naval Victories

The American victories at sea were strategically unimportant but gave a huge boost to American morale and took some of the sting out of the military disasters on the Canadian frontier. "Our brilliant naval victories," commented an army officer, "serve, in some measure, to wipe out the disgrace brought upon the Nation by the conduct of our generals."[21] The victories were especially sweet because they came against the Mistress of the Seas in her own element. "British arms cannot withstand American upon the sea," exulted a Republican congressman. "The bully has been disgraced by an infant."[22] Although Americans distorted the relative strength of the opposing ships in each duel to magnify the American victories, there was no denying that the Royal Navy had been embarrassed.

In Great Britain, on the other hand, the naval losses, particularly the three frigate defeats, went down hard. In 20 years of warfare with France and Spain, the British navy had waged some 200 single-ship duels, and the number of times they had lost could be counted on one hand. By contrast, Americans had won the first five naval engagements of the War of 1812, and in the process they had taken one frigate as a prize of war and sent two others to the bottom of the sea. "It is a cruel mortification," said a cabinet official, "to be beat by these second-

CAPTURE of H.B.M. FRIGATE MACEDONIAN, Captᵗ JOHN S. CARDEN by the U.S. FRIGATE UNITED STATES, STEPHEN DECATUR Esqʳ Commander.

Under the command of Captain Stephen Decatur (1779–1820), the heavy frigate *United States* defeated the light frigate *Macedonian*. Decatur managed to get his prize to an American port, and for many years thereafter the U.S. Frigate *Macedonian* sailed the seas as an American trophy ship. (Engraving by Benjamin Tanner based on a painting by Thomas Birch. Library of Congress)

hand Englishmen upon our own element."[23] Although some British observers, most notably the London *Times*, acknowledged the merits of American ships and sailors, most assumed that the Royal Navy had been defeated by some form of trickery. There was no shame in losing to a more powerful ship, which in every case was what actually happened, but the British preferred to believe that American frigates were ships-of-the-line in disguise and that American crews consisted of picked men who were heavily British. None of this was true.

Criticism of the British government mounted with every defeat, and the ministry responded by launching a crash program to build heavy frigates. The Admiralty also confidentially advised its frigate commanders not "to engage, single handed, the larger Class of American Ships; which, though they may be called Frigates, are of a size, Complem[e]nt and weight of Metal much beyond that Class, and more resembling Line of Battle Ships."[24] This order was by itself an extraordinary admission that, small as it was, the U.S. Navy now commanded considerable respect in Great Britain.

Privateering

If U.S. warships performed well in 1812, so, too, did American privateers. Also called "letters-of-marque," privateers were privately owned vessels that secured a commission from their government to carry arms and cruise against enemy commerce. Although privateers might be built expressly for commerce raiding, in most cases they were simply fast merchant vessels that were pierced to carry naval guns. Privateers needed speed not only to run down enemy merchant vessels but also to elude enemy warships, whose firepower and manpower they could rarely match.

Privateering came of age in the Second Hundred Years War (1689–1815), and practically every belligerent nation issued commissions. Governments liked privateering because it gave employment to ships and seamen at a time when normal trade might be disrupted or risky. It also enabled nations without much of a navy to wage warfare at sea on the cheap. Far from requiring any public funds, privateers actually brought in revenue because governments took a portion of the proceeds when prize goods were sold.

In the United States, privateers were known as "the militia of the sea." Privateering was immensely popular in the young republic because it represented a kind of democratic entrepreneurialism well suited to the rugged individualism of the age. Once war was declared in 1812, privateering commissions were eagerly sought. "The spirit of privateering prevails," an observer in the nation's capital pointed out.

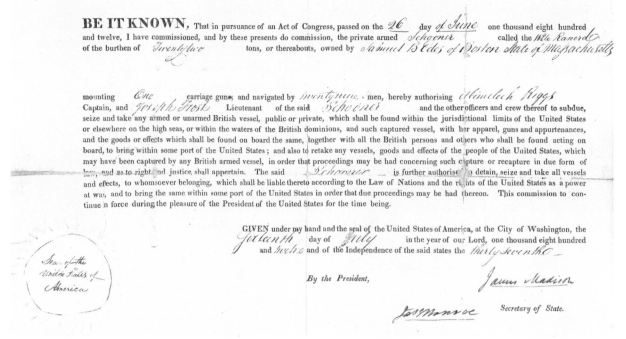

BE IT KNOWN, That in pursuance of an Act of Congress, passed on the *26* day *of June* one thousand eight hundred and twelve, I have commissioned, and by these presents do commission, the private armed *Schooner* called the *Wile Ranerd* of the burthen of *Twenty two* tons, or thereabouts, owned by *Samuel B Edes of Boston State of Massachusetts*

mounting *One* carriage guns; and navigated by *twenty nine* men, hereby authorising *Abimelech Riggs* Captain, and *Joseph Frost* Lieutenant of the said *Schooner* and the other officers and crew thereof to subdue, seize and take any armed or unarmed British vessel, public or private, which shall be found within the jurisdictional limits of the United States or elsewhere on the high seas, or within the waters of the British dominions, and such captured vessel, with her apparel, guns and appurtenances, and the goods or effects which shall be found on board the same, together with all the British persons and others who shall be found acting on board, to bring within some port of the United States; and also to retake any vessels, goods and effects of the people of the United States, which may have been captured by any British armed vessel, in order that proceedings may be had concerning such capture or recapture in due form of law, and as to right and justice shall appertain. The said *Schooner* is further authorised to detain, seize and take all vessels and effects, to whomsoever belonging, which shall be liable thereto according to the Law of Nations and the rights of the United States as a power at war, and to bring the same within some port of the United States in order that due proceedings may be had thereon. This commission to continue in force during the pleasure of the President of the United States for the time being.

GIVEN under my hand and the seal of the United States of America, at the City of Washington, the *Fourteenth* day of *July* in the year of our Lord, one thousand eight hundred and *twelve* and of the Independence of the said states the *Thirty seventh*

By the President,

James Madison

Jas Monroe Secretary of State.

Seal of the United States of America

A privateering commission, issued less than a month after the declaration of war, authorized the schooner *Wile Ranerd* of Boston to cruise against British commerce. The privateer carried only one gun, but that was enough against unarmed British merchantmen at the beginning of the war. (Courtesy of Peabody Essex Museum)

"Young men crowd in this Metropolis for commissions."[25] The first commissions were issued at the end of June, about ten days after the declaration of war.

The first privateers were mostly small pilot boats equipped with one large center pivot gun, known as a "Long Tom." These vessels carried 50 or 60 men armed with muskets, sabers, boarding pikes, and the like. According to one privateer captain, this "was quite enough to capture almost any British merchantman, at this stage of the war."[26] Later, when British merchants armed their ships, Americans had to increase the manpower and firepower of their privateers.

American privateers found a rich harvest in 1812. Cruising mainly in the Gulf of St. Lawrence and the West Indies, letters-of-marque took 450 prizes in the first six months of the war. "Our Privateers," reported a Richmond merchant in September, "bring in Prizes to almost every Port & many of these of great value."[27] Several armed ships enjoyed a particularly rich haul. The *Yankee* (15 guns) out of Bristol, Rhode Island, took eight prizes valued at $300,000, and the *Rossie* (15 guns), commanded by Joshua Barney of Baltimore, captured 18 vessels worth almost $1,500,000.

A Halifax newspaper reported in July that American privateers "were swarming round our coast" and that it was "very imprudent" for any vessel to sail except

The American privateers that raced to sea early in the war usually carried just one gun, known as a "Long Tom." (Edward S. Ellis, *The History of Our Country*)

American privateers sent to sea before British merchants learned of the declaration of war did considerable damage to British trade. Shown here, the *America,* sailing out of Salem, was considered one of the fastest and reportedly took 26 prizes in three successful cruises. (Library of Congress)

in convoy.[28] Reports from the West Indies were similar. A letter from Guadeloupe said that the waters there were infested with American privateers and that "the navy force upon the station is not sufficient for the protection of the islands."[29] Although British warships operating in the New World captured 150 American privateers in the first eight months of the war, the western Atlantic had nonetheless become dangerous for any unarmed British vessel sailing without an escort.

Privateering, however, cut both ways. Although British warships constituted the biggest menace to American merchantmen, privateers commissioned in the mother country or in the Maritime Provinces of Canada also preyed on American shipping. Because technically any prizes captured before Great Britain declared war on the United States on October 13, 1812, belonged to the Crown, Canadian privateers were slow to act. Only six were commissioned in 1812, and they took only 24 prizes, mainly by cruising along the nearby American coast. Sailing out of Liverpool, Nova Scotia, the successful *Liverpool Packet* (5 guns), which already had a commission to cruise against French ships, decided in August to target American ships. As a result, she had to fight for some of her prizes twice, first at sea and then in the British courts. By the end of the year, privateering was having a visible economic impact on the Maritime Provinces. Halifax was busy preparing ships for cruises and adjudicating prizes, and the British naval base there provided a ready market for captured food, naval stores, and ships.

Conclusion

Despite their successes on the high seas, Americans had every reason to be disappointed with the outcome of the campaign of 1812 and the British every reason to be satisfied. Not only did Canada remain in British hands, but in the West the British and their Indian allies controlled Michigan Territory and posed a significant threat to settlers on the frontier in Illinois, Indiana, and Ohio. Moreover, the clock was now ticking against the United States. Napoleon's invasion of Russia in the summer of 1812 had ended in disaster, and by the end of the year the tide appeared to be turning against the once invincible French emperor. If the war in Europe ended before the War of 1812, all hope of achieving American war aims would vanish, and the United States might find itself alone in the field against a powerful and relentless foe.

CHAPTER THREE

Don't Give Up the Ship

By the end of 1812 Republican leaders were in a somber mood. Not only had the campaign gone badly, but Federalists remained implacable in their opposition, and even some Republicans were now grumbling. Republican leaders had hoped that the decision for war would force everyone to rally to the flag, but that had not happened. Most Republicans had fallen into line, and some moderate Federalists in the middle and southern states had talked of dropping their opposition, too. But Federalists in New England had remained intransigent, and a host of Republican missteps shortly after the declaration of war had driven other Federalists back into New England's camp.

First of all, Republicans had refused to jettison the non-importation act of 1811 even though the restrictive system had always been defended as an alternative to war. Trade restrictions still had the support of many Republicans, including some War Hawks. "If you cling to the restrictive system," said Henry Clay, "it is incessantly working in your favor," and "if persisted in, the restrictive system, aiding the war, would break down the present [British] Ministry, and lead to a consequent honorable peace."[1] In addition, Republicans had embraced a discriminatory tax policy, doubling the customs duties (to 33%) while postponing any action on the proposed internal taxes. Since Federalists dominated many of the coastal areas that consumed imported goods, this looked like an attempt to saddle those who opposed the war with its costs. No less galling, Republicans in Congress conceded publicly that they had postponed the internal taxes for political reasons. "It was admitted by the ruling party in debate," said an exasperated Virginia Federalist, "that to impose [the internal taxes] now would endanger their success in the next election."[2]

Most disturbing of all, a series of vicious pro-war riots in the summer of 1812 had targeted the *Federal Republican,* an anti-war newspaper in Baltimore, leaving one Federalist dead and a half dozen others with serious injuries. Among the victims were two Revolutionary War heroes, Brigadier General James M. Lingan, who was stabbed to death, and Major General Light-Horse Harry Lee (the father of Robert E. Lee), who sustained internal injuries from which he never recovered. Nor was this incident unique. Republican mobs drove other Federalist newspapers out of business in Savannah, Georgia, and Norristown, Pennsylvania, and Federalist editors elsewhere in the middle and southern states were warned to tone down their opposition or risk a similar fate. To Federalists, this violence put the war in an entirely new light. "The war, pretendedly for freedom of the seas," complained the *Connecticut Courant,* "is valiantly waged against the freedom of the press."[3]

The Election of 1812

Dissatisfaction with the war effort was a matter of considerable import in late 1812 because the nation was in the middle of a presidential election. In those days, national elections were less uniform and more decentralized than they are today. It was not until 1848 that all states chose their presidential electors on the same day and not until 1860 that all the electors were chosen by popular vote. In 1812, each state followed its own timetable and had its own system for selecting presidential electors. About half of the states put the choice of presidential electors in the hands of the voters; the remainder left the selection up to the legislature.

The Virginia legislature launched the campaign in February 1812 by selecting presidential electors committed to Madison. In the ensuing months, seven other state legislatures followed suit. At a widely publicized congressional caucus in May (a month before war was declared), about two-thirds of the Republicans endorsed Madison for the presidency and John Langdon for the vice presidency. (When the elderly Langdon declined, Elbridge Gerry, the former governor of Massachusetts, was substituted.) Republican congressmen from New York and other northern states withheld their support. Disillusioned with the restrictive system and unhappy with the administration's lack of support for a navy, they believed that Virginians had held the presidency long enough. Hoping to capitalize on this sentiment, the New York legislature endorsed De Witt Clinton, the handsome and popular mayor of New York City who was nicknamed "Magnus Apollo." Although many Federalists distrusted Clinton, they realized that they had no chance of electing one of their own. At a Federalist convention held in

New York City in September, the delegates stopped short of openly endorsing Clinton but urged support for electors "most likely by their votes to effect a change in the present course of measures."[4] The Federalist convention offered no one for the vice presidency, but Jared Ingersoll, onetime attorney general of Pennsylvania, became the accepted candidate after being nominated by friends in his home state.

Candidates in the early republic usually tried to give the impression that they were not seeking office but that the office was seeking them. Thus, they "stood" for office rather than running for it. In accordance with this practice, Madison and Clinton did no campaigning and made no public appearances soliciting votes. Instead, the case was made by their followers. The campaign focused on the wisdom of the war and how it was waged. Madison's supporters argued that the war was necessary, that the president

In the election of 1812, New Yorker De Witt Clinton (1769–1828) appealed to those northerners who had grown weary of the Virginia Dynasty and to people everywhere who thought that, one way or another, he would put a speedy end to the war. Despite the support of Federalists and northern Republicans, Clinton came up short. (Library of Congress)

could not be blamed for setbacks in the field, and that Clinton was a Cromwell or Judas who had betrayed the party by joining forces with the Federalists. Clinton's followers retorted that Madison was a weak leader and that his supporters had embraced the British doctrine that the king could do no wrong. They portrayed Clinton as a bold and energetic man who was friendly to the navy and commerce. In pro-war states, he was presented as one who would shorten the war by prosecuting it more vigorously; in anti-war states, he would achieve this end by negotiating with the British. This was too much for Madison's followers, who accused Clinton of inconsistency. As a character in a contemporary play put it, "He cannot have *war* and *peace at the same time*."[5]

The election was determined by state action over a two-month period in late 1812, and the outcome was by no means certain. The voting followed the same sectional pattern as the vote on the declaration of war. Clinton did well in the North, Madison in the South and West. To win, Clinton needed New York's 29 electoral votes and Pennsylvania's 25. He had no trouble winning the former, thanks to shrewd maneuvering in the legislature by 29-year-old Martin Van Buren, who thenceforth would be known as the "Little Magician." But Madison prevailed in the Keystone State, aided in no small part by a booming economy fueled by large military contracts and a rich overseas trade. It was "pretty close work," commented Richard Rush, who was Madison's comptroller of the treasury, "and Pennsylvania,

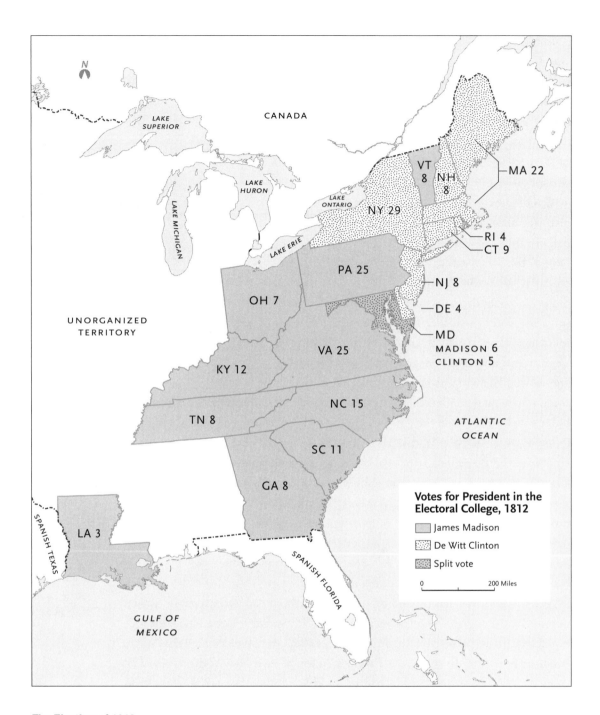

The Election of 1812

In the closely contested presidential election of 1812, James Madison (Republican) received 128 electoral votes from 11 states and De Witt Clinton (Independent) received 89 from 7 states. If Pennsylvania had voted for Clinton, he would have unseated Madison.

as usual, carries the union on her back."[6] Madison ended up with 128 electoral votes to Clinton's 89.

If the presidential election indicated dissatisfaction with the Republican administration, so, too, did the congressional and state elections. Although Republicans retained control of both houses of Congress, the proportion of seats they held slipped from 75 to 63 percent in the House, and from 82 to 78 percent in the Senate. On paper, the Republicans still had comfortable majorities in both houses, but factionalism within the party often doomed administration proposals. Republicans also saw the number of states they controlled decline from 14 (out of 17) to 11. In addition, Republicans lost their majority in the New York Assembly and sustained small to moderate losses in almost every other state east of the Appalachian Mountains. Republicans had every reason to be disappointed with these results, and Federalists every reason to rejoice.

Men and Money

Shortly after the outcome of the election was known, President Madison shored up his cabinet by getting rid of his secretary of war, William Eustis, and his secretary of the navy, Paul Hamilton, neither of whom had shown much capacity for their wartime duties, and both of whom had come under growing criticism. "The clamor against the gentlemen who are at the head of the War and Navy Departments," reported a congressional Republican in early October, "is loud & very general."[7]

Madison had trouble finding a replacement for Eustis because the War Department was known to be an administrative nightmare. He finally settled on John Armstrong of New York, an experienced public servant not without ability but who was given to indolence and intrigue. It was well known that Armstrong had authored the Newburgh Letters at the end of the American Revolution, inciting the Continental Army to mutiny, and now as head of the War Department he feuded with two other cabinet officials, Albert Gallatin and James Monroe, which greatly weakened the administration. Madison had better luck with his choice for the Navy Department. William Jones, a Philadelphia merchant, did a good job running the navy, although several years after the war he was discredited for mismanaging the National Bank.

On November 2, 1812, while the election was still in doubt, the Twelfth Congress met for its second and last session. In his opening address, Madison tried to put the best face on the war and recommended a number of measures to promote the war effort. Before any action could be taken, however, a full-scale debate on

(*left*) John Armstrong (1758–1843) replaced the incompetent William Eustis as secretary of war in late 1812. Although Armstrong had talent, he also had a penchant for intrigue that undermined his effectiveness in this crucial cabinet position. Later, when the nation's capital was burned, he took the heat and was forced to resign. (Portrait by John Wesley Jarvis. National Portrait Gallery, Smithsonian Institution)

(*right*) William Jones (1760–1831) replaced Paul Hamilton in the Navy Department in late 1812. He proved a capable administrator who deserves some of the credit for the naval victories that ensued on the northern lakes. (Portrait by Gilbert Stuart. Courtesy of Naval History & Heritage Command, Washington, DC)

the war erupted, pushing all other business aside for two weeks. House Federalists, who had remained silent during the secret proceedings on the war bill the previous June, now made their case, and Republicans responded in kind. The speeches were so long-winded that they tested everyone's patience. Even John Randolph, who was no fan of brevity, conceded that the debate in the House had become "unnecessarily protracted."[8]

The debate, which centered on the merits of the war and the wisdom and justice of targeting Canada, never really ended, although eventually it subsided enough to allow Republicans to push through war legislation. To increase the army, Congress authorized 22,000 one-year recruits, bringing the authorized level of the regular force to 57,000. The basic pay of troops was raised from $5 to $8 a month and the cash bounty from $31 to $40. In addition, Congress prohibited arresting soldiers for debt. In the flush of the navy's success, Congress also embraced naval expansion, authorizing the construction of four 74-gun battleships and six 44-gun frigates. Although none of these ships was put into service before the war was over, the law committed the nation to a long-term naval construction program. On tax measures, however, Republicans remained divided. Despite the nation's deteriorating finances, Congress still refused to consider internal taxes, and it took intense lobbying from the administration to get the body to endorse a special session (set for May) of the newly elected Thirteenth Congress to consider additional revenue measures.

The new Congress met for its special session on May 24, 1813. With reduced Republican majorities, this congress was more obstreperous than its predecessor. John C. Calhoun claimed that party spirit "was more violent than I ever knew," and another observer thought that in the Senate independent Republicans— "the malcontent junto of self-called Republicans"—were worse than the Federalists.[9] Congress was unaccustomed to meeting in the summer, and the Washington heat got to almost everyone. A New York congressman claimed that by June it was "hotter in this house than purgatory" and that during secret proceedings in July "the doors were closed and we were boiled and roasted three hours longer, almost to suffocation."[10]

Even in the best of times, President Madison was not a commanding leader, and during this session he was bedridden with dysentery and appeared to be near death. In the cabinet, there was much bickering and backbiting, and Postmaster General Gideon Granger, who was a Clintonian, was openly hostile to the administration. Even without these distractions, many Senate Republicans were unwilling to follow the administration's lead. Fortunately, good sense prevailed on public finance, and the long-delayed internal taxes were finally adopted, although their operation was put off until the end of the year. No doubt everyone was anxious to flee Washington once the session ended in early August, although factionalism afflicted the Republican party to the end. Fearing that the Senate might select an anti-administration Republican as president pro tem, Vice President Elbridge Gerry refused to follow custom by vacating his seat as the presiding officer. This ensured that if anything happened to the ailing Madison and to Gerry (who was 69 years old and in poor health), the presidency would go to the reliable Henry Clay, who as speaker of the house was next in the line of succession.

John C. Calhoun (1782–1850) was emerging as a force to be reckoned with in the House of Representatives. At this stage in his career, the South Carolina leader was a strong nationalist who was part of the coterie of War Hawks who pushed the nation into war and favored a vigorous prosecution of the contest. (Benson J. Lossing, *Pictorial Field-Book of the War of 1812*)

American and British Strategy in 1813

For the campaign of 1813, the United States could count on about 30,000 regulars, while the British had about 20,000 regulars and quasi-regulars (that is, locally raised fencible and provincial units). The United States again took the offensive and planned another multi-pronged invasion of Canada, while the British remained on the defensive. Although the new secretary of war, John Armstrong, sometimes issued vague or contradictory orders, the broad outlines of the campaign were laid down in the spring. American forces in the West would try to

(*left*) Commodore Isaac Chauncey (1779–1840) was put in charge of Lake Ontario and Lake Erie in the fall of 1812 when the administration realized that it needed to control these waterways to achieve any success in Canada. Chauncey was a decent but cautious and uninspired commander. (Benson J. Lossing, *Pictorial Field-Book of the War of 1812*)

(*right*) Commodore Sir James Yeo (1782–1818) was Chauncey's counterpart on Lake Ontario and Lake Erie. Like Chauncey, he was cautious, but this made more sense for the British because their strategy was largely defensive. (Benson J. Lossing, *Pictorial Field-Book of the War of 1812*)

retake the Michigan Territory and then invade Upper Canada across the Detroit River. To the east, American troops would target Kingston and York on Lake Ontario and then assault British positions on the Niagara River. If all went well in the earlier operations, Montreal might be targeted, although initially Armstrong envisioned no more than a demonstration there to tie up British troops.

The campaign of 1812 had demonstrated that the conquest of Canada would not be a cakewalk and that it was crucial to control the waterways to facilitate the movement of men and material through the wilderness. Hence, all eyes were on the lakes, particularly Erie and Ontario. The British had undisputed control of both lakes in 1812, and this had contributed to their military success. If the United States was to avoid failure again, it needed to seize control of the lakes. "The success of the ensuing campaign," said the new U.S. secretary of the navy, "will depend absolutely upon our superiority on all the Lakes—& every effort & resource must be directed to that object."[11]

To assume command of American forces on the Great Lakes, the United States chose Commodore Isaac Chauncey, a 40-year-old veteran naval officer. Chauncey took charge of Lake Ontario. To take command on Lake Erie, Chauncey relied initially on 30-year-old Lieutenant Jesse D. Elliott before replacing him with the younger but more seasoned Oliver H. Perry, a 27-year-old master commandant eager to escape gunboat service in Newport, Rhode Island. The British, whose own forces on the two lakes had been under the command of the Provincial Marine, an antiquated army transport service, countered by putting the Royal Navy in charge. Thirty-year-old Commodore Sir James Yeo took command of Lake

Ontario and put 26-year-old Acting Commander Robert H. Barclay in charge of Lake Erie. Both men were experienced Royal Navy officers who had seen considerable combat and had the wounds to prove it. Barclay, who had served with Lord Nelson at Trafalgar, had lost an arm in the service and had sustained numerous other combat wounds.

In the shipbuilding contest that ensued, the United States had the edge. There were experienced shipbuilders and plenty of out-of-work shipwrights on the eastern seaboard who could be recruited to work on the lakes; all the necessary building materials were readily available in the United States; and the supply lines to the lakes from the principal manufacturing centers (mainly New York, Philadelphia, and Pittsburgh) were relatively secure. The British, by contrast, had to ship most of their men and material across the Atlantic and then up the St. Lawrence River, which was in a war zone. Although the United States was able to capitalize on its advantages and win the building contest on Lake Erie, it was unable to duplicate the feat on Lake Ontario. As a result, the outcome of the conflict on the two lakes was very different.

The Appearance of Uncle Sam

Before the campaign of 1813 was fairly under way, an important figure made his first appearance on the American stage. The campaign of 1812 had illustrated the critical importance of logistics, and by 1813 the U.S. government was signing ever more supply contracts. The result was a growing number of manufactured goods that were stamped with the initials "U.S." This, in turn, produced one of the first references to Uncle Sam, who is now the universally recognized symbol for the United States government.

In early 1813 a broadside, apparently published in eastern New York, perhaps near Troy, contained doggerel that made two references to Uncle Sam. In the first case, Napoleon says: "If uncle Sam needs, I'd be glad to assist him,/ For it makes my heart bleed we live at such a distance." In the second, Commodore John Rodgers, alluding to an Anglo-Indian alliance, says: "He builds on the Indians that now with him join'd,/ But if Uncle Sam lives, they will all be Burgoyn'd"—a reference to the fate of Major General John Burgoyne in the Battle of Saratoga during the American Revolution.[12]

"Uncle Sam" seems to have grown out of the term "U.S." and may owe something to an army supplier in Troy, New York, who was named Samuel Wilson and was affectionately known as "Uncle Sam." Initially the phrase was heard only in the army, but newspapers quickly picked it up, and by the fall of 1813 the Troy *Post*

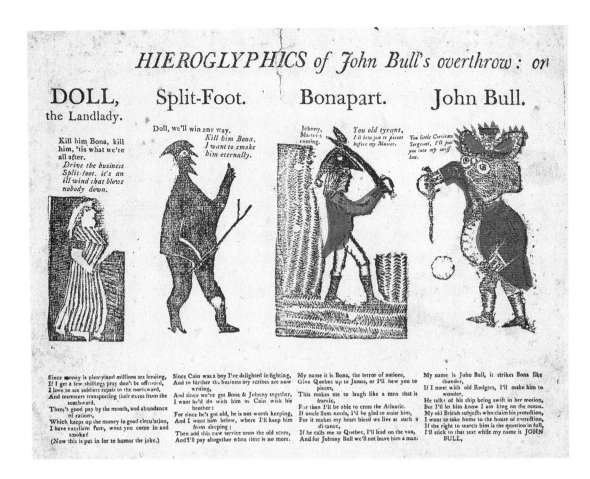

HIEROGLYPHICS of John Bull's overthrow: or

DOLL,
the Landlady.

Kill him Bona, kill him, 'tis what we're all after.
Drive the business Split-foot. it's an ill wind that blows nobody down.

Since money is plenty and millions are lending,
If I get a few shillings pray don't be offended,
I love to see soldiers repair to the northward,
And teamsters transporting their stores from the southward.
There's good pay by the month, and abundance of rations,
Which keeps up the money in good circulation,
I have excellent fum, wont you come in and smoke?
(Now this is put in for to humor the joke.)

Split-Foot.

Doll, we'll win any way.
Kill him Bona, I want to smoke him eternally.

Since Cain was a boy I've delighted in fighting,
And to further the business my scribes are now writing,
And since we've got Bona & Johnny together,
I want he'd do with him as Cain with his brother:
For since he's got old, he is not worth keeping,
And I want him below, where I'll keep him from sleeping;
Then add this new service unto the old score,
And I'll pay altogether when time is no more.

Bonapart.

Johnny, Master's coming.
You old tyrant, I'll hew you to pieces before my Master.

My name it is Bona, the terror of nations,
Give Quebec up to James, or I'll hew you to pieces,
This makes me to laugh like a man that is frantic,
For then I'll be able to cross the Atlantic.
If uncle Sam needs, I'd be glad to assist him,
For it makes my heart bleed we live at such a distance,
If he calls me to Quebec, I'll lead on the van,
And for Johnny Bull we'll not leave him a man.

John Bull.

You little Corsican Sergeant, I'll put you into my snuff box.

My name is John Bull, it strikes Bona like thunder,
If I meet with old Rodgers, I'll make him to wonder,
He talks of his ship being swift in her motion,
But I'll let him know I am king on the ocean,
My old British subjects who claim his protection,
I want to take home to the house of correction,
If the right to search him is the question in full,
I'll stick to that text while my name is JOHN BULL,

(*above and opposite*)
A broadside, probably produced in the spring of 1813 in eastern New York, celebrates American victories. It has early references to "Uncle Sam" (see the verses under the third and eighth illustrations). Tradition holds that "Uncle" Sam Wilson, a government contractor in Troy, New York, was the inspiration for using this phrase for the American government, but the evidence is far from conclusive. (The Granger Collection)

claimed: "This cant name for our government has got almost as current as 'John Bull' (for the British). The letters U.S. on the government waggons, etc. are supposed to have given rise to it."[13] An image of Uncle Sam did not appear until 1832, and he did not assume his modern form—as a gaunt and aging man decked out in striped pants and a top hat—until the 1870s, when Thomas Nast depicted him in cartoons for *Harper's Weekly,* Nevertheless, Uncle Sam made his debut during the War of 1812, and he has been an American fixture ever since.

The Assault on Fort Meigs and Fort Stephenson

Early in the campaign of 1813, the British took advantage of their control of Lake Erie to launch two operations into Ohio in the hope of disrupting American preparations in the West and pushing them further back from the frontier. As a base for his operations, Major General William Henry Harrison had built a new

A View of the Northern Expedition in Miniature.

James War. Tom Patriot. John Adams. John Rogers:

Kill him Bona, kill him & I'll take Canada.

Here comes No. 1. Let me at him Bona & I'll take him down

Kill him Bona, & I'll pay all damages.

Let me at him Bona, and I'll blow him to atoms.

Columbia, Columbia, to glory arise,
Fly quick to the north, make Canada a prize,
While it's mine to command, it is your's to obey,
Then all hands make ready to seize on the prey.
We'll repair to the northward, sick close by the lines,
Lest we get too far in those northerly climes,
When the winter sets in, to Greenbush we'll retire,
And smoak our long pipes by the side of the fire.

Starvation's the fate of the British empire,
My destructive machine will soon make them expire,
Methinks I will make them come under my thumb,
With my little bark that mounts only one gun,
I will bring them to terms by the force of this measure,
Then we'll go abroad & return home at pleasure,
We'll sail to sweet France, & in ev'ry direction,
And no British tyrant demand our protection.

My name is Taxation—in my introduction,
Some people I vext, to prevent their destruction,
Had I in the place of some others been sitting,
I'd built me a navy to cope with Great Britain.
But now I'm retir'd, sees the states in a bustle,
And all I'm afraid, paid too dear for the whistle,
One caution I'd give you before that I leave you,
I'd send Barlow to Bona, and borrow a navy.

My fleet to John Bull no true homage will pay,
Though his orders in council forever should stay ;
He talks of a right for to search for his slaves,
Before I grant that I shall sink in the waves :
He had better be silent and send me no threat,'
Lest I catch his fish in my old yankee net,
He builds on the Indians that's now with him, join'd,
But if Uncle Sam lives, they will all be Burgoyn'd.

fort on the east bank of the Maumee River at the rapids in present-day Perrysburg, Ohio. Named after Return J. Meigs, the popular governor of the state, the fort was exceptionally strong. It was ringed by log pickets, earthworks, and abatis and was protected by batteries and blockhouses that commanded all approaches. Huge interior earthworks, called traverses, offered additional protection to the soldiers inside.

In the spring of 1813, Henry Procter, who had been promoted to brigadier general after his victory on the River Raisin, invaded Ohio with a force of 1,000 regulars and militia. At the Maumee River he was joined by Tecumseh and upwards of 1,200 Indians. His target was Fort Meigs, which was defended by 1,100 regulars and militia under Harrison's command. Procter mounted a siege on May 1, but his artillery was no match for the earthworks. On May 5, Brigadier General Green Clay arrived from Kentucky with a relief force of some 1,200 volunteer militia. Although Clay drove some of the British away and captured their batter-

The first phase of the nine-day siege of Fort Meigs, which culminated in the arrival of Green Clay's relief force on May 5. Clay's men, ignoring orders, pursued the retreating British and ran into a powerful counterattack that destroyed the force. Still, the fort survived the siege, which was lifted on May 9. (Alexander C. Casselman, *Richardson's War of 1812*)

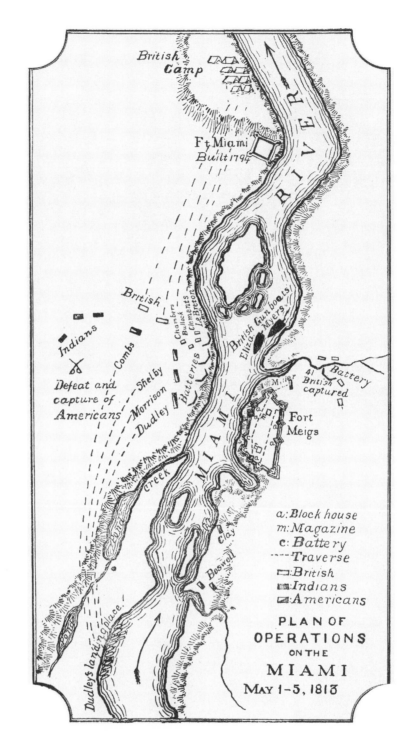

British Camp

Ft Miami
Built 1794

British

Indians

Defeat and capture of Americans

Combs

Shelby

Morrison

Dudley

Chambers
Bullock
Clements
LeBreton

Batteries

British Gun boats

Eliza

Myers

41 British captured

Battery

Miller

Fort Meigs

Creek

Clay

Boswell

Dudley's landing place.

MIAMI

RIVER

a: Block house
m: Magazine
c: Battery
----- Traverse
British
Indians
Americans

PLAN OF
OPERATIONS
ON THE
MIAMI
MAY 1–5, 1813

ies, his undisciplined militia recklessly continued their pursuit and ran into the jaws of a large and determined Anglo-Indian counterattack. About half of the Kentuckians were killed, wounded, or captured. Some 40 of the prisoners were then massacred by Indians, and only Tecumseh's intervention prevented further carnage. Procter called off the siege on May 9 after his Indian allies began to drift off with their plunder and his militia officers told him that their men (many of whom had already left) needed to return home to plant their corn. The British (excluding Indians) had sustained about 100 losses compared to 900 for the United States, but Fort Meigs remained in American hands.

In July 1813, Procter (now a major general) returned to Ohio with a force of 500 regulars and militia and 3,000 Indians. The invaders again targeted Fort Meigs, but since they lacked the necessary siege artillery, they hoped to lure the Americans into the open by staging a mock battle nearby. Green Clay, who was now in command of the fort, knew that no reinforcements were headed his way and refused the bait. Rather than attempt a costly assault, Procter detached 400

After the battle of Fort Meigs, some Indians at Fort Miami started killing American prisoners until Tecumseh intervened to halt the slaughter. (Robert Tomes, *Battles of America by Land and Sea*)

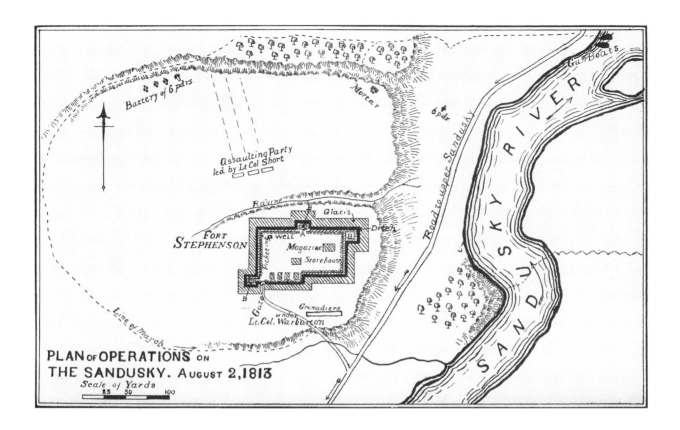

PLAN OF OPERATIONS ON THE SANDUSKY. AUGUST 2, 1813

The assault on Fort Stephenson. The British approached from the north but were cut down before they could breach the fort. (Alexander C. Casselman, *Richardson's War of 1812*)

regulars and a large body of Indians for an attack on Fort Stephenson on the Sandusky River in present-day Fremont, Ohio. The fort was held by 160 men under the command of 21-year-old Major George Croghan. Convinced that the fort was indefensible, Harrison ordered it abandoned, but Croghan demurred. "We have determined to maintain this place," he told Harrison, "and by heavens we can."[14] Facing this determination, Harrison relented.

On August 1, the British demanded the surrender of Fort Stephenson, but Croghan refused. The next day an artillery bombardment was followed by an attempt to storm the fort. When the British reached a ditch at the edge of the fort, they were cut down by Kentucky sharpshooters and a French 6-pounder that was nicknamed "Good Bess." Calling this "the severest Fire I ever saw," Procter called off the assault and marched his army back to Canada.[15] The attack had cost him close to 100 men, while Croghan had suffered only eight casualties. This marked the end of British offensive operations in the Old Northwest.

The Battle of Lake Erie

To challenge the British for control of Lake Erie, Commodore Isaac Chauncey in the late summer of 1812 ordered Lieutenant Jesse Elliott to Black Rock near Buffalo on the Niagara River. There Elliott was to develop a base and purchase small schooners that could be outfitted as gunboats. The following month Elliott led a mixed force of seamen, regulars, and local militia in a successful night attack on two small British brigs, the *Detroit* (6 guns) and *Caledonia* (3 guns) anchored under the guns of Fort Erie. Although the *Detroit* had to be burned after she ran aground, the Americans got the *Caledonia* safely across the river, contributing to the small but growing American naval presence at Black Rock.

Meanwhile, the administration had dispatched Daniel Dobbins, a sailing master, to the region with orders to construct gunboats. Much to Elliott's dismay, Dobbins had convinced the Navy Department that Presque Isle at Erie, Pennsylvania, was the best site for a base. There, under the direct command of Chauncey, Dobbins began constructing four gunboats. He was joined in early 1813 by Noah Brown, a master shipbuilder from New York who was authorized to oversee the

This illustration, from a late nineteenth-century textbook, shows the British assault on Fort Stephenson. The real damage in the battle was done by a small American fieldpiece and small arms fire, which cut the British down in a depression near the fort. (Engraving by Knapp. William Cullen Bryant and Sidney Howard Gay, *A Popular History of the United States*)

Master Commandant Oliver H. Perry (1785–1819) contributed to the capture of Fort George in the spring of 1813 and then engineered America's victory on Lake Erie late that summer. The latter, coupled with his terse after-action report, forever fixed his reputation in the annals of U.S. naval history. (Alexander C. Casselman, *Richardson's War of 1812*)

construction of two brigs that would be larger than anything then in service on the lake. Thus, when Chauncey sent Perry to take command in the spring of 1813, the young officer found that some of his warships—four schooners and the *Caledonia*—were at Black Rock while other vessels were under construction 100 miles away at Presque Isle.

In June 1813 Chauncey ordered Perry to consolidate his forces by moving his vessels from Black Rock to Presque Isle. Although Commander Barclay cruised the shoreline with part of his squadron, a fog enabled Perry to evade detection and accomplish his mission. This was the first of several instances of good luck that the young American naval officer enjoyed during the campaign. Despite recurring bouts of "bilious fever"—probably dysentery—Perry worked tirelessly with Brown and Dobbins to complete the ships under construction at Presque Isle.

The British had their own construction program under way at Malden on the Detroit River under the direction of Barclay and an able shipwright named William Bell, but because of chronic supply problems, their program was necessarily more modest and had to rely on makeshift expedients. Most of their resources went into building the *Detroit*, which had to be armed with artillery taken from Fort Amherstburg and outfitted with a set of improvised sails. Moreover, because of a failure to stock the *Detroit* with slow match, the British had to improvise to fire their artillery. Barclay also faced daunting problems manning his ships. Perry faced similar problems but had more success in overcoming them. Although both commanders had to fill out their ship crews with volunteers from the land forces, Perry had a larger number of experienced seamen on his ships.

By the end of July Perry's ships were ready to sail, but the young commander still faced the difficult and risky task of getting his two largest vessels over the sandbar that protected his base. The water there was so shallow that Perry had to strip the ships of their guns and use "camels" (floats) to lift the vessels so that they could be towed across the bar to open water. The ships were vulnerable during this maneuver, but once again Perry's luck held. Although Barclay's squadron had been nearby, it had withdrawn to the British side of the lake, probably to resupply.

Once Perry got his ships over the bar and properly armed, he sailed to Put-in-Bay on South Bass Island at the western end of the lake. This served as Perry's base for interdicting British shipping on the lake. Perry had two identical brigs, the *Lawrence* (his flagship) and the *Niagara* (commanded by Elliott), each carrying 20 guns, and seven smaller vessels, mostly gunboats. The total weight of his broadside was 912 pounds. Barclay had two ships, the *Detroit* (which was his flagship and carried 19 guns) and the *Queen Charlotte* (17 guns), and four smaller vessels. The total weight of Barclay's broadside was 494 pounds.[16]

Although clearly overmatched, Barclay had little choice but to challenge Perry because the British and their Indian allies on the Detroit River were running low on food. The only way to keep British supply lines open was to regain control of the lake. Hence, late in the evening of September 9, 1813, Barclay sailed his squadron from its anchorage at Malden down the Detroit River into Lake Erie to challenge Perry. The following morning he spotted the American squadron. As he approached, Barclay enjoyed the weather gauge (which meant that the wind was at his back and he could choose the distance for the engagement). But once again Perry got lucky, and a shift in the wind gave him the weather gauge.

With the wind at his back, Perry ordered his ships to close to take full advantage of his superior firepower. Flying a battle flag with the motto "Don't Give Up the Ship," Perry sailed the *Lawrence* into the heart of the British squadron and repeatedly exchanged broadsides with the *Detroit* and *Queen Charlotte*. With metal projectiles and wood splinters flying everywhere, an American tar reported so much carnage that "it was impossible to take the wounded below as fast as they fell."[17] The two British ships also sustained considerable damage, and Barclay was twice wounded and had to be taken below.

Perry remained unscathed, but his situation was desperate. Nearly all of the *Lawrence*'s guns were knocked out of action, and 80 percent of its crew was either killed or wounded. But instead of surrendering, Perry hauled down his battle flag and boarded a small boat. Despite a hail of British fire aimed at him, Perry enjoyed more good luck and made it safely to the *Niagara,* which was largely untouched by battle because for reasons that have never been satisfactorily explained Elliott had kept his distance and barely engaged the enemy.

Perry took command of the *Niagara* and sailed it back to the British squadron, while Elliott followed with the gunboats. As Perry approached, the two main

Perry emblazoned Captain James Lawrence's words on his Lake Erie battle flag, and when he defeated the weaker British squadron, the U.S. Navy adopted this motto for its slogan. (Facsimile from Benson J. Lossing, *Pictorial Field-Book of the War of 1812*)

The most common illustration of Perry's victory on Lake Erie shows the young officer shifting his command from the U.S. Brig *Lawrence* to its sister ship, the U.S. Brig *Niagara*. This particular version, which dates from 1865, shows oversized seamen rowing Perry to the *Niagara*. (Print of a painting by N. H. Powell. Library of Congress)

British ships tried to wind around to bring undamaged batteries to bear, but in the process the *Charlotte* rammed the *Detroit*, rendering both ships immobile. With a full crew and fresh batteries and with supporting fire from his gunboats, Perry shot the two British ships to pieces. Shortly thereafter, the British squadron surrendered, ending the bloody three-hour battle.

Elliott was the first American officer to board the British flagship. The deck was so saturated with blood that he slipped and fell. After righting himself, he visited Barclay below and then ordered one of his men to climb the ship's mast and cut down the royal ensign. That flag, along with Perry's battle flag, is now at the U.S. Naval Academy in Annapolis, Maryland. Meanwhile, on the back of an old letter Perry wrote Major General Harrison one of history's shortest and most memorable after-action reports: "We have met the enemy and they are ours: two ships, two brigs, one schooner, & one sloop."[18] With Perry now in firm control of Lake Erie, the initiative in the Old Northwest shifted to the United States.

We have met the enemy and they are ours: Two Ships, two Brigs one Schooner & one Sloop.

Yours, with great respect and esteem

O H Perry.

Perry's famous after-action report to Major General William Henry Harrison has been lost, but not before Benson J. Lossing prepared this facsimile of the text. (Benson J. Lossing, *Pictorial Field-Book of the War of 1812*)

A contemporary song celebrating Perry's victory on Lake Erie. (Library of Congress)

BRILLIANT NAVAL VICTORY.

YANKEE PERRY, BETTER THAN OLD ENGLISH CIDER.

"TUNE---THREE YANKEE PIGEONS."

HUZZA! for the brave Yankee boys,
  Who touch'd up John Bull on lake Erie,
Who gave 'em a taste of our toys,
  From the fleet of brave Commodore *Perry.*

They were not made of 'lasses but lead,
  And good solid lumps of cold iron,
When they hit JOHNNY BULL in the head,
  They gave him a pain that he'll die on.

Now the *Niagara* bore down,
  To give 'em a bit of a whacking,
The *Lawrence* came up and wore round,
  And set her nine pounders a cracking.

They soon felt the *Scorpion's* sting,
  And likewise the *Æriel's* thunder,
The *Porcupine* give 'em a quill,
  And made the Queen Charlotte knock under.

The *Somers* now gave 'em a touch,
  And the *Tygress* she gave him a shock sir,
Which did not divert Johnny much,
  For it put him in mind of the BOXER.

The *Trip* she was hammering away,
  The *Oris[ ]on* made 'em smell powder,
The brave *Caledonia* that day
M ade her thunder grow louder and louder.

We gave 'em such tough yankee blows,
  That soon they thought fit to surrender;
That day made 'em feel that their foes,
  Were made in the masculine gender.

Poor Johnny was sick of the gripes,
  From the pills that we gave them at Erie,
And for fear of the stars and the stripes,
  He struck to brave Commodore PERRY.

Now as for poor old Johnny Bull,
  If we meet him on land or on Sea sir,
We'll give him a good belly full,
  Of excellent gun powder tea sir.

Old England is fam'd for her perry and beer,
  Which quickly bewilders the brain,
But such PERRY as she's taken here,
  She never will wish for again.

Huzza! for our brave Yankee Tars,
  Who pepper'd the British so merry,
Who fought for the stripes and the stars,
  Under brave Commodore PERRY.

☞ Printed by N. COVERLY, Milk-Street.

The Battle of the Thames

When he learned of Barclay's defeat, Procter realized that he could no longer supply his troops and that he risked being cut off if an American force was moved across the lake to his rear. "I do not see the least Chance," the British officer concluded, "of occupying to advantage my present extensive Position."[19] Determined to withdraw to the east, Procter met with furious resistance from his Indian allies, who saw this as a betrayal of the British promise to protect their lands. Tecumseh tried to shame Procter into holding his ground by comparing him to "a fat animal that carries its tail upon its back but when affrighted . . . drops it between his legs and runs off."[20] With the Indians openly threatening to turn on him, Procter promised to make a stand somewhere to the east. The British were slow to abandon their positions on the Detroit River, their withdrawal east was unhurried, and they failed to destroy all the bridges they crossed so that the trailing Indians could use them. This proved fatal to Procter's army.

Meanwhile, Harrison had been calling for volunteer militia from Ohio and Kentucky to take part in offensive operations. Some 3,000 Kentuckians responded, including 63-year-old Governor Isaac Shelby, who was known as "Old King's Mountain" because he had participated in a battle of that name during the Revolutionary War. The response from Ohio was equally enthusiastic, but much to their chagrin, many of the Ohio volunteers had to be sent home because there were not enough supplies to sustain them. By September Harrison had amassed an army of over 5,000 men (including some Indians) at the mouth of the Portage River at present-day Port Clinton, Ohio. While Perry transported most of the men across the lake and to the British side of the Detroit River just south of Fort Amherstburg, some 1,200 mounted volunteers under Colonel Richard M. Johnson rode overland to Detroit and then were ferried across the river to join their comrades.

Although Harrison never expected to catch Procter, he began his pursuit with about 3,500 regulars and militia, including 1,000 of Johnson's mounted men, and about 200 Indians. The Americans came across baggage and supplies abandoned by the retreating British and captured some stragglers. They also took

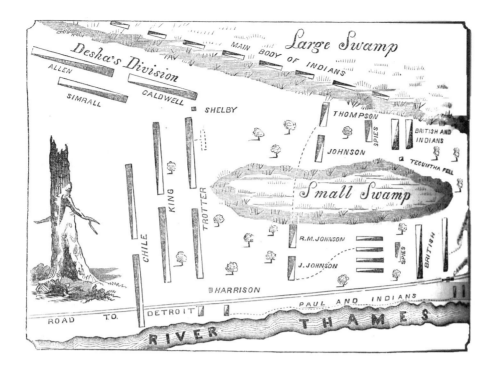

A map of the Battle of the Thames, which re-established American hegemony in the Old Northwest. (Alexander C. Casselman, *Richardson's War of 1812*)

two gunboats on the Thames River loaded with Procter's spare ammunition. With the Americans closing in, Procter decided to make his stand near Moraviantown, about 50 miles east of Detroit. The British general arrayed 600 men in two thin lines extending from the Thames into a marshy swampland to the north. Some 500 Indians anchored Procter's right flank in the thick underbrush of the swamp.

On October 5, 1813, as the Americans approached the British lines, Harrison gave Johnson permission to make a frontal attack with his mounted men. Shouting "Remember the Raisin!"—a reference to the Indian massacre the previous January—Johnson's men galloped toward the enemy. About 500 men led by Lt. Colonel James Johnson (Richard Johnson's brother) burst through the thin British lines and then dismounted and caught the British in a crossfire. After resisting for only a few minutes, most of the British surrendered, although Procter and some soldiers escaped to the east. Meanwhile, the rest of the mounted Kentuckians under Richard Johnson charged the Indians to the north. Johnson himself led the "forlorn hope" (an advance party expected to draw fire and expose enemy positions). Johnson was wounded four times but was credited, accurately it appears, with killing Tecumseh. When the Indians learned that Tecumseh was dead, they melted away, and the battle was over. It was a stunning defeat for the British and their Indian allies. Although casualties on both sides were light, Tecumseh was dead and some 600 British soldiers were now prisoners of war.

BATTLE OF THE THAMES.
5th Oct. 1813.
Respectfully Dedicated to Andrew Jackson Esq, President of the United States.

Made during Andrew Jackson's presidency in the 1830s, this print shows (with considerable artistic license) the Battle of the Thames. At center stage are Richard M. Johnson and Tecumseh. (Lithograph by John Dorival. Library of Congress)

John Naudee, a Chippewa leader also called Oshawahnah, was reportedly Tecumseh's second in command at the Thames. He survived the battle and sat for this daguerreotype many years later. (Alexander C. Casselman, *Richardson's War of 1812*)

Richard M. Johnson (1780–1850) was credited with killing Tecumseh in the Battle of the Thames even though he himself was wounded four times. Johnson's feat helped elevate him to the vice presidency in 1837. More remarkable was this Kentuckian's commitment to racial equality. He lived with a slave, Julia Chinn, and tried to introduce their two daughters into polite society. (Library of Congress)

The next day the dead were buried in mass graves. Kentuckians identified Tecumseh's body and took his hair, clothing, and even patches of his skin for souvenirs. "I [helped] kill Tecumseh and [*helped*] *skin him*," a veteran of the campaign recalled many years later, "and brot Two pieces of his yellow hide home with me to my Mother & Sweet Harts."[21] Americans also captured a large amount of war material, including a small fieldpiece that originally had been taken in the Battle of Saratoga in 1777 and then lost in the surrender of Detroit in 1812. Part of the booty was property taken from Moraviantown. When some of Procter's papers were found in a house there, the town was looted and burned on the grounds that it was a British garrison.

Procter was convicted by a military court of mismanaging the campaign and reprimanded. As was customary in such cases, the reprimand was read before every regiment in the British army. Procter never held another command. Harrison's military career ended not long after as well. Although lionized by the public for his victories at Tippecanoe and the Thames, he resigned his commission in a huff in the spring of 1814 when Secretary of War John Armstrong sought to keep him on a short leash and undercut his authority by sending orders directly to his subordinate officers.

The Battle of the Thames (known in Canada as the Battle of Moraviantown) was a significant American victory. Besides regaining control over the Michigan Territory, the United States now extended its reach across the Detroit River into the Western District of Upper Canada. Moreover, with the death of Tecumseh any hope of forging a broad Indian confederacy had vanished. Most Indians in the region had no interest in supporting a loser; they came to terms with the United States and turned against the British and those natives who remained loyal to them. For the rest of the war, the United States controlled the Old Northwest. But as impressive as the Perry/Harrison triumph was, it did not bring the United States any closer to conquering Canada or to winning the war. The whole theater of operations was simply too far west and too remote for that.

The Contest for Lake Ontario

The struggle for naval supremacy on Lake Ontario was more intense than the contest on Lake Erie because this body of water was closer to the centers of population and thus of greater strategic importance. Taking command on Lake Ontario in early September 1812, Commodore Isaac Chauncey ordered Lieutenant Melancthon T. Woolsey to buy, refit, and arm merchantmen at the naval base at Sackets Harbor, New York. Woolsey was soon joined by Chauncey's longtime friend, New York shipbuilder Henry Eckford, who oversaw the construction of new warships. The British had their own construction programs at Kingston and York, and once Commodore Sir James Yeo took charge and the Royal Navy committed resources, these programs gained momentum.

In the competition to build ships for service on Lake Ontario, the United States enjoyed a huge logistical advantage, but it did not fully capitalize on this advantage, nor did it seriously threaten the British pipeline on the St. Lawrence River. As a result, the British were able to match the American construction program, and control of the lake shifted back and forth as each side brought ever larger ships into service. But the growing squadrons never fought a decisive engagement. Unlike Commander Barclay on Lake Erie, neither commander on Lake Ontario was desperate enough to fight when he was at a disadvantage. Hence, even though there was some skirmishing, the results were inconclusive, and the most important service that each squadron performed was to support land forces in amphibious operations and to transport troops and supplies.

The Capture of York

In the spring of 1813, Major General Dearborn and Commodore Chauncey held a council of war to plan their campaign. Fearing that Kingston was too well defended, they decided to target York first. Departing from Sackets Harbor on April 25, the American squadron (13 vessels, each towing army bateaux) reached York two days later with a force of some 1,800 men plus 800 naval personnel. To resist the invasion, Major General Roger Sheaffe had only about 1,000 men (regulars, militia, volunteers, and Indians). Using army bateaux and ships' boats to reach the shore, the invaders were led by Major John Forsyth's riflemen and under the overall command of Brigadier General Zebulon Pike.

Forsyth's riflemen pushed back the Mississauga, Ojibwa, and Chippewa Indians who contested their landing. Aided by heavy fire from those U.S. warships that could get close enough to offer support, more troops poured ashore. After securing the landing area, the Americans routed the British force they now faced and pushed east against resistance toward the garrison in York. British forces rallied around a battery of 18-pounder guns, but a mishandled match accidentally blew it up, killing and wounding the gun crews. The British militia who had gathered here quickly decamped, and the regulars soon had to follow suit.

Sheaffe did not provide very effective leadership during the attack, and when he realized that he could not halt the American onslaught, he ordered his men to abandon York and retreat towards Kingston. He also burned a ship on the

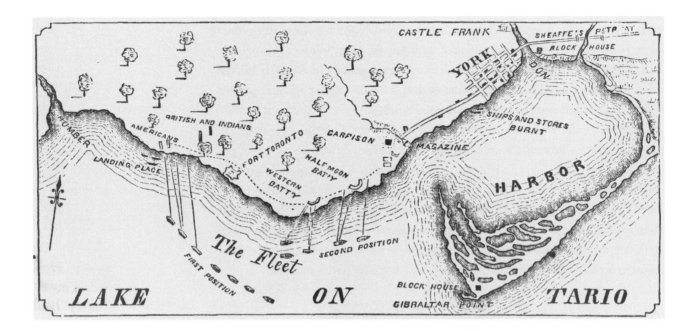

Map labels:
CASTLE FRANK — SHEAFFE'S RETREAT — BLOCK HOUSE — YORK — DON — SHIPS AND STORES BURNT — MAGAZINE — HARBOR — BRITISH AND INDIANS — AMERICANS — FORT TORONTO — GARRISON — HALF MOON BATTY — WESTERN BATTY — LANDING PLACE — HUMBER — The Fleet — FIRST POSITION — SECOND POSITION — BLOCK HOUSE — GIBRALTAR POINT — LAKE ONTARIO

As a result of the Battle of York, the United States occupied the capital of Upper Canada and burned its public buildings. (Benson J. Lossing, *Pictorial Field-Book of the War of 1812*)

The Rev. John Strachan (1778–1867), the rector of York, was one of Canada's heroes in the war. Not only did he help protect York from looting after it had fallen, but he ministered to the sick and wounded and raised money for war-related causes. Later he shaped Canada's public education system and served as the first Anglican bishop of Toronto. (Messotint after G. T. Verthon. Toronto Reference Library.)

stocks (the *Sir Isaac Brock*) and all the naval stores and blew up the grand magazine, which was made of stone and housed 300 barrels of powder. The ensuing explosion was tremendous, shaking windows in Fort Niagara more than 30 miles away. Some 265 Americans were killed or wounded by the explosion. Among the victims was Pike, who died when a large flying stone crushed his spine. In all, the Americans sustained 310 casualties. The British, by contrast, lost about 200 killed and wounded, although another 275 were captured.

Enraged by the explosion, Americans burned the public buildings (including the provincial parliament), looted the town, and harassed the townspeople. They were joined in the looting by locals, including some released from jail by the occupation force and others who came in from the countryside. Major General Dearborn, who had remained on his ship during the operation, was now ashore and in command but was slow to assert control over his men. Because the naval yard and the ship had been torched after negotiations to surrender had been initiated by officials representing the city, Dearborn refused to ratify the agreement. He was finally shamed into acting by an influential local clergyman, John Strachan, who later became the first Anglican bishop of Toronto.

Bad weather delayed the American departure from York for a week. Confined to their crowded ships while they waited for the weather to break, the Americans suffered further losses from disease. As for Sheaffe, he was excoriated by the people of York for botching the defense of the town. His effectiveness at an end, he was removed from command and became the scapegoat for misfortunes that visited York after its fall.

The Capture of Fort George

After reaching Fort Niagara, the American force from York took three weeks to convalesce before joining additional troops from Sackets Harbor in another amphibious operation, this time against Fort George across the Niagara River. The British fort was bombarded for two days before the Americans launched their assault in the early morning hours of May 27. Commodore Chauncey again provided the transportation and naval support, and Dearborn again chose to remain in the background. The army, about 4,000 strong, was nominally under the command of Major General Morgan Lewis, but most of the preparations had been overseen by Colonel Winfield Scott, one of the army's rising stars. Scott was assisted by Master Commandant Oliver H. Perry, who had not yet won a name for himself on Lake Erie. Landing north of the fort, the Americans were met

Like so many other capable young officers during the War of 1812, Winfield Scott (1786–1866) rose quickly up the command ladder, moving from the rank of captain in 1811 to brigadier general at the end of the war. He was a superb trainer of men, led by example, and developed a reputation for being a fearless, even reckless, battlefield commander. (Wikipedia)

This view of Fort George, from just outside Fort Niagara on the American side of the Niagara River, shows how close the two posts guarding the mouth of the river were to one another. (Painting by Edward Walsh. Library and Archives of Canada)

by 1,400 British regulars, militia, and Indians under the command of Brigadier General John Vincent.

Overwhelmed by sheer numbers and pummeled by artillery fire both from the American shore and Chauncey's ships, the British fell back toward Fort George. Fresh American troops crossed the Niagara River to cut Vincent off, but they did not move quickly enough to catch him. Retreating to the southwest, Vincent ordered Fort George blown up and all British positions on the Niagara River (including Fort Erie) abandoned. When one of Fort George's magazines exploded, Scott was knocked off a horse he had commandeered, injuring a shoulder. But he quickly regained his feet and was the first American to enter the fort. He prevented the other magazines from exploding and personally cut down the British flag. He then led the pursuit of Vincent until the overly cautious Lewis ordered him to halt. American losses in the battle were about 150. The British, by contrast, lost as many as 450 men, but Vincent still managed to muster some 1,600 men at Burlington Heights (in present-day Hamilton). Americans had won the day, but the failure to destroy Vincent's army came back to haunt them in the months that followed.

The Assault on Sackets Harbor

Commodore Chauncey was understandably worried about being away from Sackets Harbor for very long, for he had information that the British planned to attack in his absence. Sir George Prevost saw an assault on the U.S. naval base as a way of destroying an irreplaceable American asset and of forcing the recall of American forces sent to the Niagara front. Accordingly, shortly after sunset on May 27, a hastily assembled squadron of 33 vessels commanded by Yeo set sail from Kingston for Sackets Harbor some 35 miles away. On board were 900 regulars and fencibles (long-term local volunteers who were essentially regulars) as well as 37 Mississauga and Mohawk Indians. Prevost himself was aboard although he gave Colonel Edward Baynes operational command.

The British reached Sackets Harbor the next day. Shortly thereafter Baynes sent an Anglo-Indian force to attack a number of American recruits who were spotted in boats heading north along the shore from Oswego to Sackets Harbor. Some of the Americans made it safely ashore, but after a brief clash with the fierce Indians, about 115 surrendered to the British. After this promising start, all the British troops were ordered into boats for the assault on Sackets Harbor. At this point, however, bad weather loomed, and Prevost—much to the dismay of Yeo—ordered a delay. While the British troops waited uncomfortably in their

Sackets Harbor was the principal American naval base on Lake Ontario and thus a beehive of construction activity throughout the war. In May 1813 the British made their one and only attempt to destroy the base but failed to do irreparable damage. (*Naval Chronicle,* 1818. Courtesy of Naval History & Heritage Command, Washington, DC)

boats, the Americans used the time to prepare their defenses and summon militia from the surrounding area.

In charge of the American defenses was Brigadier General Jacob Brown of the New York militia. A local entrepreneur and land speculator, Brown had forsaken the pacifism of his Quaker upbringing to pursue a military career. At Sackets Harbor he had at his disposal 1,450 men, mostly regulars and militia but with a smattering of marines, sailors, and shipwrights in the mix.

After daybreak on May 29, the British boats approached Horse Island, which was connected to the shore by a partially submerged but fordable neck. Landing on the island, the invaders marched to the neck and then slogged toward the mainland. They took heavy fire from muskets and artillery (much of the latter from nearby Fort Tompkins), and they had to detour around abatis. Brown's militia was nearest to the shore, and these men fired several volleys before fleeing. But the British were still under heavy fire from Fort Tompkins as well as from regulars under the command of Lieutenant Colonel Electus Backus. The invading force got little support from Yeo's ships or the British gunboats because of contrary winds.

Believing that the battle was lost, an American midshipman put the shipyard and naval stores to the torch. A partially built ship, later christened the *General Pike,* was threatened by the conflagration but was saved by a hastily organized fire brigade commanded by Brown's brother. Meanwhile, Baynes had concluded from the smoke that the shipyard was in flames and that his mission had been accomplished. In addition, heavy losses now made it difficult, if not impossible, for his men to overcome the stout resistance they continued to face, especially from American forces in and around the fort. After conferring with Prevost, he ordered a retreat. This decision, which was attributed to Prevost and has been criticized ever since, ended the battle.

Despite the botched defense of the shipyard, the United States had prevailed, preserving a base that was vital to future operations on Lake Ontario. The British lost roughly 260 men in the engagement. Counting those recruits who were killed or surrendered en route from Oswego, American losses were about the same. Since Backus was killed, Brown wrote the only American report and thus received the lion's share of credit for the victory. He was rewarded with a brigadier general's commission in the regular army. Chauncey rued the damage done to his shipyard and thereafter was reluctant to cooperate with the army if it meant leaving Sackets Harbor exposed.

Jacob Brown (1775–1828) was a brigadier general in the New York militia when he oversaw the successful defense of Sackets Harbor against a British amphibious attack in 1813. He was rewarded with a commission in the regular army, and his willingness to slug it out with the British on the bloody Niagara front in 1814 earned him the nickname "the fighting Quaker." (Engraving based on a painting by Alonzo Chappel. Library of Congress)

The Battles of Stoney Creek and Beaver Dams

The American position on the British side of the Niagara River, which seemed so secure after the capture of Fort George, soon began to deteriorate, mainly because the British army had escaped intact. In early June, Major General Dearborn decided to send a force to challenge Vincent's army at Burlington Heights. Brigadier General William Winder marched west from Fort George with 1,400 men and was soon joined by another 1,100 men under Brigadier General John Chandler, who assumed command of the combined force. After skirmishing with the British, the Americans on June 5 made camp at Stoney Creek, about 40 miles west of Fort George. Although Chandler expected to be attacked and his army occupied a strong position on high ground, he did not deploy his men to the best advantage.

Brigadier General William Winder (1775–1824) was captured in the Battle of Stoney Creek and later mismanaged the defense of Washington, which opened the door to the British occupation. Despite these failures, the genial Winder remained popular, and his law practice in Baltimore flourished after the war. (Engraving by Charles de Saint-Mémin. Library of Congress)

Meanwhile, Lieutenant Colonel John Harvey, a British officer who had reconnoitered the American position, persuaded Vincent to let him hazard a night attack with some 750 men. In the confused battle that ensued on the night of June 5–6, there were some casualties from friendly fire on both sides. The British were nearly routed by heavy artillery fire but turned the tide when they captured four American guns as well as both American generals, who accidentally stumbled into enemy units. The Americans lost 170 men in the battle, the British 215. The Battle of Stoney Creek was a clear British victory. The Americans had failed to achieve their objective, they had lost two generals, and they withdrew so precipitously the day after the battle that they left their dead unburied and their equipment and supplies behind.

Less than three weeks later, the United States suffered another setback in the hinterland of Fort George, this time some 18 miles to the southwest near Beaver Dams. The British maintained one of several posts here from which they harassed Americans. This particular post had a force of only about 50 men under Lieutenant James FitzGibbon, but not far away was an Indian camp of more than 450 warriors. Ordered to wipe out FitzGibbon's camp, Lieutenant Colonel Charles Boerstler marched some 600 men from Fort George under cover of darkness to Queenston on June 23 and then on to Beaver Dams the next morning. FitzGibbon had been warned that enemy troops were on the way by Laura Secord, who trekked more than 20 miles to deliver the warning, and by Indian scouts, who monitored the Americans' progress. Before reaching his camp, however, the Americans were ambushed by 400 Indians at Beaver Dams. The Americans fought well, but after three hours they were running low on ammunition and found themselves surrounded. At this point FitzGibbon arrived and, by greatly exaggerating the size of his force and raising the specter of an Indian massacre, he persuaded Boerstler to surrender.

FitzGibbon always credited the Indians with the victory at Beaver Dams. "They beat the American detachment into a state of terror," he said, "and the only share I claim is taking advantage of a favorable moment to offer them protection from the tomahawk and scalping knife."[22] But FitzGibbon received the lion's share of credit for the victory. As the Mohawk leader John Norton put it, "The *Cognawaga Indians* fought the *battle*, the *Mohawks* . . . got the *plunder*, and *Fitzgibbon* got the credit."[23] This was the last offensive action undertaken by American troops from Fort George. It was also the last straw for Dearborn's critics in Washington. The hapless and aging general had provided uninspired leadership from the beginning of the war and had shown no taste for battle. He was relieved of his command, ostensibly until he recovered his health.

The Abandonment of Fort George and the Burning of Newark

After the twin defeats at Stoney Creek and Beaver Dams, many of the American regulars on this front were transferred east to take part in a campaign against Montreal and to garrison Sackets Harbor. The remaining troops at Fort George hunkered down and remained on the defensive. Seizing the initiative, the British moved in with their Indian allies and for several months maintained a loose siege of the fort, harassing American outposts, skirmishing with detachments sent from the fort, and conducting raids across the river. Eventually, however, most of the British troops were withdrawn to deal with more pressing threats elsewhere.

Laura Secord (1775–1868) walked some 20 miles through rough country in June 1813 to warn Lieutenant James FitzGibbon that an American attack was imminent. Secord's warning, coupled with intelligence provided by Indians, led to the U.S. defeat at Beaver Dams. On a visit to Canada in 1860, the Prince of Wales took notice of the now elderly Secord's trek of almost a half century earlier, and thereafter she was recognized as one of Canada's heroes of the war. (Benson J. Lossing, *Pictorial Field-Book of the War of 1812*)

By the fall, command of Fort George had devolved on Brigadier General George McClure, a New York militia officer who realized that his position was far from secure. Most of the regulars were now gone, and the tour of duty of the New York militia would soon be up. McClure tried to persuade the militia to remain, but as was so often the case, the men refused because their pay was in arrears.

With his army melting away, McClure decided to abandon Fort George. As the last of the Americans departed on December 10, they were supposed to destroy the fort, but the return of British troops from Burlington Heights caused panic, and the post remained largely intact. Probably following the counsels of renegade Canadian Joseph Willcocks, McClure ordered the nearby town of Newark (also known as Niagara) burned. The inhabitants were given only a few hours to leave in the winter weather. This act was heartless and unnecessary, and it invited retaliation, which was not long in coming.

The Capture of Fort Niagara and the Burning of Buffalo

Furious with the needless destruction of Newark and convinced that Fort Niagara was vulnerable, Lieutenant General Gordon Drummond, now in charge of all the British forces on the Niagara front, was determined to retaliate. Late on December 18, 1813, Colonel John Murray led a British force of more than 550 men across the river under cover of night. Securing the sign and countersign from a

In late December 1813, the British burned the American side of the Niagara River in retaliation for the American burning of Newark on the British side. Buffalo, then a village of 1,500, was the largest town to go up in smoke. (John H. Spears, *The History of Our Navy*)

captured American picket, the British entered Fort Niagara after midnight and, making good use of their bayonets, soon gained the upper hand. The defenders were caught by surprise, and their commanding officer, Captain Nathaniel Leonard, a notorious drunkard, was not present during the attack. The British offered no quarter to those who refused to surrender. In all, 80 Americans were killed or wounded and almost 350 captured, including Captain Leonard, who returned to the fort the next morning. The British, by contrast, lost fewer than a dozen men. The fort remained in British hands for the remainder of the war.

Leaving a detachment at Fort Niagara, British troops, accompanied by their Indian allies, laid waste to American settlements, including Buffalo and Black Rock, all along the Niagara River. At Lewiston, some of the Indians got drunk and evidently left a gruesome scene. "The sight we have witnessed," said an American who returned to the town shortly after the attack, "was shocking beyond description. Our neighbors were seen lying dead in the fields and roads, some horribly cut and mangled with tomahawks, others eaten by the hogs."[24]

The destruction of the New York towns on the American side of the river marked a sad end to the campaign on the Niagara frontier in 1813. A campaign that had begun with such promise with the British abandonment of Fort George and other strong points on the Niagara River had ended with the British in control of key forts on both sides of the river and with virtually all the settlements on the American side in ruins. "The whole frontier from Lake Ontario to Lake Erie," lamented Governor Daniel D. Tompkins of New York, "is depopulated & the buildings & improvements, with a few exceptions, destroyed."[25]

In a proclamation, Sir George Prevost made it clear that the British were willing to give up this kind of warfare if the Americans followed suit, and the American government seemed receptive to the overture. The United States apologized for the burning of Newark and did not retaliate for the destruction of Buffalo and its sister towns. But American commanders in the field followed their own counsels. The kind of warfare that devastated the Niagara frontier in 1813 continued in 1814, ultimately contributing to the British decision to burn Washington.

Montreal Targeted

One of the reasons that the United States was so vulnerable on the Niagara frontier in late 1813 was that many of the U.S. regulars at Fort George had been ordered east to take part in an assault on Montreal. This important city—the largest in British North America—was one of the anchors of British defenses on the St. Lawrence River, but the United States had made only a halfhearted attempt against it in 1812, and in 1813 it was initially not even on the target list. It was not until the summer that an attack on the city received serious consideration, and not until October that the attack was finally launched. This was dangerously late in the campaigning season for such a major operation.

The plan for taking Montreal called for a two-pronged assault. One army would depart from Sackets Harbor and move by boat down the St. Lawrence River to threaten the city from the west, while a second army would move north from Plattsburgh. Not only was much of this plan developed late and on the fly, but neither Armstrong nor his two commanding generals had much faith in it.

In charge of the entire operation was Major General James Wilkinson, a onetime Spanish spy with a reputation for corruption and intrigue. Wilkinson was the ranking officer in the U.S. Army from 1796 to 1812, but because of his unsavory reputation, the War Department had bypassed him in making command assignments in 1812. Instead, he was left in New Orleans, while the assignments on the northern frontier went to newly appointed generals. By 1813, however, Wilkinson had worn out his welcome in Louisiana. By then it was said that militia in many parts of the state would not serve under him and that the state's two

Major General James Wilkinson (1757–1825) mismanaged his command at New Orleans before the war and then bungled the campaign against Montreal in 1813. It was not that he lacked talent but rather that he was incapable of putting any cause before his own venal interests. Although he never won a battle, he never lost a court martial either, and thus he flourished in peacetime. The War of 1812 purged the army of officers like Wilkinson. (Benson J. Lossing, *Pictorial Field-Book of the War of 1812*)

Republican senators had threatened to go into opposition if he were not ordered out of the state. The War Department responded by posting him to New York to serve under Dearborn, but when Dearborn was relieved, Wilkinson—promoted to major general several months before—assumed command of the entire theater of operations.

Wilkinson contracted dysentery in New York and during the operation took large amounts of laudanum, a drug that consisted of opium and alcohol. Although this was standard treatment for intestinal disorders, the drug left Wilkinson unfit for command. He conceded that he had "a giddy head," and one officer said that during the descent down the St. Lawrence "the general became very merry, and sung and repeated stories."[26] Even under the best of circumstances, Wilkinson had no taste for hard campaigning, and anticipating defeat, he was eager to avoid blame. "In case of Misfortune," he told Armstrong shortly after the operation began, "having no retreat, the army must surrender at discretion."[27]

In charge of the other wing of the attack was 59-year-old Major General Wade Hampton, a haughty and rich South Carolina planter who had served in the Revolution and rejoined the army in 1808. Armstrong persuaded Hampton to serve on the northern frontier with Dearborn, but only by giving him a separate command. Hampton would take orders from Dearborn only if their two armies acted in concert. When Hampton learned that Wilkinson, a longtime enemy, had succeeded Dearborn, he made it clear to Armstrong that under no circumstance would he serve under him. To pacify the temperamental general, Armstrong promised that all his orders would come from Washington. This dubious command structure did not bode well for what proved to be the largest American offensive of the war.

The Battles of Châteauguay and Crysler's Farm

Hampton assembled his army on Cumberland Head just north of Plattsburgh. His force consisted of more than 6,000 men, but most of his regulars were raw recruits, his officers were untested, and his militia (about a quarter of his force) would not serve outside the country. Although Hampton had not yet received orders from the War Department, he planned at the very least to make a demonstration against Montreal. Hence, on September 19, he moved his army into boats and sailed from Cumberland Head to the northern end of Lake Champlain. Disembarking, the American troops crossed into Canada and fought their way into Odelltown.

Here Hampton paused to consider his options. Not only did he face further British resistance ahead but a prolonged drought had dried up the local wells.

With the approval of his officers, he decided to veer off to the west toward the Châteauguay River, which drained into the St. Lawrence west of Montreal. After a tough four-day march, he reached the Châteauguay. Making camp at Four Corners (present-day Chateaugay, New York), he spent the next three weeks improving his lines of communication, particularly the road that brought supplies in from Plattsburgh, and waited for further orders.

In mid-October Hampton finally received orders from Armstrong to march to the mouth of the Châteauguay River so that he might threaten Montreal. Departing from Four Corners on October 21, Hampton's troops made slow progress. Besides battling cold and rainy weather, they had to contend with a crude and muddy river road that had to be cleared of trees felled by the British. With the militia refusing to cross the border, Hampton's effective force when he re-entered Canada was about 3,800 men.

By October 25, Hampton found himself facing some 1,800 men, mostly French Canadian fencibles and militia, under the command of Lieutenant Colonel Charles de Salaberry, an able 35-year-old combat veteran. The British defensive works were strong, and the principal French Canadian units, the Canadian Voltigeurs, were battle-tested. Salaberry also made good use of about 150 native warriors, mostly Abenakis and Nipissings, who were part of his force.

Hampton knew that Salaberry's force was small, but he also knew that his defenses were formidable. On October 25 he dispatched Colonel Robert Purdy with 2,300 men to the east side of the river in the hope of getting around Salaberry to attack him from the rear. Hampton's plan was to advance against the British on the west bank the following day. When he got back to his headquarters that evening, however, he found orders from Armstrong to build winter quarters in the rear. From this he concluded that the administration had no real interest in pursuing the assault on Montreal. Although this sapped his own enthusiasm for the operation, he decided to go ahead with the planned attack anyway.

About 10:00 a.m. on October 26, Hampton's advance, under the command of Brigadier General George Izard, came into contact with Salaberry's force and deployed for battle. Izard was reinforced, and the engagement dragged on fitfully until mid-afternoon. Meanwhile, Purdy's progress on the east bank had been slow,

Lieutenant Colonel Charles de Salaberry (1778–1829) was a French Canadian who engineered the victory against a much larger American force at Châteauguay. Because the victory was won mainly by soldiers of French descent, it was later used to bolster the myth that a united Canada had met and defeated the American invaders. (William Wood, *Select British Documents of the Canadian War of 1812*)

hampered by darkness, a lack of good guides, stormy weather, and thick undergrowth. By 11:00 a.m. he had barely made it to a position opposite Salaberry's main force on the other side of the river. Here he was stymied, first by a small force of militia and Indians on the east bank and then by galling enemy fire from Salaberry's main force on the west bank. Early in the fighting, many of Purdy's junior officers deserted, seeking refuge along the river bank.

By 3:00 p.m. Hampton had concluded that the entire operation was a failure and ordered forces on both sides of the river to retreat to Chateaugay, New York. Casualties in the Battle of Châteauguay were light, about 50 for the United States and 25 for the British. It was a clear and convincing British victory, one that was due mainly to some 350 French Canadian Voltigeurs and militia and their Indian allies.

The other prong of the attack got under way when Wilkinson departed with his army from Sackets Harbor for Grenadier Island in mid-October. High winds and rough seas made for a difficult passage, and on the way the army lost many of its provisions and medical supplies and much of its ammunition. The need to secure more supplies and repair damaged boats delayed the departure from Grenadier Island, and it was early November before the bulk of Wilkinson's army sailed into the St. Lawrence River. A squadron of Commodore Isaac Chauncey's ships had covered the army's movement from Sackets Harbor to Grenadier Island and now convoyed it down the river to French Creek (now Clayton, New York).

Brigadier General Jacob Brown had arrived at French Creek earlier with an advance force and was twice attacked by a squadron of warships under the command of Captain William H. Mulcaster of the Royal Navy. Brown's artillery beat off the British vessels, the second time with hot shot heated in a furnace constructed for that purpose. The main American army, about 7,300 strong, arrived on November 3. Two days later the army headed for Morrisville, New York, although in the darkness, the American boats ended up depositing their human cargo over a four-mile stretch of the American shore. The following day, the army marched overland through Ogdensburg, while under cover of night the boats were rowed past the British batteries at Prescott. Undeceived, the British opened fire, but darkness obscured their aim, and they did little damage to the passing boats.

Wilkinson moved his force further down the St. Lawrence, but on November 10 he ordered a halt at a set of rapids then known as Long Sault (but now called the International Rapids). To clear the north shore ahead, Wilkinson dispatched a large force, 2,600 strong, under General Brown. With the assistance of Colonel Winfield Scott, Brown accomplished his mission, first driving British militia from Hoople's (or Uphold's) Creek and then occupying Cornwall.

An image taken from a larger panoramic view of the Battle of Crysler's Farm, which turned back the American campaign against Montreal in 1813. (Climax of the Action at Crysler's Farm, mural by Adam Sheriff Scott. Courtesy of Upper Canada Village, Ontario)

Two days before, Wilkinson had learned that he faced a new threat from the rear. Following him down the river, first in ships and then in boats, was a mixed British force of regulars, fencibles, and Mohawk Indians under the command of 30-year-old Lieutenant Colonel Joseph W. Morrison, a British officer who was well respected but had little combat experience. To protect his rear from Morrison's force, Wilkinson detached a large force that ultimately came under the command of 48-year-old Brigadier General John P. Boyd, a onetime mercenary who had fought in India before returning to the United States and rejoining the army in 1808. Boyd had taken part in the Battle of Tippecanoe in 1811 and then had feuded with Harrison over whether militia or regulars deserved credit for the American victory.

Morrison's men had left their boats and now harassed the American army on the north shore of the river. With some 1,200 men, Morrison next settled into a good defensive position at Crysler's Farm and waited for an attack. On November 11, Boyd obliged, bringing around 3,000 men into action. Although Boyd's men fought well, they were sent into battle piecemeal and ran out of ammunition. As a result, Morrison's troops delivered a stinging rebuff to the larger American force. The British first beat off an attack on their left and then one on their right. At this point Boyd, who had not provided much guidance during the battle, ordered a withdrawal, leaving many wounded on the field. Thus ended the engagement. American losses in the Battle of Crysler's Farm were 400 killed, wounded, or missing, while British losses were a little over 200. One of the Americans killed was a well-regarded officer, Leonard Covington, who had just passed his forty-fifth birthday and been promoted to brigadier general of the U.S. Army.

The day after this defeat, Wilkinson moved his demoralized army down the river to the foot of the rapids west of Cornwall. At this point, Wilkinson received word that Hampton would not join him but instead was marching his army back to Plattsburgh. This was the only excuse that Wilkinson needed to call off the operation and order his men into winter quarters at French Mills (now Fort Covington), New York. Here the men suffered from exceptionally harsh winter conditions, bad provisions, and a shortage of medical supplies and other necessities. "Under these circumstances," reported an army doctor, "sickness and mortality were very great."[28] Most of the officers, including Wilkinson, chose to take up residence elsewhere, and it was not until General Brown took charge that conditions improved.

It was impossible to put a good face on the failed American offensive against Montreal. Although this double-barreled operation included the largest assemblage of U.S. regulars prior to the Civil War, it ended in disgrace with both American armies suffering defeat at the hands of much smaller forces and with neither getting anywhere near Montreal. Since the British took the threat seriously and had amassed some 6,000 troops at Montreal, the prospects for a successful American assault were slender anyway.

The Creek War

The United States fought one Indian war in the Old Northwest that started at Tippecanoe in 1811 and blended into the war with Great Britain. The nation fought a second Indian war in the Old Southwest that was also inseparable from the War of 1812. In this case, the war was fought against the Creeks. As in the Northwest, the British offered to assist the Indians, but they were slow to act, and by the time they established a presence on the Gulf Coast, the United States had already won the decisive battle of the conflict.

The Creeks, or Muskogees, occupied most of present-day Alabama and a large part of Georgia. They were loosely allied to neighboring tribes in a large confederation. Many of the Creeks had adopted white ways, and a large number of mixed-bloods lived among them. By white standards of the day, they were comparatively advanced. Although they still hunted, they also practiced agriculture and raised livestock, they owned slaves, and they had developed an effective form of tribal government.

The Creek War grew out of a civil war among Indians that pitted the accommodationists (who embraced white ways and sought peace with the United States) against a militant faction known as Red Sticks (because they favored the use of red war clubs). The Red Sticks bitterly resented encroachments on their lands and were determined to end them. A visit in 1811 from Tecumseh, the great Shawnee leader, emboldened the Red Sticks, who began attacking white settlements on the frontier in the Southwest. Americans were particularly outraged by a massacre of women and children on the Duck River south of Nashville in May 1812. To keep peace with the United States, the old Creek chiefs ordered the perpetrators hunted down and killed. This precipitated a civil war in the confederation. The Red Sticks got the upper hand in this war, forcing the old chiefs and their followers to flee to the American Indian agent for protection.

The Battle of Burnt Corn and the Fort Mims Massacre

In July 1813 a group of Red Sticks visited Pensacola to buy arms, ammunition, and other supplies from the Spanish. On July 27, they were ambushed about 80 miles north of Pensacola by 180 militia from the Mississippi Territory in what is known as the Battle of Burnt Corn. Although the Mississippi troops made off with most of the pack animals carrying the supplies, they were driven from the field in disorder by the Indians. The fighting lasted for three hours, but the casualties on both sides were light. The Battle of Burnt Corn was the opening round of the Creek War. It transformed what had been a civil war in the Creek confederacy into a larger and more devastating conflict with the United States.

The Red Sticks retaliated on August 30 by assaulting Fort Mims, a stockade 40 miles north of Mobile. The fort was occupied by 200 troops under the command of Major Daniel Beasley, who took his duties lightly and ignored signs that an Indian attack was imminent. Caught by surprise with the stockade gate jammed open by blowing sand, the defenders were overwhelmed. They took a heavy toll on the Indians—perhaps 200—but lost about 250–300 men, women, and children in the process. The only survivors were some whites who escaped into the wilderness and some slaves carried off by the victorious Indians. American casualties were bad enough, but contemporary reports exaggerated their number, and the "Fort Mims Massacre" stirred up hostility against Indians in the Old Southwest every bit as much as the River Raisin Massacre had in the Old Northwest.

Andrew Jackson (1767–1845) forged his reputation as an indomitable military leader and campaigner during the Creek War. Refusing to let dysentery slow him down, he earned a reputation for being as hard as hickory. Thus was born the nickname "Old Hickory." Jackson looked after his men, but in return he expected unquestioned obedience to orders. (Library of Congress)

Andrew Jackson Takes Charge

The whole southwestern frontier was soon in flames as roving bands of Creeks raided exposed settlements. In response, expeditions were mounted from Georgia and the Mississippi Territory. Although they took a heavy toll on the Red Sticks, they failed to deliver a knockout blow. Andrew Jackson, a major general in the Tennessee militia, mounted a similar expedition with some 2,500 volunteers and militia that included young Sam Houston and Davy Crockett, who reportedly kept "the camp alive with his quaint conceits and marvelous narratives."[29] A tough frontier brawler and Indian fighter who was already known as "Old Hickory," Jackson planned to crush the Indians and then seize Spanish Florida.

Marching south from Tennessee, Jackson built Fort Strother on the Coosa River as a forward base. From here, Jackson's able lieutenant, 42-year-old Brigadier General John Coffee, launched a successful attack against hostile Creeks in the Battle of Tallushatchee on November 3, and Jackson duplicated the feat six days later in the Battle of Talladega. The Creeks suffered at least 500 killed in these two battles, while American losses were only about 150 killed and wounded.

At this point, Jackson had to suspend operations because he was running out of supplies and his men were clamoring to return home. Jackson repeatedly clashed with his men, volunteers and militia alike, who insisted that their term of service was up. On more than one occasion, the feisty general threatened to fire on units to prevent them from leaving camp, and no one doubted that he would make good on this promise if anyone defied him. In the end, however, Jackson had to release many of the men, which greatly depleted his ranks.

By early 1814, Jackson's strength was back up to 1,000 again, and he resumed offensive operations. Marching deep into the heart of Creek country, he fought two additional engagements with the Indians, at Emuckfau on January 22 and then at Enitachopco Creek two days later. Although the engagements were inconclusive, Jackson lost only about 100 men compared to 200 for the Indians. Returning to Fort Strother, Jackson stockpiled supplies and waited for reinforcements.

As news of Jackson's victories spread, recruitment picked up, so that by February his army had grown to 4,000 men, including some 600 regulars. Jackson hoped that the presence of regulars would give "strength to my arm & quell mutiny," but his independent-minded Tennessee militia remained obstreperous.[30] When one young man, John Woods, refused to obey orders, Jackson ordered him court-martialed. He was convicted of disobedience and mutiny and shot by a firing squad—the first citizen soldier executed since the American Revolution. According to one of Jackson's aides, "a strict obedience afterward characterized the army."[31] Jackson's draconian discipline was unusual among militia officers, but it had the desired effect.

The Battle of Horseshoe Bend and the Treaty of Fort Jackson

In March 1814 Jackson learned from friendly Indians that about 1,000 enemy Creeks occupied a peninsula of the Tallapoosa River known as Horseshoe Bend. Protected from a land assault by strong fortifications, the Creeks kept canoes on the river in case they needed to escape. Marching 2,700 of his men plus 600 Indians (including 100 friendly Creeks) to Horseshoe Bend, Jackson carefully laid plans for an attack. On March 27 Jackson started pounding the Indians' breastworks with his small field artillery. At the same time, friendly Indians swam across the river and made off with the canoes, which deprived the Creeks of their means of escape. Jackson's artillery proved ineffective. Hence, while some of his men used the Creek boats to cross the river and mount an assault from the rear, Jackson mounted a frontal assault. After some fierce fighting at the breastworks, Jackson's men, led by Sam Houston, poured over the top. Their defenses breached, the Creeks fled, seeking refuge wherever they could among the trees and along the riverbank. Jackson's men then systematically hunted them down. Few of the Creeks sought quarter, and those who tried to escape in the river were shot down. The "*carnage,*" Jackson conceded, "*was dreadfull.*"[32] Some 800 Creeks were killed, while Jackson's own casualties were only about 200. "The fiends of the Tallapoosa," the victorious Jackson publicly intoned, "will no longer murder our Women and Children or disturb the quiet of our borders."[33]

As a result of this fierce campaign, the Creeks called Jackson "Sharp Knife" or "Pointed Arrow." Although Jackson had enjoyed invaluable assistance from

Brigadier General John Coffee (1772–1833) was Andrew Jackson's right-hand man in the Creek War and the Gulf Coast Campaign. A surveyor by trade, he was badly wounded in the Battle of Emuckfau but recovered enough to perform vital service in the defense of New Orleans. (Benson J. Lossing, *Pictorial Field-Book of the War of 1812*)

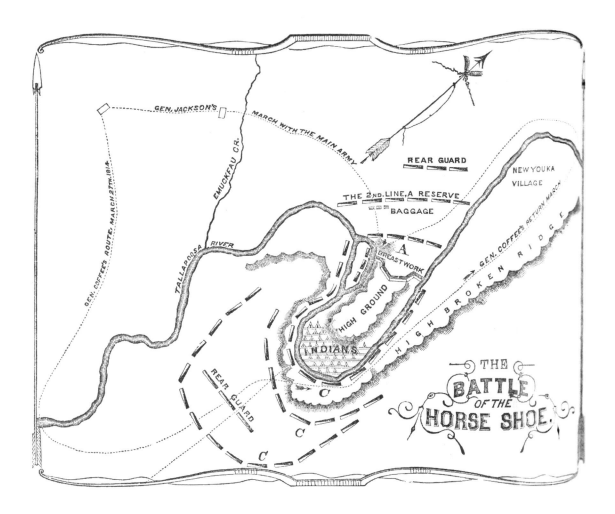

THE
BATTLE
OF THE
HORSE SHOE.

The Creeks thought that they had established an impregnable position at Horseshoe Bend, but it proved to be a deadly killing ground from which there was no escape. This was the climactic and decisive battle of Jackson's Creek War. (Benson J. Lossing, *Pictorial Field-Book of the War of 1812*)

friendly Creeks, who served as scouts and combat allies, he did not reward their loyalty. On August 9, 1814, the victorious general forced all the Creek leaders, friend and foe alike, to sign the Treaty of Fort Jackson, which compelled them to surrender 23 million acres, over half of their land. This massive land grab pleased Jackson's friends in the West, although it left many officials in Washington aghast. The treaty was nonetheless allowed to stand. The once powerful Creek Confederation had been humbled, its mighty empire dismantled. While many surviving Red Sticks joined the Seminoles in Florida to fight another day, the friendly Creeks who accepted the new order were eventually forced to march to Oklahoma, a trek remembered as the Trail of Tears.

The War at Sea

The British had been slow to exploit their advantage at sea in 1812, but that changed in 1813. The Admiralty gradually increased British naval strength in American waters and put Admiral Sir John Borlase Warren in charge of all its forces in the North Atlantic and Caribbean. Warren was ordered to neutralize the U.S. navy either by destroying its ships or by bottling them up in port. In the fall of 1812 Warren already had established a naval blockade that extended from Charleston, South Carolina, to Spanish Florida, and that blockade was gradually expanded in 1813 to include all the middle and southern states. New England was exempted, both to reward the Federalist stronghold for opposing the war and to keep up the flow of foodstuffs to Canada.

The war took a heavy toll on the maritime economy all along the Atlantic seaboard. Even though New England remained unblockaded, its ships could not venture safely to sea, which was a heavy blow to a region so dependent on shipping and the carrying trade. South of New England, the British blockade wreaked even more havoc. Merchants could not get their ships to sea, nor could farmers send their commodities to market. The coasting trade was thoroughly disrupted, and the primitive roads of the day did not offer an efficient alternative. Transporting anything overland was slow and expensive, and the increased traffic only worsened conditions. By 1813, the roads in Virginia had become so bad that one observer claimed that it took 38 hours to travel between Fredericksburg and Alexandria, a distance of only 50 miles, and a traveler in New Jersey reported that there was so much traffic between Trenton and New York that "the road is literally cut hub deep."[34]

Gluts and shortages appeared everywhere. Prices of overstocked items plummeted, while those in short supply soared. Rice that sold for $3 a hundredweight in Savannah or Charleston commanded $9 in New York and $12 in Philadelphia. Flour selling for $4.50 a barrel in Richmond went for $8.50 in New York and almost $12 in Boston. Tropical goods that were normally imported—sugar, coffee, tea, molasses, cotton, and spices—doubled, tripled, or even quadrupled in price. American foreign trade (exports plus imports), which stood at $115 million in 1811 declined to less than $50 million in 1813. This affected government revenue, which was heavily dependent on the import trade. Between 1811 and 1813, government expenditures quadrupled from $8 million to almost $32 million. Although the customs duties were doubled in 1812 to cover the cost of the war, government revenue in this two-year period actually remained flat at about $14 million.

British Raids in the Chesapeake

The British also used their naval power to conduct coastal raids, especially in the Chesapeake. Their aim was to draw off American troops from Canada and to bring the war home to Americans. Admiral Warren, who had no stomach for this sort of petty warfare against civilians, assigned the duty to Rear Admiral Sir George Cockburn (pronounced Co-burn), a gifted combat leader with a flair for amphibious operations. In late April Cockburn sailed into the Upper Chesapeake, where he burned Frenchtown, Maryland. Several days later, he burned three additional Maryland towns: Havre de Grace, Georgetown, and Fredericktown. He also sailed up Principio Creek in Cecil County and destroyed a foundry that made cannons under government contract. This was a severe loss to the United States. Cockburn was rebuffed at Elkton, Maryland, and the British met with considerable resistance at Queenstown and St. Michaels as well, but mostly they had their way. There were no regulars near any of their targets, and the local militia units were usually slow to respond and quick to retreat.

The Battles of Craney Island and Hampton

On June 1, Admiral Warren arrived in the Chesapeake with reinforcements under the command of Colonel Thomas Sidney Beckwith, a Peninsula War veteran who was considered one of the best leaders of light infantry in the British army. Thus reinforced, Warren determined to attack Norfolk, which harbored the American frigate *Constellation* and Gosport Navy Yard. Warren had a sizeable attack force, about 2,400 men, but this included two Independent Companies of Foreigners consisting of French deserters and prisoners of war who were notoriously difficult to control. These men were especially unruly because their French officers were stealing their pay. To defend Norfolk, Brigadier General Robert B. Taylor had less than 800 men (a mixture of soldiers, sailors, and marines), but he fortified Craney Island, which commanded the approaches. In addition, Captain John Cassin of the Gosport Navy Yard deployed a squadron of gunboats to block access to the harbor should the British get around Craney Island.

On June 22, 1813, Beckwith landed men two and a half miles to the west for an overland march along the shore to Craney Island. At the same time, Captain Samuel J. Pechell guided 50 boats loaded with men in the same direction just off the shore. Beckwith's men came under heavy artillery fire and had to retreat. The tide was in, which made it impossible for them to reach Craney Island by fording anyway. Artillery fire also took a toll on Pechell's squadron of boats. The lead boats got trapped in deep mud far from the shore and had to be abandoned. The other boats withdrew. In the Battle of Craney Island, the British suffered less than 20 killed or wounded but another 62 (mostly Frenchmen who had deserted) were missing. The United States reported no casualties in the engagement.

Three days later the British targeted Hampton, Virginia. A large force, perhaps 2,400 men, attacked from two directions. The defending militia, less than 450 men under the command of Major Stapleton Crutchfield, had several artillery pieces and offered surprisingly stout resistance before being overwhelmed and forced to retreat. British losses were 12 killed, 45 wounded, and 22 missing, while the Americans sustained about 30 casualties. Claiming that Americans had massacred some of their men when one of their boats ran aground in the attack at Craney Island, the French soldiers now ran amok, perpetrating a host of crimes on the civilian population. "Every horror was committed with impunity," their commanding officer reported, "rape, murder, pillage: and not a man was punished!"[35] The Independent Foreigners were shipped to Halifax, where they remained unruly until their units were finally sent to Europe and disbanded.

The entire campaign in the Chesapeake seemed punitive in nature, designed to punish the civilian population, encourage slaves to run away, and enrich British soldiers and sailors with the loot they carried off. *Niles' Register* called Warren the "spoiler of the Chesapeake" and labeled his troops "water-*Winnebagoes*"—a reference to the militant tribe of that name in the Old Northwest. Cockburn came in for even sharper criticism. "The wantonness of his barbarities," said *Niles*, "have gibbetted him on infamy."[36] As for the despoiling of Hampton, it was not soon forgotten. The very name of the town became a byword for British atrocities committed during the war.

Rear Admiral Sir George Cockburn (1772–1853) perfected the art of amphibious warfare in the Chesapeake in 1813–14 and was largely responsible for the attack on Washington. Although reviled in the local press, he bore the American people no animosity, and he obeyed the rules of war as he understood them. (Portrait by W. Greatbatch. Library and Archives of Canada)

The Chesapeake-Shannon Engagement

Because the British blockade kept most American warships in port, there were fewer naval engagements in 1813 than in 1812. Some U.S. ships still managed to get to sea, either from unblockaded ports in New England or from other ports

(*left*) Captain James Lawrence (1781–1813) earned the command of the U.S. Frigate *Chesapeake* after leading the U.S. Sloop *Hornet* to victory over the British sloop *Peacock*. But the *Chesapeake* was defeated in 15 minutes by the superbly trained crew of the British frigate *Shannon* under Captain Philip Broke. Lawrence was honored with a huge funeral in New York City, and his words, "Don't give up the ship," were immortalized by Oliver H. Perry on Lake Erie and became the slogan of the U.S. Navy. (Benson J. Lossing, *Pictorial Field-Book of the War of 1812*)

(*right*) Captain Philip Broke (1776–1841) restored the honor of the Royal Navy after a series of stinging defeats when he led the *Shannon* to a victory over the U.S. Frigate *Chesapeake*. Broke was showered with gifts and accolades and ever thereafter was known as "Broke of the *Shannon*." (Benson J. Lossing, *Pictorial Field-Book of the War of 1812*)

where British blockading squadrons were understrength or were blown off station. In May 1813, Captain James Lawrence, a 31-year-old officer who had made a name for himself several months before when he had commanded the U.S. Sloop *Hornet* (20 guns) in its victory over the British sloop *Peacock* (20 guns), was given command of the U.S. Frigate *Chesapeake* (50 guns), which was then refitting in Boston. Waiting for the *Chesapeake* to emerge was the British frigate *Shannon* (52 guns), commanded by Captain Philip Broke, a superb 35-year-old commander who (unlike other British naval commanders after Trafalgar) had carefully trained his crew in gunnery with live ammunition.

Broke sent Lawrence a challenge for a meeting "Ship to Ship, to try the fortunes of our respective Flags."[37] Lawrence never received the challenge because he had already sailed, but he needed no invitation to do battle. Flying a banner that read "Free Trade and Sailors Rights," he headed directly for the British ship. In the bloody engagement that ensued, superior gunnery carried the day for the *Shannon*. The *Chesapeake* was disabled, subjected to murderous fire, and then boarded. Lawrence, mortally wounded, cried out to his men, "Don't give up the ship" or words to that effect. But his shipmates had sustained such heavy casualties that they had little choice but to surrender. Lawrence lingered on for several days before dying. The British sailed the *Chesapeake* to Halifax and then sent the prize to England, where it was ultimately broken up, its timbers used to construct a flour mill.

Smarting from earlier naval defeats, the British treated Broke, who had sustained a nasty head wound from which he never fully recovered, like a hero. The

A view of the British capture of the *Chesapeake*. Note the flying bodies and the banner proclaiming "Free Trade and Sailors Rights." (Drawing by G. Webster based on artwork by Jeakes. Courtesy of William L. Clements Library, University of Michigan)

The death of Captain James Lawrence of the U.S. Frigate *Chesapeake*. Lawrence actually died several days later. (J. A. Spencer, *History of the United States*)

Naval Chronicle credited Broke with "the most brilliant act of heroism ever performed," and news of the victory was received in Parliament with the "loudest and most cordial acclamations from every part of the House."[38] As far as the British were concerned, Broke's victory vindicated the Royal Navy, showing that, in spite of earlier U.S. victories, Brother Jonathan (as the British called the United States) was no match for John Bull in a fair fight on the high seas.

As for Lawrence, he, too, was treated like a hero—the only American naval officer whose reputation rose even in defeat. His funeral in New York City reportedly drew 50,000 people, and he was memorialized across the nation. Master Commandant Oliver H. Perry named his flagship on Lake Erie after Lawrence, and his battle flag—"Don't Give Up the Ship"—immortalized Lawrence's words. This slogan became the motto of the young navy and replaced "Free Trade and Sailors' Rights" as the rallying cry of the war. Having sustained such a one-sided defeat in what was arguably a pointless battle, Lawrence could hardly have asked for more.

The Cruise of the Essex

The most impressive cruise for the United States in 1813 was probably that of Captain David Porter aboard the U.S. Frigate *Essex.* Overloaded with 46 guns—all powerful short-range carronades—the *Essex* was not a good sailer, but Porter in late 1812 rounded Cape Horn and took her into the Pacific. The *Essex,* which in 1800 had been the first American warship to show the flag in the Indian Ocean, now became the first to venture into the Pacific. For over a year Porter cruised in those waters, destroying British whaling ships, taking prizes, challenging thinly veiled pirates flying dubious foreign flags, and living off his captures. Although Porter greatly exaggerated the impact of the cruise (which was only a tenth of the $5 million that he claimed), he did enough damage to British interests in the Pacific to attract the attention of the Admiralty, which in late 1813 dispatched three warships to the Pacific under the command of Captain James Hillyar.

In early 1814 Hillyar caught up with Porter at Valparaiso, Chile, with two of his warships, the *Phoebe* (46 or 53 guns) and the *Cherub* (26 guns). Porter tried to

Captain David Porter (1780–1843) led the *Essex* on the first U.S. Navy cruise into the Pacific in 1813. After doing considerable damage to British whaling operations, he was tracked down and defeated by the British ships *Phoebe* and *Cherub.* Although taken prisoner, Porter emerged from the war as a hero. (Benson J. Lossing, *Pictorial Field-Book of the War of 1812*)

persuade Hillyar to fight a ship-to-ship duel at sea, but the British captain refused to surrender the advantage of his second ship and was content to patrol the waters off Valparaiso and wait for Porter to emerge. On March 28, 1814, Porter slipped out of port and made a run for open waters, but a sudden squall destroyed his topmast, forcing him to seek sanctuary in a small bay. Although the U.S. ship was in Chilean waters, the British ships closed in for the kill. After a hard-fought contest, the *Essex* was forced to surrender. The battle left hard feelings, with Porter accusing the British of continuing to fire after he had struck his colors and the British accusing him of facilitating the escape of his crew after he had surrendered. The defeat of the *Essex* put an end to American operations in the Pacific.

The British ships *Cherub* and *Phoebe* are shown battering the crippled U.S. Frigate *Essex* into submission. (John H. Spears, *The History of Our Navy*)

Privateering

American and British privateers faired much worse in 1813 than 1812. Since American trade had been driven from the seas, there were few prizes available to British cruisers. And since British merchant ships now traveled in convoy, protected by a Royal Navy escort, the pickings were thinner for American privateers, too.

The commander of one American privateer reported "vexing the whole Atlantic" without seeing a single British vessel.[39] To seek out prizes, American privateers had to cruise near the British Isles or in the West Indies, where merchantmen were not required to sail in convoy.

The *Scourge* (15 guns) and *Rattlesnake* (16 guns) enjoyed successful cruises in the North Sea, taking 23 prizes that were sent into Norwegian ports for condemnation. Even more successful was the *True-Blooded Yankee* (16 guns), which had been outfitted by an American in Paris. In a spectacular 37-day cruise, this privateer took 27 British prizes, burned seven vessels in a Scottish port, and occupied an Irish island for six days. "She outsailed everything," marveled a British naval officer; "not one of our cruisers could touch her."[40] Despite bringing in fewer prizes, American privateers continued to annoy British trade, and British merchants continued to demand better protection from their government.

Conclusion

American leaders had every reason to be disappointed with the outcome of the campaign of 1813. Although the United States was now dominant in both the Old Northwest and the Old Southwest, the real losers had not been the British but the Indians. Success in the West brought the new nation no closer to the conquest of Canada nor to anything that resembled victory over the British. Moreover, the signs from Europe were increasingly ominous. The Sixth Coalition (which included Britain, Russia, Austria, and Prussia) now challenged Napoleon, and an allied army defeated the French emperor at Leipzig in the "Battle of the Nations" in October 1813. This victory not only opened up the whole of northern Europe to British trade, but it made the British confident enough of final victory to begin cautiously redeploying forces to the New World. This boded ill for the United States and suggested that the next year of campaigning might be more problematic for the young republic than the first two had been.

In the wake of the *Chesapeake* affair, U.S. warships were ordered to be vigilant in upholding American sovereignty and protecting American rights, especially along the coast. This led to an armed clash in 1811 between the U.S. heavy frigate *President* and the much smaller British sloop *Little Belt*. Many Americans considered this fitting retaliation for the British attack on the *Chesapeake* in 1807. (Engraving by William Elmes. William L. Clements Library, University of Michigan)

An illustration showing the deadly close combat of the Battle of Tippecanoe, although most of the fighting actually took place before dawn. This battle touched off an Indian war in the Old Northwest that blended into the War of 1812 seven months later. It also launched William Henry Harrison's military career. (Print by Kurz & Allison. Library of Congress)

A Scene on the FRONTIERS as Practiced by the HUMANE BRITISH and their WORTHY ALLIES

Bring me the Scalps and the King our master will reward you—

Reward for Sixteen Scalps

Arise Columbia's Sons and forward press,
Your Country's wrongs call loudly for redress;
The Savage Indian with his Scalping knife,
Or Tomahawk may seek to take your life,

By bravery aw'd they'll in a dreadful Fright,
Shrink back for Refuge to the Woods in Flight;
Their British leaders then will quickly shake,
And for those wrongs shall restitution make.

American troops found British weapons in Prophet's Town after the Battle of Tippecanoe, which only served to reinforce the widely held (but inaccurate) view, depicted here, that the British were behind Indian raids on the American frontier before the War of 1812. In truth, the British sought to restrain their native allies but were not always successful. (Watercolor etching by William Charles. Library of Congress)

This early-twentieth-century rendition of the chase of the U.S. Frigate *Constitution* in the summer of 1812 shows how the American ship's boats were used to pull the frigate in a dead calm. The British ships in pursuit were actually further away. (Painting by Anton Otto Fischer. Naval History & Heritage Command, Washington, DC)

A dramatic picture that served to publicize the River Raisin Massacre, thus fueling American hatred, especially in the West, against Indians. (William L. Clements Library, University of Michigan)

MASSACRE of the AMERICAN PRISONERS, at FRENCH-TOWN, on the River Raisin, by the SAVAGES Under the Command of the British Genl PROCTOR: January 23d 1813.

Hand-to-hand combat that took place after tars from the British frigate *Shannon* boarded the U.S. Frigate *Chesapeake*. The Americans are on the defensive and the ship's colors are already coming down. (Engraving by M. Dubourg based on artwork by Heath. William L. Clements Library, University of Michigan)

BOARDING and TAKING the AMERICAN SHIP CHESAPEAKE, by the Officers & Crew of H.M.Ship Shannon, Commanded by Capt. Broke, June 1813.

The second phase of the Battle of
Lake Erie, when Master Commandant
Oliver H. Perry, now in command of
the *Niagara,* challenged the two British
ships, *Queen Charlotte* and *Detroit.*
Perry's banner, "Don't Give Up the
Ship," is flying from the mast of the
American ship. (Painting by Peter
Rindlisbacher. Courtesy of the artist)

No decisive naval battles were fought
on Lake Ontario. The closest thing
was "the Burlington Races" in 1813,
when Commodore Isaac Chauncey's
squadron chased the British squadron
across the lake in gale force winds. The
British ships took refuge in Burlington
Bay at the western end of the lake,
and Chauncey, fearing his vessels
might be blown ashore, chose not to
follow. (Painting by Peter Rindlisbacher.
Courtesy of the artist)

The basic uniforms of the U.S. Army and the U.S. Navy during the war.
(Edward S. Ellis, *The History of Our Country*)

Two panels from a panoramic view of the Battle of Crysler's Farm.
The British victory on this field turned back the American campaign
against Montreal in 1813. The battlefield has been under water
since the 1950s because of the St. Lawrence Seaway project.
(Climax of the Action at Crysler's Farm, mural by Adam Sheriff
Scott. Courtesy of Upper Canada Village, Ontario)

Sackets Harbor in 1813. This painting, by Peter Rindlisbacher, shows an American frigate under construction. (Courtesy of the artist)

Captain Richard Coote of His Majesty's Ship *Boxer* led a British raid on Pettipaug, Connecticut, on April 7–8, 1814. In this illustration, which is part of a larger mural, Coote and his men are shown after they have landed and started burning ships in the harbor. (Painting by Russell Buckingham. Courtesy of the Connecticut River Museum)

Hoping to disrupt the American supply line to Sackets Harbor, the British stormed Fort Ontario in Oswego, New York, in May 1814. They carried off some war material but missed a much larger cache that was stored 12 miles upriver above Oswego Falls. (Engraving by R. Havell based on a drawing by L. Hewett. William L. Clements Library, University of Michigan)

REPULSION OF THE BRITISH AT FORT ERIE,
On the 15th of August 1814, at 2 O'Clock A. M.

Americans.
1. Capt. A. I. Williams
2. Lieut. McDonough
3. Lieut. Watmough

British.
4. Col. Drummond
5. Col. Scott
6. Midshipman Hyde

This illustration of the defense of Fort Erie during the British night attack in August 1814 was prepared by one of the American participants in 1840. Lieutenant E. C. Watmough placed himself in the center of the picture between his fellow officer, Lieutenant Patrick McDonough, and one of the British commanders, Lieutenant Colonel William Drummond, who was killed in the assault. This phase of the battle probably took place at 3:00 a.m. rather than at 2:00 a.m. (*United State Military Magazine,* 1841)

Black seamen formed a significant part of the transatlantic maritime community, serving extensively aboard British and American warships and privateers. Black tars like this one were a particularly important part of the crews of American gunboats because so many white seamen eschewed flotilla service. (Courtesy of Fort McHenry National Monument and Shrine)

American cities and towns that were threatened by British amphibious operations on the Atlantic seaboard had to decide whether to resist or seek terms. On August 29, 1814, Alexandria, Virginia, a prosperous Federalist port city on the Potomac, chose submission and as a result surrendered all of its public stores and maritime property. As this cartoon suggests, the city was sharply criticized for its decision. (Etching by William Charles. Library of Congress)

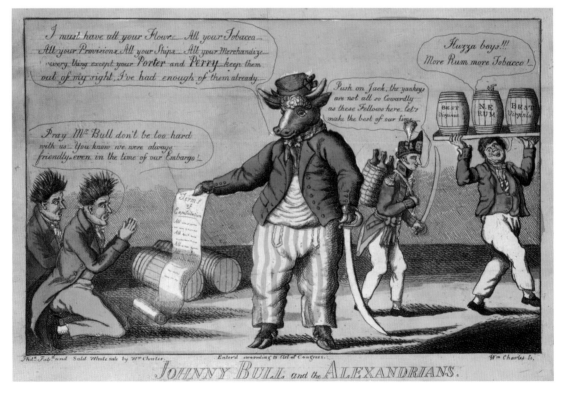

Like the White House, the Capitol Building was torched by the British, and all that survived
was the shell. Congress met elsewhere, first in the patent office and then in a building called
the Old Brick Capitol, until the Capitol Building was once again ready for occupation in 1819.
(Ink and watercolor by George Munger. Library of Congress)

Maryland militia (infantry and cavalry) are seen here gathering to challenge the British approach
to Baltimore. What ensued was the Battle of North Point, which took a heavy toll on the British
invaders. (Painting by Thomas Ruckle. Courtesy of Maryland Historical Society)

A modern depiction of the Battle of North Point that shows Maryland's 5th Regiment of Infantry engaging the advancing British along the road to Baltimore. (Painting by Don Troiani www. historicalimagebank.com.)

Personnel at Fort McHenry manned the water battery during the British bombardment of the post. During most of the bombardment, the British bomb and rocket ships were beyond the range of the American guns. (Courtesy of Fort McHenry National Monument and Shrine)

A VIEW of the BOMBARDMENT of Fort McHenry, near Baltimore, by the British fleet taken from the Observatory under the Command of Admirals Cochrane & Cockburn on the morning of the 13th of Sepr 1814 which lasted 24 hours & thrown from 1500 to 1800 shells in the Night attempted to land by forcing a passage up the ferry branch but were repulsed with great loss.

This illustration from 1816 shows the British squadron bombarding Fort McHenry with explosive shells. The British ships actually were much farther away. Their mortars and rockets could reach the fort, but the fort's garrison guns did not have the range to respond. (Aquatint by John Bower. The Granger Collection)

This dramatic painting shows Francis Scott Key (1780–1843) spotting the Fort McHenry flag after the British bombardment, thus inspiring "The Star-Spangled Banner." However, the flag that Key saw was little more than a speck on the horizon, and he was on an unarmed truce ship, not a warship. (Painting by E. Percy Moran. Library of Congress)

THE AMERICAN PRIVATEER "GENERAL ARMSTRONG" CAPT. SAM. C. REID.

In the Harbor of Fayal (Azores) Oct.ʳ 26ᵗʰ 1814. Repulsing the attack of 14 boats containing 400 men from the British Ships Plantagenet 74., Rota 44. and Carnation 18 Guns. The General Armstrong was 246 tons burthen Carried 6 Nine pounders and a Long Tom (42 pounder) amid ships and a crew of 90 men. The British loss was 120 killed and 130 wounded. Americans lost 2 killed and 7 wounded.

On September 26–27, 1814, the American privateer *General Armstrong* was attacked by the boats of a British squadron in the Azores. The Americans inflicted heavy casualties on the British before being forced to abandon and torch the *General Armstrong* and flee to the shore. (Lithograph by N. Currier. Library of Congress)

His Majesty's Ship *St. Lawrence*, which was put into service on Lake Ontario in October 1814, carried 104 guns and was the largest ship on the northern lakes. As this painting illustrates, the *St. Lawrence* was struck by lightning on her maiden voyage. (Painting by Peter Rindlisbacher. Courtesy of the artist)

On December 14, 1814, some 45 British boats carrying 1,000 seamen and marines overwhelmed the small American flotilla of gunboats that Major General Andrew Jackson had ordered to protect the entrance to Lake Borgne. The British victory opened the door to a land attack on New Orleans but bought Jackson valuable time to strengthen his defenses. (Painting by Thomas L. Hornbrook. Courtesy of Historic New Orleans Collection)

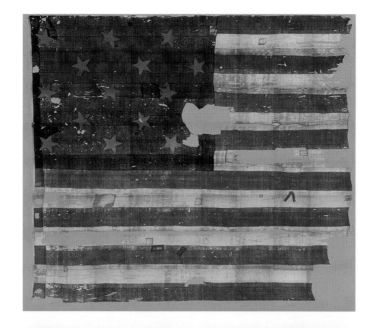

The Fort McHenry flag remained in the Armistead family until 1907, when it was given to the Smithsonian. Over the years the family cut off swatches for souvenirs so that today the flag is eight feet shorter on the fly end. A star is also missing; it is unknown what became of it. The flag has been the subject of several conservation efforts over the years and is now on display in a state-of-the-art, climate-controlled glass chamber. (Military History, National Museum of American History, Smithsonian Institution)

Although few people at the time thought that the War of 1812 would be the last Anglo-American war, this contemporary image, with symbolic representatives of the two nations joining hands upon the conclusion of peace, provided a prophetic vision of the future. (Ink and watercolor by John Rubens Smith. Library of Congress)

CHAPTER FOUR

Don't Give Up the Soil 1814

By the time the Thirteenth Congress convened for its second session on December 6, 1813, Republicans were understandably discouraged by the course of the war. "The result of the last campaign," commented a Republican congressman in January 1814, has "disappointed the expectations of every one."[1] Except in the West, the news from every front was bad and appeared to be getting worse. As a result, victory seemed as elusive as ever. "In spite of some gleams of success," observed a Federalist, "we are further off our object than at first."[2]

President Madison, who had recovered from his summer ailment, tried to sound upbeat in his opening message to Congress. He insisted that the recent campaign had "been filled with incidents highly honorable to the American arms" and that "the war, with its vicissitudes, is illustrating the capacity and the destiny of the United States to be a great, a flourishing, and a powerful nation."[3] The president's rosy outlook seemed to be vindicated when a truce ship arrived on December 30 with news that, although the British had rejected a Russian mediation proposal, they had offered to negotiate directly with the United States. Madison lost no time in accepting this proposal. To represent the United States in the negotiations, he appointed a strong delegation that included Speaker of the House Henry Clay; Secretary of the Treasury Albert Gallatin; and John Quincy Adams, a former Federalist who had been kicked out of the party for supporting the embargo in 1807.

Personnel Changes and Debate on the War

Clay's departure necessitated selecting a new speaker of the house. Although the administration backed Felix Grundy of Tennessee, he was defeated by Langdon Cheves of South Carolina, a strong supporter of the war but also an outspoken opponent of the restrictive system. Madison also needed to replace two cabinet officials: William Pinkney, who had resigned as attorney general, and Gallatin, who was on the peace commission. The president's nomination of young Richard Rush for attorney general was a good choice, but his selection of Senator George W. Campbell of Tennessee as secretary of the treasury was not. The administration lost a valuable spokesman and ally in the Senate and in exchange got a secretary of the treasury who showed little capacity for managing the nation's increasingly chaotic finances. Madison also took the occasion to replace the disloyal Gideon Granger as postmaster general. Granger had held this office since 1801 but for many years had been doling out postal jobs to enemies of the administration. He was also considered lukewarm, if not openly hostile, to the war. He was replaced by Return J. Meigs, the popular governor of Ohio.

Whether the president came out ahead with all the job shuffling is unclear. Certainly Congress, particularly the Senate, continued to ignore or reject many presidential recommendations, and Federalists remained relentless in their opposition. "There is every appearance," said a Republican congressman, "that the minority will contest every inch of ground."[4] Federalists wasted no time, offering two proposals in the House to restrict military operations to defending the nation's borders pending the outcome of the peace negotiations. This led to another extended debate on the merits of the war, a debate that went on for weeks and even spilled over into routine spending bills. Tempers on both sides flared, and Republicans showed a growing impatience with the opposition. James Fisk of Vermont accused Federalists of accepting British gold, and Felix Grundy claimed that they were guilty of "moral treason."[5] Such was the personal nature of some of these exchanges that on two occasions John C. Calhoun nearly engaged in duels with Federalists.

Army Measures and Trade Restrictions

Eventually, Congress got down to the business of war-related legislation. Although army strength had reached 30,000 the previous spring, many enlistments were due to expire. To maintain troop levels, Congress retained the 160-acre land bounty while increasing the cash bounty from $40 to $124, which was as much as many unskilled laborers made in a year. This handsome bounty boosted American troop levels to around 40,000 by the spring of 1814.

Congress also had to deal with the divisive issue of trade restrictions. In the summer of 1812, Congress had voted to retain the non-importation law, the last peacetime trade restriction, and had added an enemy trade act that prohibited any commerce with Great Britain or its colonies. As a concession to the anti-restrictionists, there was no ban on the use of British licenses. This meant that American merchants could continue to supply grain to British armies in the Spanish Peninsula, a large and lucrative trade that was conducted under British licenses. Madison was never very fond of this trade, and he became alarmed when he learned in early 1813 that the British were favoring anti-war New England with the coveted licenses. The president tried to get Congress to act, but that body was unwilling to ban the use of enemy licenses until the following summer. By then the British were no longer issuing licenses to trade with the Peninsula, and U.S. courts had upheld the condemnation of an American ship carrying a British license.

Madison also had trouble getting Congress to move against trade with the enemy in North America, which steadily increased during the war. It was no secret that British troops in Canada and British seamen along the coast were feasting on American provisions. "We have been feeding and supplying the enemy," complained a Republican newspaper in January 1814, "both on our coast and in Canada ever since the war began."[6] Some of the trade was carried on legally in neutral vessels, but any such traffic conducted overland or in American vessels violated the enemy trade act. Neither the Treasury Department nor the War Department had the personnel needed to patrol all the roads and waterways that linked the United States to Canada, nor could they prevent the flow of American provisions to British squadrons off the coast. Smugglers came up with various ruses to cover their trade, and even when caught, they often escaped conviction in local courts. The illegal traffic knew no social or political bounds, and in some cases whole communities were implicated, making it nearly impossible to stamp out the trade.

Determined to reduce this trade and to exert broader economic pressure on Great Britain, Madison asked for additional trade restrictions, but throughout most of 1813 Congress turned a deaf ear. Presidential proposals to ban exports in foreign ships or to impose an embargo on all exports went down to defeat. By the end of 1813, however, the illegal traffic to British forces in war zones had become so scandalous that Congress was finally moved to act. When Madison renewed his request for an embargo in December, a bill that banned all exports and gave government officials broad enforcement powers sailed through Congress in a week.

Although the president finally got the sweeping embargo that he sought, any

Throughout the Napoleonic Wars, many British officials—at home, in the colonies, and on the high seas—issued licenses permitting trade with the enemy to secure badly needed food and other supplies. The license featured here, issued by Lieutenant Governor Sir John Sherbrooke of Nova Scotia in 1813, authorized Halifax merchant John Moody to import food from the United States. (Record Group 8, Halifax Prize Cases, Library and Archives of Canada)

IMPORT No. 122

Lieutenant-General
Sir JOHN COAPE SHERBROOKE,

Knight of the Moſt Honourable Order of the Bath, Lieutenant Governor in or over the Province of Nova-Scotia, and the Territories thereunto belonging in America,

IN Purſuance of the Authority given to me by an Order of Council bearing date the Thirteenth Day of October, 1812, Do hereby grant this Licence, and do hereby Authoriſe and Permit *John Moody & Co of Halifax Mercht* to IMPORT, in any Ship or Veſſel, excepting a Ship or Veſſel belonging to FRANCE, or the Subjects thereof, into the Port of HALIFAX, in NOVA-SCOTIA, from any Port in the UNITED STATES OF AMERICA, from which Britiſh Veſſels are excluded, a Cargo of Wheat, Grain, Bread, Biſcuit, Flour, Pitch, Tar or Turpentine, without Moleſtation, on account of the preſent Hoſtilities, and notwithſtanding the ſaid Ship or Goods ſhall be the Property of any Subject or Inhabitant of the UNITED STATES OF AMERICA, or of any Britiſh Subject Trading therewith.

GIVEN under my Hand and Seal at Arms, at HALIFAX, this *Sixteenth* day of *April* 1813, in the Fifty-Third Year of His Majeſty's Reign.

J. C. Sherbrooke

THIS LICENCE TO CONTINUE IN FORCE FOR *three* MONTHS.

By His EXCELLENCY's Command,

H. H. Cogswell

D. Fey

satisfaction he felt was short lived. Two weeks after the passage of this measure, a ship arrived with news of the allied victory at Leipzig, which opened the whole of northern Europe to British trade, and of the British proposal to discuss peace, which suggested that an end to the War of 1812 might not be that far off. Britain's new commercial opportunities in Europe undercut the broader coercive purposes of the embargo, and a growing number of Republicans wondered if maybe trade restrictions did more harm than good by undermining American prosperity and government revenue at a critical stage in the war.

Federalists clamored for the repeal of both the embargo and the non-importation law, but they got nowhere. Then, at the end of March in 1814, the president stunned nearly everyone by recommending that these measures be repealed. The president's change of heart, which one newspaper described as a "political earthquake," was greeted with "utter astonishment" in Washington because Madison had been the architect of the restrictive system and was one of its most faithful supporters.[7] Madison's message was all that many wavering Republicans needed, and despite bitter opposition from die-hard restrictionists, a bill repealing the embargo and non-importation laws was approved by large majorities in both houses of Congress.

Although other laws remained on the books that prohibited trading with the enemy or using enemy licenses, the repeal of the broader measures marked the end of the restrictive system as a coercive instrument. The nation would now rely exclusively on military force to achieve its war aims. Whether those aims were within reach, however, remained an open question, for the nation's military prospects appeared to be dimming with each passing month.

American and British Strategy in 1814

Strategic planning for 1814 was shaped by the news from Europe, which for the United States got steadily worse. The armies of the Sixth Coalition gradually increased the pressure on Napoleonic France. After the Battle of Leipzig in October 1813, the allies pursued Napoleon into France. At the same time, a British army under the Duke of Wellington, which had defeated French troops in the Spanish Peninsula, invaded France from the south. On March 31, 1814, the allies marched into Paris. A week later Napoleon abdicated and was soon exiled to the Mediterranean island of Elba. For the first time in more than a decade, there was peace in Europe.

Federalists rejoiced at the defeat of the "Anti-Christ," and some Republicans did, too. Even Thomas Jefferson welcomed the downfall of "this scourge of the world."[8] Many Federalists believed that the end of the war in Europe would pave the way for peace with Great Britain, but Republicans were skeptical. Most expected the British to be unyielding, if not vindictive, and the British press seemed to bear them out. "Our demands," said the *Times*, "may be couched in a single word, *Submission.*"[9]

With the United States now alone in the field against Britain, the nation was forced on the defensive. "We should have to fight hereafter," predicted Joseph H. Nicholson, a Maryland judge and banker, "not for 'free trade and sailors rights,' not for the conquest of the Canadas, but for our very existence."[10] As the character of the war changed, so, too, did the nation's perspective. "Don't Give Up the Soil" joined "Don't Give Up the Ship" as a popular slogan.

By the time the campaigning season opened in 1814, the United States had about 40,000 regulars. The British army in North America had only about 30,000 (counting regiments of the line as well as locally raised units), but these soldiers continued to be more seasoned and more experienced than their American counterparts, and their numbers were steadily growing. One significant improvement on the American side was in the quality of army leadership. The junior officers had acquired valuable experience in the first two years of the war, and at all levels those ill suited for combat had been swept away. This was especially true at the top. Hull, Smyth, Dearborn, Lewis, and Hampton were gone, and Wilkinson would soon follow. In their place there was a new set of leaders, such as Brown, Jackson, and Scott, who had proven their fitness for command and knew how to win on the battlefield.

Although events in Europe forced the United States on the defensive, American leaders were not yet prepared to give up their war aims and hence they remained on the offensive, at least in the West. American control of Lake Erie and the destruction of Tecumseh's Indian confederacy had left the United States dominant in this region, but Britain still retained the loyalty of many Indian and French Canadian residents. In the hope of ending British influence in the West, the United States planned to recapture Mackinac. The young republic also hoped to sweep the British from the Niagara peninsula. Fort Niagara and Kingston were on the target list as well, but in the end no attempt was made against these British strongholds or against any British positions further east.

The British planned a winter campaign in the West, but it never materialized; they remained on the defensive in that region as well as on the Niagara frontier. Further east they could take the offensive. Their ascendancy on Lake Ontario meant that they could menace American positions at Oswego and Sackets Harbor, and their growing strength around Montreal meant they could threaten upper

New York. Their strategy called for undertaking additional raids on the Atlantic Coasts and seizing territory—in northern New York and on the Atlantic and Gulf coasts—that might be used as bargaining chips in the forthcoming peace negotiations.

The Assault on Mackinac

To dislodge the British from Mackinac, an American force of 700 regulars and volunteer militia under Lieutenant Colonel George Croghan, the hero of Fort Stephenson, left Detroit on July 3 aboard an impressive squadron of U.S. warships under the command of Captain Arthur Sinclair, who was now the ranking naval officer on the western lakes. Fighting contrary winds, the squadron slowly made its way into Lake Huron and then sailed north, where it destroyed an unoccupied British fort on St. Joseph Island and then seized British property at Sault Ste. Marie. On July 26 the Americans reached Mackinac Island only to find that it had been heavily fortified by Lieutenant Colonel Robert McDouall. Sinclair could not elevate his naval artillery enough to hit the British fortifications, and they were too strong to be taken by storm.

Croghan decided to land on the western side of the island and to establish a base there from which to annoy the British and their Indian allies. The position chosen for the fort lay next to a forest, and here McDouall lay in wait with perhaps 450 regulars, militia, and Indians. On August 4 Croghan came under fire. Although he counterattacked, he was unable to dislodge the enemy and thus called off the assault. Croghan had not shown much enthusiasm for the operation and seemed unwilling to press the attack after he lost several key officers. The Americans had sustained about 60 casualties; the British and their Indian allies perhaps a dozen. The failure of this operation left Fort Mackinac in British hands until the war was over.

On August 13, 1814, Sinclair's naval force sailed to the Nottawasaga River on Georgian Bay to destroy Britain's lone warship on Lake Huron, H.M. Schooner *Nancy,* a supply ship carrying three guns that was commanded by an enterprising 23-year-old Royal Navy officer, Lieutenant Miller Worsley. In the engagement that ensued the following day, Sinclair accomplished his mission and then sailed back to Lake Erie. Convinced that the British could mount no naval challenge on Lake Huron, he left only two schooners, the *Tigress* (1 gun) and the *Scorpion* (2 guns), to cruise those waters.

Although Worsley had escaped into the wilderness when the *Nancy* was destroyed, he was far from done. After leading a small force in a canoe and two

H.M. Schooner *Nancy* was a British supply ship on Lake Huron. Although destroyed by the United States in a raid on the Nottawasaga River in 1814, the hull was recovered in the twentieth century and is now on display in Wasaga Beach, Ontario. (Painting by Peter Rindlisbacher. Courtesy of the artist)

bateaux on a heroic six-day, 380-mile voyage across Lake Huron, he secured reinforcements from Fort Mackinac and then on the night of September 3 surprised and captured the *Tigress* after a brief but fierce fight. Three days later, with the *Tigress* still flying the American flag, he surprised and took the *Scorpion*. In less than 72 hours, Worsley had changed the balance of power on Lake Huron. Although Britain's hold on the lake remained tenuous, the capture of the American schooners meant that the British could resupply their troops at Fort Mackinac and thus solidify their influence over Indian allies scattered across the region. This, in turn, emboldened the natives to launch raids into present-day Illinois, Iowa, and Missouri. Americans were unable to consolidate their hold over the region until the War of 1812 had ended and the Indians were at last at their mercy.

American Raids into Western Upper Canada

Taking advantage of their naval control of Lake Erie and a strong military presence on the Detroit River, Americans were also active in the western districts of Upper Canada. Since the British defeat at the Thames in 1813, much of this region had been a kind of no man's land subject to predatory raids. Although conducted under the American flag, these raids were often spearheaded by renegade Canadians who had joined the Canadian Volunteers under the leadership of Joseph Willcocks, Abraham Markle, and Andrew West-brook. Frequently the raids were little more than a pretext for pillage and plunder and for settling old scores. Like the victims of British raids in the Chesapeake, Canadian settlers had to rely for protection on local militia and a few scattered regular units, who invariably arrived after the damage had been done.

On May 14 Colonel John B. Campbell landed with 700 troops at Dover (now Port Dover), one of several communities located on Long Point on Lake Erie's north shore. The raiding party included a detachment of Canadian Volunteers led by Markle. Campbell claimed that Dover was inhabited by "revolutionary tories and halfpay officers," some of whom had taken part in the destruction of Buffalo the previous winter.[11] Doubtless he got this idea from the Canadian Volunteers. With Markle's band leading the way, the raiders entered the town on May 15 and went on a burning spree. "A scene of destruction and plunder now ensued," said one American soldier, "which beggars all description."[12] The invaders torched not only Dover but also other settlements on Long Point.

The British vigorously protested this wanton disregard for private property, and they were far from satisfied when a court of inquiry mildly rebuked Campbell for torching private homes in Dover. The destruction of Dover and the other settlements in Upper Canada was later used to justify the burning of Washington as well as other British depredations in the Chesapeake in the summer of 1814.

Americans launched yet another predatory raid into the region in the fall. In the late summer of 1814, Brigadier General Duncan McArthur raised 720 mounted soldiers. Most of the recruits were Kentucky and Ohio volunteer militia, but some 50 U.S. Rangers and 70 Indians were also part of the force. McArthur put out the word that his target was Potawatomi Indians in the Old Northwest, but his real intention was to conduct an extended raid into Upper Canada to destroy economic resources.

Departing on horseback from Detroit on October 22, McArthur's force headed east along the Thames River. Traveling lightly and moving quickly, the mounted men lived off the land and burned mills and other buildings along the way. On November 5, the raiders arrived at the Grand River. After exchanging fire with an Anglo-Indian force on the other side, McArthur turned south toward Malcolm's Mills (near present-day Oakland), 20 miles from Dover. Here the Americans ran into 400 inexperienced but entrenched militia. In the ensuing battle, the

Brigadier General Duncan McArthur (1772–1839) fought the war's last battle on the northern border at Malcolm's Mills. McArthur's deep raid into Upper Canada anticipated the extended mounted raids of the Civil War. (Benson J. Lossing, *Pictorial Field-Book of the War of 1812*)

Americans routed the defenders with a frontal assault on foot. Casualties on both sides in the Battle of Malcolm's Mills were slight. After the battle, the Americans torched and plundered their way back to Detroit. McArthur blamed some of the excesses of the raid on his Indian allies, "whose customs in war impel them to plunder after victory."[13]

Targeting mills had some military justification because British troops depended on the foodstuffs they processed, but the losses worked a real hardship on the civilian population. British officials were livid over the destruction of so much private property, and Sir George Prevost ordered Lieutenant General Gordon Drummond to retaliate against American mills east of the Niagara River. The war ended, however, before Drummond could carry out this order.

The Battles of Chippawa and Lundy's Lane

To prepare for the campaign on the Niagara River in 1814, Brigadier General Winfield Scott laboriously trained American regulars for seven hours a day at his camp near Buffalo. Everyone, even the hard-nosed Scott, was impressed with the results. "I have a handsome little army," the brigadier said, "The men are healthy, sober, cheerful, and docile."[14] In the early summer, other forces arrived, including regulars under Major General Brown, a brigade of New York and Pennsylvania volunteer militia commanded by Major General Peter B. Porter, about 50 Canadian Volunteers under Lieutenant Colonel Joseph Willcocks, and some 500 Iroquois under the leadership of the aging, celebrated Seneca chief, Red Jacket. In all, Brown had an army of about 5,500 men.

On July 3, Brown moved his army across the river to invest Fort Erie, a small stone fort defended by less than 140 men under Major Thomas Buck. Much to the chagrin of his own officers and men, Buck surrendered after putting up only token resistance. Brown next ordered Scott to lead an American advance north along the river road. He followed with the main force shortly afterward.

Major General Phineas Riall, who had been expecting the invasion, had about 4,000 men under his command. Most were experienced regulars, although his force included some reliable fencible and militia units as well as 500 or 600 Indians. Most of the Indians were refugees from the West, but there was also a band of Grand River Iroquois led by the redoubtable Mohawk leader, John Norton.

As soon as he learned of the American invasion, Riall reinforced the British position at Chippawa and sent a force under Lieutenant Colonel Thomas Pearson to harass Scott's advancing force. Pearson slowed the Americans by tearing up the bridges and periodically skirmishing as he withdrew to the north, but by late afternoon on July 4 Scott had reached the Chippawa River. Brown joined him with the main force around midnight. Storms that day had left the clay ground wet, but both sides bedded down for a few hours of sleep, the British north of the Chippawa River and the Americans south of Street's Creek (now called Ussher's Creek).

The skirmishing resumed on July 5. That afternoon Brown ordered Porter and Red Jacket to lead a detachment of militia and Indians into a forest of pines on the west to drive off British and Indian skirmishers. Porter accomplished his mission, but when his men emerged from the woods at the Chippawa River, they faced the flank of a large Anglo-Indian force that Riall had brought across the river to attack the American army. Several volleys were exchanged before the Americans and their Indian allies were overwhelmed and fled back to Street's Creek. Brown, who now realized that the British were advancing in force along the river road, ordered Scott to attack. The ensuing battle pitted about 1,300 Americans against a British force of roughly equal strength.

While Captain Nathan Towson employed his artillery battery to good effect against the British, Scott's men coolly maneuvered under heavy British fire and took up a position along a farm lane. The British advanced to within musket range but got the worse of several volleys that were exchanged, forcing Riall to order a withdrawal to the north side of the Chippawa River and thence to Fort George. The British retreat ended the two-hour battle.

In the Battle of Chippawa, the Americans lost 325 killed, wounded, and missing, while British losses were about 500. The battle was a watershed for the U.S. Army, which for the first time in the war had defeated a British force of equal strength on an open battlefield. Scott's men, who were wearing gray jackets because the traditional blue cloth was unavailable, did not look like regulars, and Riall assumed that he was facing militia from Buffalo that he could easily drive from the field. Stunned by the cool professionalism under fire that he witnessed, Riall reportedly exclaimed, "Why, these are regulars!"—thus contributing to the birth of an American legend.[15]

After the Battle of Chippawa, there was a brief lull in major operations, but vicious petty warfare erupted in the vicinity that angered people on both sides. On July 12, John Swift, a Revolutionary War veteran and brigadier general in the New York militia, was mortally wounded by a British picket who the Americans claimed had already surrendered. Less than a week later, a group of Americans led by Lieutenant Colonel Isaac Stone of the New York militia, probably egged on by Canadian Volunteers, burned the village of St. Davids to the ground. Brown was furious and ordered Stone home, but the damage had been done.

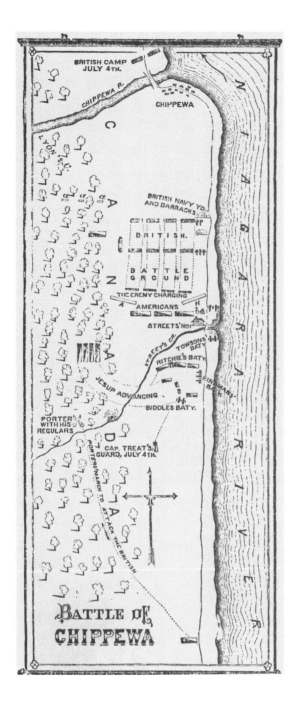

Brigadier General Winfield Scott's brigade showed remarkable poise under fire in the Battle of Chippawa, a direct result of weeks of training. The outcome was an American victory. (Benson J. Lossing, *Pictorial Field-Book of the War of 1812*)

Brown hoped that Commodore Chauncey would cooperate in the reduction of British strongholds on the Niagara peninsula by bringing heavy guns from Sackets Harbor and providing other logistical support, but Chauncey was ill and refused to allow a subordinate to take the squadron out. He was unlikely to help anyway because he considered the defeat of Yeo's squadron his top priority, and he had no desire to turn his warships into army transports. Even without naval support, Brown was determined to engage the British, but he was unable to draw them out from Fort George. Hence, he withdrew temporarily to the Chippawa River.

Although General Riall was reluctant to take on the larger American army, Lieutenant General Gordon Drummond, who sent reinforcements and later arrived to take command, was more aggressive. Determined to engage the enemy, Drummond gradually assembled British troops on a hill at Lundy's Lane. Hearing reports of the British presence, Brown on July 25 ordered Scott to head north to seek out the enemy. That evening Scott found himself at Lundy's Lane with 1,200 men facing a British force 1,600 strong. Ever aggressive, he attacked. Both armies were reinforced, and Brown and Drummond arrived to take charge. In the end, about 3,000 men were engaged on each side. The confused and bloody six-hour battle dragged into the night, drowning out the roar of nearby Niagara Falls.

Scott's brigade was shredded by heavy British artillery fire before getting within effective musket range. Everyone on the American side realized that the British artillery, which was located on the southern slope of the hill in front of the main British force, had to be neutralized. Colonel James Miller led a determined attack against the artillery, delivering a volley of musket fire at close range and then charging with fixed bayonets. This forced the British gunners to withdraw. The British repeatedly counterattacked, but despite ferocious fighting, they were unable to retake their guns.

Two perspectives of the climax of the bloody Battle of Lundy's Lane when the Americans attacked the British batteries. The second engraving, which is often mislabeled "Miller at Chippawa," is highly stylized but nonetheless captures the fierce close combat that ensued when Colonel James Miller (who is featured on horseback) reached the British lines. (First engraving by William Strickland. Courtesy of William L. Clements Library, University of Michigan. Second engraving from Robert Tomes, *Battles of America by Land and Sea*)

Drummond withdrew to regroup and then launched three attacks across a broad front. Scott had reformed his brigade, but it was again cut to pieces, first when it marched across the front line and took fire from both sides and then when it advanced on the British right and took more heavy fire. Despite inflicting heavy casualties, however, Drummond was unable to break the American line or to recover his guns, and he called off his attack. At this point, Brown ordered an American withdrawal. The battle ended with both sides thoroughly exhausted and unable to mount another attack.

Miller characterized the Battle of Lundy's Lane as "one of the most desperately fought actions ever experienced in America."[16] The casualties on both sides were heavy. Each army suffered around 850 killed, wounded, and missing, but the Americans suffered twice as many deaths, mainly because British artillery fire was so deadly before darkness set in. Among the wounded were the four senior officers engaged in the battle—Drummond and Riall on the British side and Brown and Scott on the American side. Riall (who was captured when he rode into an American unit on the British flank) received a nasty arm wound, and Scott sustained a shoulder wound that knocked him out of the war. The battle ended in a draw, although the British retained control of the field and recovered their field guns when the Americans failed to carry them off.

The Siege of Fort Erie and the Battle of Cook's Mills

After Lundy's Lane, the Americans, now about 2,200 strong, retired to Fort Erie. About ten days later, Brigadier General Edmund P. Gaines arrived and took command. The Americans had been strengthening this post since its capture, and it was now greatly enlarged with earthworks to accommodate all the troops. Fully expecting an attack because of intelligence supplied by British deserters, Gaines made sure his men were ready, and his vigilance paid off.

General Drummond first tried to force the evacuation of Fort Erie by attacking its supply base at Black Rock and Buffalo. On August 3, Lieutenant Colonel John Tucker led 600 men across the river but was forced to retreat after being ambushed by Major Lodowick Morgan's regiment of American riflemen in the Battle of Conjocta Creek. Another operation ordered by Drummond nine days later was more successful. On the night of August 12 Captain Alexander Dobbs of the Royal Navy led a successful raid against American schooners anchored off Fort Erie, capturing the *Somers* (2 guns) and the *Ohio* (1 gun). This deprived the defenders at Fort Erie of valuable artillery support from the river. The following morning Drummond opened an artillery bombardment on Fort Erie from batteries erected north of the post. Although the guns were at the extreme limit of their effective range, they nonetheless took a toll on the Americans inside the fort.

In the early morning hours of August 15, Drummond launched an ambitious and risky three-pronged night attack against Fort Erie with around 2,500 men. The plan was to distract the Americans before the assault with an Indian demonstration to the west, but Britain's native allies arrived only after the battle had begun. The main British column, about 1,300 men under Lieutenant Colonel Victor Fischer, assaulted the south end of the fort at 2:30 a.m. In the hope of surprising the Americans, most of the British troops were ordered to remove their flints, but this made it difficult for them to respond when they discovered that their scaling ladders were too short to get over the fort's wall and the defenders opened fire. American artillery and musket fire took a heavy toll before the British finally retreated.

Two other British columns—300 men led by Lieutenant Colonel William Drummond and 650 led by Colonel Hercules Scott—assaulted the north end of the fort around 3:00 a.m. Although they sustained heavy casualties and both of their commanding officers were killed, the British eventually forced their way into one of the fort's bastions. Here they engaged the Americans in close combat for at least half an hour before being blown up when a powder magazine was accidentally detonated. "The Explosion was tremendous," reported Gaines. "It was decisive."[17] The surviving British withdrew, ending the battle. British losses in the assault on Fort Erie, mostly from the explosion, were staggering. Over 900 were killed, wounded, or missing. The Americans, by contrast, lost only 85 men.

The month after the Battle of Fort Erie was punctuated by artillery exchanges and skirmishing around the fort. In one skirmish, Joseph Willcocks, leader of the renegade Canadian Volunteers, was killed, and in one of the British bombardments, General Gaines was seriously wounded, forcing Brown, who had not yet recovered from wounds sustained at Lundy's Lane, to resume command. The British began erecting a battery within 500 yards of the fort, and Brown's officers advised him to evacuate the post. But the arrival of 2,000 volunteer militia under General Porter strengthened Brown's hand, and "the fighting Quaker" wanted to see if he could capture or destroy the British batteries.

On September 17, during a heavy fog that was followed by yet another of the many rainstorms that pelted the region that summer, Porter and Colonel James Miller led about 2,000 regulars and New York militia against the British batteries. Although they caught the British by surprise and spiked the guns in two batteries, they soon met with heavy resistance and were forced to withdraw. Casualties in the sortie from Fort Erie were heavy, about 500 on each side.

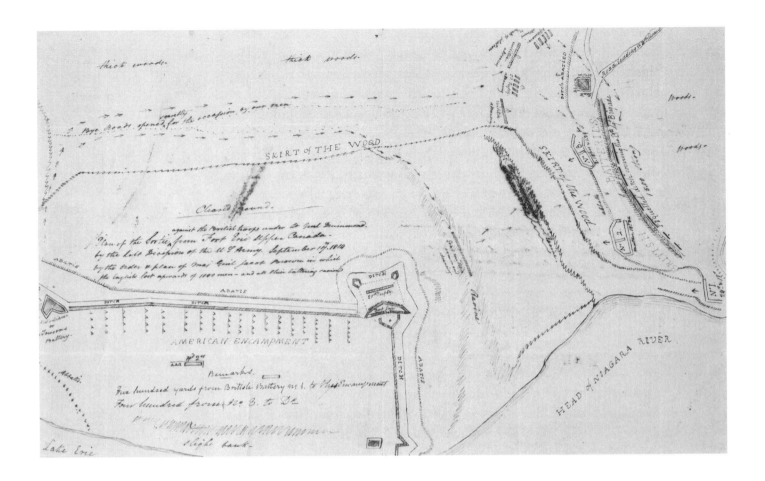

A contemporary map, prepared by Captain Loring Austin (1790–1827), an aide to Major General Jacob Brown, showing the American assault on the British artillery batteries in the sortie from Fort Erie in September 1814. (Courtesy of William L. Clements Library, University of Michigan)

After this engagement, the British withdrew to the north side of the Chippawa River, Drummond having ordered this move before the American sortie. Not only had he lost faith in the campaign, but his men were running low on food and ammunition, and the lack of tents coupled with the frequent rains left them more vulnerable to disease.

In early October Major General George Izard arrived with a large, well-trained force of regulars from Plattsburgh. Despite his lack of combat experience, Izard outranked Brown and took command of their combined force, which totaled more than 6,000 men. Izard slowly moved north from Fort Erie along the river road, rebuilding bridges as he went. Although Drummond was greatly outnumbered, he was in a very strong position behind the Chippawa, and Izard was unable to draw him into the open for a set-piece battle.

Learning that a large quantity of grain had been stockpiled at Cook's Mills on Lyon's Creek (about 12 miles west of the British position), Izard ordered Brigadier

General Daniel Bissell and 1,000 men to seize or destroy the grain. Drummond responded by sending 750 regulars and Glengarry Light Infantry (a fencible unit) to intercept the Americans. On October 19, the opposing forces clashed in an engagement known as the Battle of Cook's Mills or the Battle of Lyon's Creek. An American frontal attack coupled with a flanking movement drove the British from the field. The Americans lost about 70 men, the British half this number. Bissell then destroyed the grain he had come for.

The Battle of Cook's Mills was the last engagement on the Niagara front in the war. American forces had performed exceptionally well during the campaign, but except for helping to forge a tradition of hard training and even harder fighting for the U.S. Army, the campaign had achieved little of significance. Most of the Niagara peninsula remained in British hands, and when the United States evacuated and blew up Fort Erie on November 5, the British faced no further threats on this front.

The Assault on Oswego and the Battle of Sandy Creek

On Lake Ontario the Royal Navy had achieved temporary naval superiority in 1814, which meant it could take the offensive. The British were reluctant to hazard another amphibious assault on Sackets Harbor because its defenses had been strengthened and there was usually a sizeable American force there. Instead, they targeted Oswego, which was an important way station on the supply route from New York City to Sackets Harbor. Most naval stores and other supplies were shipped up the Hudson River to the Mohawk River, then along a mostly water route to Oswego, and from there to Sackets Harbor via Lake Ontario. If the British could interrupt the flow of supplies at Oswego, they could materially disrupt the naval construction program at Sackets Harbor.

On May 4, a British force of 900 men, mostly soldiers and marines commanded by General Drummond, left Kingston for Oswego in a squadron of ships under Commodore Yeo. Fort Ontario, the dilapidated post that protected Oswego, was manned by 300 men, mainly artillerymen, under Lieutenant Colonel George E. Mitchell. With Colonel Victor Fischer in command, the British sought to make a landing on May 5, but contrary winds denied them covering fire from their ships, and they were driven off by artillery fire from the fort. The following day they renewed their attack with naval support, and this time they routed the defenders that met them on the beach and then captured the fort. The British suffered 90 casualties, the Americans about half that number, although an additional 25 Americans were taken prisoner.

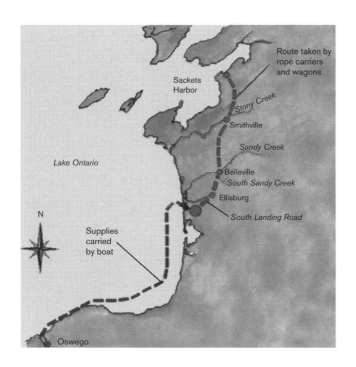

When they departed from Oswego, the British carried off naval guns and ammunition and a considerable quantity of naval stores and provisions. Spared from the British raid was a large cache of naval guns and rope that had been moved to Oswego Falls, about 12 miles from the fort up the Oswego River. The British raid was damaging, but it could have been far worse.

Later that month Master Commandant Melancton Woolsey guided a number of boats that were carrying 35 large naval guns and rope from Oswego to Sackets Harbor. With a large British squadron under Commodore Yeo nearby, Woolsey left Oswego at night on May 29, taking refuge the next day in Sandy Creek. Here Woolsey's flotilla was met by 130 U.S. Riflemen under Major Daniel Appling and 120 Oneida Indians, who took cover in the forest downriver from the boats. Another 300 men arrived from Sackets Harbor with artillery to provide additional security for the boats and their precious cargo.

Unaware that there was such a large land force present, Captain Stephen Popham, who was on detached duty from the main British squadron, led a force of 200 British soldiers, marines, and seamen in boats up Sandy Creek on May 30 to attack the American flotilla. When he spotted the masts of the American boats, Popham landed some men on shore and advanced further upriver with the artillery from his boats providing covering fire. Although the Oneida fled from the British artillery, Applington's riflemen, with support from American artillery, cut the British force to shreds. After sustaining more than 70 casualties, the British surrendered. Only one American and one Indian were wounded in the Battle of Sandy Creek. Popham's defeat had an ancillary effect. Deprived of the manpower lost in the engagement, Commodore Yeo called off a planned Congreve rocket attack on Sackets Harbor.

Since it was unsafe to venture back into the lake, the American guns and naval stores were moved overland from Sandy Creek to Sackets Harbor 20 miles away,

After the Battle of Sandy Creek, the American supplies that were headed for Sackets Harbor were moved overland in wagons. Part of a huge cable, weighing nearly five tons, was put in a wagon, but the bulk was carried by a regiment of New York militia—like a giant centipede (*below*). (Illustration by Robert McNamara, The Art of Wilderness. Courtesy of the Great Lakes Seaway Trail)

but there was a huge cable that was too large for any wagon. The cable, which was 7 inches in diameter, 300 feet long, and weighed a staggering 9,600 pounds, was slated to be used on a heavy frigate under construction at Sackets Harbor. Colonel Allen Clarke's 55th Regiment of New York militia offered to carry the cable to Sackets Harbor. Part of the rope was lifted into a large wagon, and the men—perhaps a hundred in all—carried the rest on their shoulders. They marched for a mile at a time and then rested. Their shoulders became so raw that they padded them with straw and grass. Although some men deserted during the march, others took their places. Thirty hours after leaving Sandy Creek, the cable arrived safely at Sackets Harbor. The men were cheered and were rewarded with a barrel of whiskey and $2 a day in bonus pay.

The Invasion of New York and the Battle of Lake Champlain

The British mounted their most significant offensive on the northern frontier against northeastern New York. The British government sent Sir George Prevost reinforcements, including several of Wellington's generals who had served in the Spanish Peninsula. Although the governor-general was urged to take the offensive, he was also cautioned not to risk getting cut off deep in American territory, which had spelled disaster for Major General John Burgoyne in 1777. Prevost was expected to seize and hold territory in upper New York to enhance Canadian security and to give the British a useful bargaining chip in the peace negotiations that were under way.

Prevost amassed an army of around 10,000 men at Montreal, and on August 31 the bulk of this force crossed the international frontier. Secretary of War John Armstrong had not expected a major British campaign here, and so on August 10 he ordered Major General Izard to march his army of about 4,000 men to the Niagara frontier. This left the defense of upper New York in the hands of Brigadier General Alexander Macomb, who had only 3,400 men at his disposal. Although some of his staff members urged him to retreat, Macomb refused. Instead, claiming that "fortune always favors the brave," he dug in at Plattsburgh.[18]

Macomb sent skirmishing parties (mostly militia) to harass the advancing British troops, but they were easily swept aside. "So undaunted . . . was the Enemy," reported Macomb, "that he never deployed in his whole march, always pressing on in Column."[19] When he reached the Saranac River at Plattsburgh, Prevost engaged the Americans on the other side, and this marked the beginning of the Battle of Plattsburgh. But before launching a full-scale attack, the British commander sent a detachment west to ford the river and approach the defenders

The victory of Master Commandant Thomas Macdonough (1783–1825) on Lake Champlain induced the British to withdraw the largest army that has ever invaded the United States. Showered with gifts, Macdonough became a rich man overnight. (Engraving by J. B. Forrest after a portrait by John Wesley Jarvis. Library of Congress)

from the rear. He also waited for the outcome of a naval engagement between the opposing squadrons on Lake Champlain.

The British had won control of Lake Champlain in early June 1813, when they captured two American 11-gun warships, the *Eagle* and *Growler,* that had ventured too deep into the shallow waters at the northern end of the lake and then found themselves unable to maneuver when they ran into trouble there. Since then, both sides had been building additional warships, and the two squadrons were now about evenly matched.

The British squadron was headed by the *Confiance* (39 guns), the flagship of 36-year-old Captain George Downie. The squadron also included the *Linnet* (16 guns), *Chub* (11 guns), and *Finch* (11 guns) as well as 12 gunboats (carrying a total of 17 guns). The *Confiance* was the most powerful ship on the lake, but it was not yet completed, and carpenters were still working on the vessel just before it went into battle. Opposing Downie was 30-year-old Master Commandant Thomas Macdonough, whose flagship was the *Saratoga* (26 guns). Macdonough's squadron also included the *Eagle* (20 guns), *Ticonderoga* (17 guns), *Preble* (7 guns), and ten gunboats (with a total of 16 guns). Although Downie had the advantage in long guns, Macomb's carronades gave him the edge at close range.

Macdonough anchored his squadron south of Cumberland Head far enough east of Plattsburgh to ensure that the advancing British army could not reach him with its field artillery. The prevailing winds favored Macdonough because the British could not easily stand off and use their long guns. In addition, before the battle Macdonough put out his kedge anchors so that, if necessary, he could wind his principal ships around to bring a fresh battery to bear on the enemy. This careful preparation played a decisive role in shaping the outcome of the battle.

At 8:00 a.m. on September 11, 1814, Downie rounded Cumberland Head and sailed for the American squadron. Macdonough used his long guns to good effect as the British squadron approached, but Downie brought his ships around in good order. Once the *Confiance* was in position, it delivered a withering broadside that shook the *Saratoga* to its keel and killed or wounded some 40 members of its crew. Although momentarily stunned, the Americans saw a rooster fly into the ship's

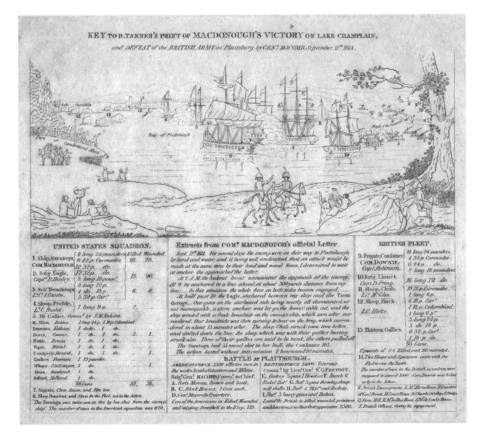

The Battle of Lake Champlain is featured here with a key to the various vessels. The opposing squadrons were actually much further from the shore. (Engraving by B. Tanner after a painting by H. Reinangle. Key by an unknown artist. Both courtesy of the William L. Clements Library, University of Michigan)

This engraving focuses more on the Battle of Plattsburgh (on land) than the more celebrated Battle of Lake Champlain (on water). Although waged across the Saranac River, the land battle was more desultory than depicted here. (Samuel G. Goodrich, *Pictorial History of America*)

shrouds and crow. With this, they let out a lusty cheer and continued the battle.

Several of the smaller vessels on each side were knocked out of action, but the heaviest casualties were on the two flagships, which relentlessly pounded one another with broadsides. Downie was crushed to death 15 minutes into the battle by a gun carriage that was blasted loose from its moorings. His flattened watch reportedly revealed the exact time of his death. Macdonough was twice knocked down and dazed, once by the flying head of a decapitated midshipman. Eventually, almost all of the *Saratoga's* guns facing the enemy were silenced, but Macdonough now performed the masterstroke of the battle by winding his ship around to bring a fresh battery into action.

Lieutenant James Robertson, who had succeeded Downie, tried to wind the *Confiance* around, but without advance preparation his lines became fouled, and the American ship pummeled his ship into submission. According to Robertson, "The Ship's Company declared they would stand no longer to their Quarters, nor could the Officers with their utmost exertions rally them."[20] Two and a half hours into the battle, the *Confiance* surrendered. Although the gunboats had already

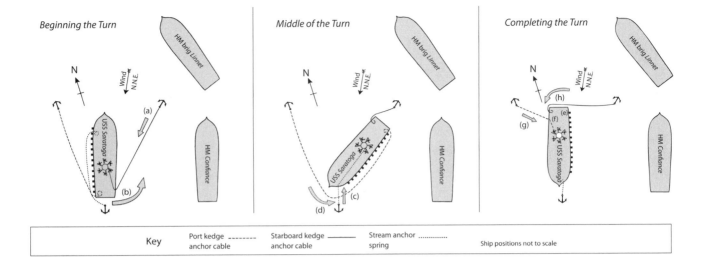

Beginning the Turn

Middle of the Turn

Completing the Turn

Key — Port kedge anchor cable -------- Starboard kedge anchor cable _____ Stream anchor spring .... Ship positions not to scale

withdrawn, the rest of the British ships followed the *Confiance*'s example, and the Battle of Lake Champlain was over.

When Prevost learned of Downie's defeat on the lake, he feared that American troops might be ferried to his rear, cutting him off. He therefore ordered his army to withdraw. The flanking force that he had sent west had trouble finding the ford across the Saranac River but had just gotten into position to attack Macomb's rear when Prevost's order to retreat arrived. There was much grumbling among the troops during the British withdrawal. The veteran officers from the Peninsula had never been happy with Prevost's strict dress code, and now they unleashed a torrent of complaints against his leadership. They were joined by Commodore Yeo and by Prevost's civilian enemies in Canada. "All ranks of people," reported a British newspaper, "were clamorous against Sir George Prevost."[21] Although Prevost had been Canada's savior early in the war, his talent was husbanding limited resources to wage defensive warfare. He had never shown much imagination on the battlefield or much of a flair for offensive operations. He was now recalled to the mother country but died before he could present his case and salvage his reputation.

The invasion of New York was the largest British offensive of the war. It was also the war's last major military operation on the northern frontier. With the approach of cool weather, both sides went into winter quarters to await the outcome of the peace negotiations and the return of warm weather. Although the British retained control of Mackinac and Fort Niagara, the war on this extended front was otherwise a stalemate.

This diagram shows how Macdonough wound the *Saratoga* around in the Battle of Lake Champlain to bring a fresh battery to bear on the British flagship *Confiance*. Winding was commonly used for moving ships in port without setting any sails. Macdonough's genius was not in devising a new tactic but in preparing his ships beforehand so that he could put this well-known technique to good use in the heat of battle. ("How Macdonough Turned the Battle Around." Diagram by Michael J. Crawford and Morgan I. Wilbur. Courtesy of Naval History & Heritage Command, Washington, DC)

The British Blockade Extended

Although the defeat of Napoleon in Europe enabled the British to concentrate on the American war, the economy-minded Admiralty was unwilling to commit the sort of massive naval force needed to completely seal off the long and irregular American coast. It did, however, send enough warships to increase the pressure. The naval blockade had been limited to the middle and southern states in 1813, but in April 1814 it was extended to New England. This was done to bring the war home to more Americans and to prevent American warships and privateers from cruising from New England's ports.

The extension of the British blockade increased the economic pain of the young republic. Total trade (exports plus imports), which had declined from $115 million in 1811 to $50 million in 1813, plunged to $20 million in 1814, and the gluts and shortages that had appeared in 1813 worsened. But not everyone suffered equally from the British blockade. Many people in the middle and western states enjoyed a measure of prosperity, which was fueled by fat government contracts and a spurt in manufacturing. Few people in New England or the southern states shared in this bounty. People living on the coast were especially hard hit because almost everyone's livelihood was tied to the sea. With farmers unable to get their crops to foreign markets and merchants unable to send their ships to sea, suffering was widespread.

People living on American islands off the coast had little choice but to come to terms with the British because trade with the mainland was their lifeline. Although Nantucket was reliably Republican, this Massachusetts island declared its neutrality in August 1814. In exchange for surrendering its public stores and agreeing to supply the Royal Navy, the island's residents were permitted to trade with the mainland and to fish unmolested in nearby waters. Block Island off Rhode Island never declared its neutrality, but people living there routinely supplied the British with so much intelligence and food that U.S. officials prohibited all trade with the island.

The British blockade had an equally profound impact on the nation's finances. Even though the customs duties (taxes on imports) had been doubled at the beginning of the war, income from this critical source of revenue, which had remained flat at $14 million from 1811 to 1813, plummeted to $6 million in 1814. With the cost of the war soaring and revenue drying up, the nation's finances were increasingly at risk.

British Raids on the Atlantic Coast

British raids up and down the Atlantic coast increased dramatically in 1814. From Maine to Georgia, British raiding parties confiscated or destroyed public stores, war material, and maritime goods and burned any settlements that offered resistance. Although these raids were designed mainly to draw off American forces from Canada, they also reflected a new policy of retaliation for American depredations in Upper Canada.

After Campbell's raid on Long Point led to the burning of Dover, Sir George Prevost asked Vice Admiral Sir Alexander Cochrane, who had replaced Sir John Borlase Warren on the American station, to "assist in inflicting that measure of retaliation which shall deter the enemy from a repetition of similar outrages."[22] Cochrane, who had little love for Americans, was happy to comply, and he ordered his commanders on the American station "to destroy & lay waste such Towns and Districts upon the Coast as you may find assailable."[23] But the British admiral was pragmatic enough to realize that he could ill afford to alienate completely a population that supplied his ships with food and other necessities. In a secret memorandum he authorized his officers to spare those places that could supply the Royal Navy or were willing to pay tribute.

Cochrane also targeted the social structure of the slave states. Runaway slaves had been seeking sanctuary with the British ever since the Royal Navy appeared in the Chesapeake the previous year. In April 1814, Cochrane issued a proclamation offering slaves a "choice of either entering into His Majesty's Sea or Land Forces, or of being sent as FREE Settlers, to the British Possessions in North America or the West Indies."[24] Many slaves who responded served as guides or scouts for the British or took part in combat as members of a special corps of Colonial Marines.

Some of the British raids on the American coast did significant damage or garnered considerable plunder. A British flotilla of boats rowed six miles up the Connecticut River to target Pettipaug (now Essex). After driving away the local militia, the British destroyed 27 vessels valued at $140,000. A much larger Royal Navy force threatened Stonington, Connecticut. Although the British did not

Vice Admiral Sir Alexander Cochrane (1758–1832) assumed command of the Royal Navy's Atlantic squadron in 1813 and stepped up the raids on the American coast, especially in the Chesapeake. Cochrane had no love for Americans and thought they needed to be taught a hard lesson for declaring war on the Mistress of the Seas. (Engraving based on a portrait by William Beechey. Library and Archives of Canada)

Joshua Barney (1759–1818) was a rare figure who distinguished himself in both the Revolution and the War of 1812. Besides a successful privateering career, he headed the flotilla of gunboats that harassed the British in the Chesapeake and then led his flotillamen in the defense of Washington at Bladensburg. His artillery pounded the advancing British before he was forced to surrender. He died en route to Kentucky three years after the war when a thigh wound received at Bladensburg flared up. (Portrait by Charles Willson Peale. Library of Congress)

attempt a landing, heavy fire from their warships destroyed a large number of buildings in the town.

Still another British force sailed up the Potomac River and compelled Alexandria to deliver up its public stores and maritime property. American artillery batteries that lined the Potomac made the return trip harrowing, and several British ships that ran aground had to be temporarily unloaded to free them. Despite these mishaps, the entire British squadron made it safely back to the Chesapeake with a huge cache of goods that included 16,000 barrels of flour, 1,000 hogsheads of tobacco, 150 bales of cotton, and $5,000 worth of sugar, wine, and other commodities. One British naval officer considered this feat "as brilliant an achievement . . . as grace the annals of our naval history."[25]

In early 1815 part of Britain's Atlantic squadron showed up at Cumberland Island off the coast of Georgia. The British occupied the island on January 10 and three days later attacked the American battery at Point Peter. The American defenders had to withdraw up the St. Marys River but took a heavy toll on a British detachment sent in pursuit. The British occupied Cumberland Island until the war was over and while there offered sanctuary to many runaway slaves, some of whom joined the Corps of Colonial Marines.

With few regulars available and no idea of where the British would strike next, local officials threatened by British raids had to rely on militia, usually without much success. In the Chesapeake, American officials took another tack. At the suggestion of Joshua Barney, a successful privateering commander, a flotilla of barges and gunboats was established that could harass the Royal Navy and engage its smaller boats in shallow waters. With Barney serving as commander, the Chesapeake flotilla enjoyed considerable success until it had to be torched on August 22 at Pig Point near Upper Marlboro on the Patuxent to keep it out of British hands.

In most cases, the British raids on the Atlantic coast did not rise above the level of petty warfare and plundering, but there were several sizeable amphibious operations that threatened a large swath of the coast or a major population center. These served to remind Americans of how formidable their foe was and how menacing the Royal Navy could be once it was freed from its commitments in Europe.

The Occupation of Maine

British officials considered the coast of Maine a good candidate for amphibious operations. Maine (which was then part of Massachusetts) was thinly populated and closer to the British naval station at Halifax than any other American territory. In addition, northern Maine was wedged between Lower Canada and New Brunswick, and because the Treaty of Paris in 1783 did not spell out the border clearly, the boundary was in dispute. The British were eager to rectify the boundary in their favor so that they could establish a direct overland route between Quebec and Halifax. In June 1814 Lord Bathurst, the secretary of state for war and the colonies, ordered Sir John Sherbrooke, the lieutenant governor of Nova Scotia, to occupy "that part of the District of Maine which at present intercepts the communication between Halifax and Quebec."[26]

Sir John Sherbrooke (1764–1830) served as lieutenant governor of Nova Scotia (the chief official in the province) during the war and oversaw the occupation of Maine in 1814. He succeeded Sir George Prevost as governor-general of Canada after the war. (Benson J. Lossing, *Pictorial Field-Book of the War of 1812*)

The Admiralty had already ordered Admiral Cochrane to seize several islands in Passamaquoddy Bay. These islands were claimed by both nations but were occupied by the United States. In accordance with this directive, the Royal Navy on July 11 landed 1,000 men under Lieutenant Colonel Andrew Pilkington on Moose Island. Pilkington threatened Eastport, which was protected by Fort Sullivan, a crudely built post garrisoned by 85 men under the command of Major Perley Putnam. Apparently at the urging of local residents, Putnam offered no resistance before surrendering to the overwhelming British force. Insisting that this was British territory, Royal officials required all permanent residents to take an oath of allegiance or leave the island. Most took the oath.

Sherbrooke followed up with the main operation on September 1, when 16 warships commanded by Rear Admiral Edward Griffith ferried some 2,500 men under the lieutenant governor's command from Halifax to Penobscot Bay. The British seized Castine, easily driving off the small American force defending the town. Some 600 British soldiers and marines were then dispatched up the Penobscot River in search of the *Adams,* a 28-gun corvette under the command of Captain Charles Morris, who was sheltering his ship at Hampden. The British scattered the local militia at Hampden, forcing Morris and his crew to burn the ship and flee. The British then sailed further up the river and occupied Bangor. A few days later, they seized Machias, which gave them effective control over about 100 miles of the Maine coast.

The British seized all public property in the occupied territory and some private property as well. The residents were given a choice: take an oath to keep the peace or leave the area. Those willing to take a second oath, pledging their allegiance to the Crown, were accorded the same commercial privileges as British subjects, which meant they could freely trade with British ports. Castine became a British port of entry and emerged as a popular resort town for British army and navy officers on leave. There was already considerable illicit trade between Maine and New Brunswick, and most residents welcomed the British occupation because it meant that trade with British North America would now be far less risky.

U.S. officials halted American trade with the occupied territory and hatched a plan for re-conquest. A mixed force of regulars and militia would march overland and attack Castine from the rear. The operation was risky and depended on securing the cooperation of Caleb Strong, the Federalist governor of Massachusetts, who was expected to provide the militia and part of the funding. Strong demurred because the state's resources were stretched thin, and his advisors told him—probably correctly—that such a campaign was unlikely to succeed without naval control of the Penobscot Bay. The plan was shelved when it was leaked to the press. Thus, northeastern Maine, like Mackinac and Fort Niagara, remained in British hands until the war was over.

The Burning of Washington

The British occupation of Maine had little lasting effect and was quickly forgotten after the war was over. Two major operations in the Chesapeake, by contrast, had a profound and enduring impact on the nation. The first was the assault on Washington, D.C. Despite the growing British force in the Chesapeake, government officials were slow to perceive the danger to the nation's capital. Secretary of War Armstrong thought that the British would bypass Washington in favor of Baltimore, a larger and more inviting target, and no one else in the administration seemed much concerned about the capital's safety.

It was not until July 1 that President Madison created a new military district embracing the capital, but he put Brigadier General William H. Winder in charge. This made good sense politically because Winder was the nephew of the Federalist governor of Maryland, whose cooperation was deemed vital to the defense of the region, but the brigadier had done nothing to distinguish himself in the field nor to indicate that he could handle a major command. He got little help from Armstrong and was soon overwhelmed by his duties. With only 500 regulars at his disposal, he had to rely heavily on militia, but instead of planning strategy

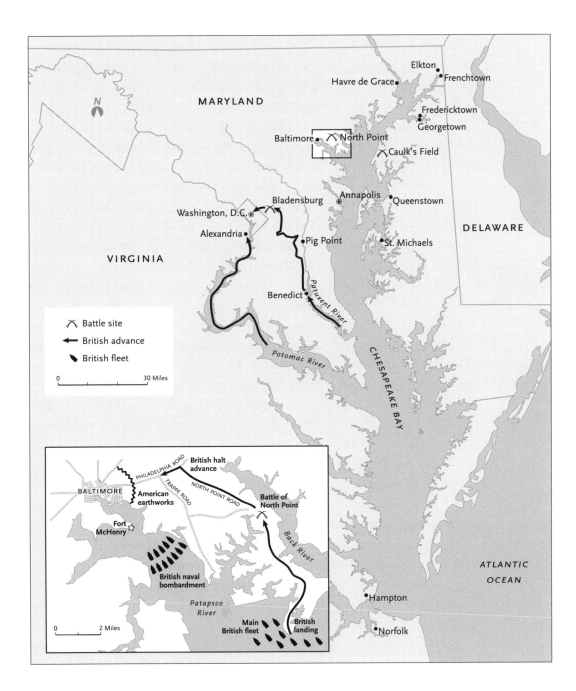

The Campaign in the Chesapeake, 1814

and preparing defenses, he spent most of his time dashing about the countryside to inspect the terrain. As a result, the capital remained exposed.

In mid-August a large British force, 4,000 strong, under the command of Major General Robert Ross arrived in the Chesapeake. Ross was an experienced and respected leader, and like most of the men who accompanied him, a veteran of the Peninsular Wars. With an eye on the capital, Ross on August 19–20 landed his army at Benedict, Maryland, and, guided by two local renegades (one of whom was racked by leprosy), headed north along the Patuxent River. By the time Ross reached Upper Marlboro, Admiral Cochrane, who was providing logistical support for the operation, got cold feet and sent a message urging withdrawal. Ross hesitated, but Rear Admiral Sir George Cockburn, who had spearheaded most of the predatory raids the previous summer, was convinced that no American force could stop them. Hence, he persuaded Ross to continue on to Bladensburg, which lay on a road to the capital from the northeast.

By this time American officials realized that the capital was in danger and made a hurried attempt to provide for its defense. Additional militia units were summoned from the surrounding area, and they were joined by 500 regulars under the command of Colonel William Scott. Commodore Barney, fresh from the destruction of his flotilla, arrived just in the nick of time with 600 U.S. sailors and marines lugging five heavy naval guns. In all, some 6,000 American troops gathered at Bladensburg. They were arrayed in two main lines, although the first line had some lead elements near the river. Secretary of State James Monroe, who was not in the chain of command and had no authority here, redeployed the second line so that it could not support the first. President Madison arrived on the scene but was warned off just as the British appeared.

At 1:00 p.m. on August 24, as the last American troops took their places, 4,000 British troops reached the opposite shore of the Patuxent. Although exhausted from their sun-baked march in temperatures that approached 100 degrees, they were unimpressed by what they saw across the river. According to one officer, the Americans "seemed [like] country people, who would have been much more appropriately employed in attending to their agricultural occupations than in standing, with their muskets, in their hands."[27]

The bridge across the river had been left intact, although the river was shallow enough to ford. Despite taking heavy casualties, first one British brigade, headed by Colonel William Thornton, and then a second, headed by Colonel Arthur Brooke, crossed the bridge to the American side. The British outflanked the first American line, forcing it to fall back. Winder, who had radiated defeatism from the outset, ordered the men in this line to withdraw down the Georgetown Road.

This made it impossible for them to support the second line, on the Bladensburg Road. Panic gripped the fleeing troops, immortalized in wit and verse as "the Bladensburg races." No doubt the British use of Congreve rockets, which did little damage but sometimes frightened even veteran troops, added to the panic.

In spite of the chaos, the second American line, which was anchored by Barney's flotillamen, held firm. With his heavy guns belching grapeshot, Barney held the British off for an hour before he ran out of ammunition, and the British routed the militia on his flank and then stormed his position. Although Barney was wounded and captured, most of his men escaped. By 4:00 p.m. the Battle of Bladensburg was over. The Americans had sustained only about 70 casualties compared to 250 for the British. This disparity suggests that with more reliable troops, the United States might have prevailed. The British made no attempt to pursue the retreating American forces. Mindful of how exhausted his men were, Ross rested them for several hours before advancing into the capital city.

Even before the battle was fought, people began leaving Washington, and with the news of the American defeat, the city took on the appearance of a ghost town. Although wagons were difficult to come by, government clerks managed to find enough to remove most official records, and First Lady Dolley Madison sacrificed her own property to haul away White House treasures, including a large portrait of George Washington. Secretary of the Treasury George W. Campbell had given the president a pair of dueling pistols, but Madison left them in the White House, and they disappeared in the chaos that ensued. Madison and Attorney General Richard Rush proceeded to Virginia and were joined en route by Monroe. Federal officials remained away from Washington for two days.

The British marched into the city around 8:00 p.m. They could find no one to arrange terms of surrender, and they took some sniper fire from a house, which they burned. They then burned the Capitol (which included the Library of Congress). A group of British officers headed by Ross and Cockburn entered the White House and ate some of the food that had been laid out for the president's usual mid-afternoon meal. "We found a supper all ready," recalled Ross's aide, "which many of us speedily consumed . . . and drank some very good wine also."[28] After taking a few souvenirs, the British burned the White House.

The British also torched the buildings housing the Treasury, War, and State Departments, and they destroyed the war material in the federal arsenal on Greenleaf Point. Several ropewalks were burned as well, and the office of the semi-official *National Intelligencer* was destroyed. Dr. William Thornton, who had designed the Capitol Building and was now superintendent of patents, persuaded the British to spare the patent office on the grounds that the samples it housed were private

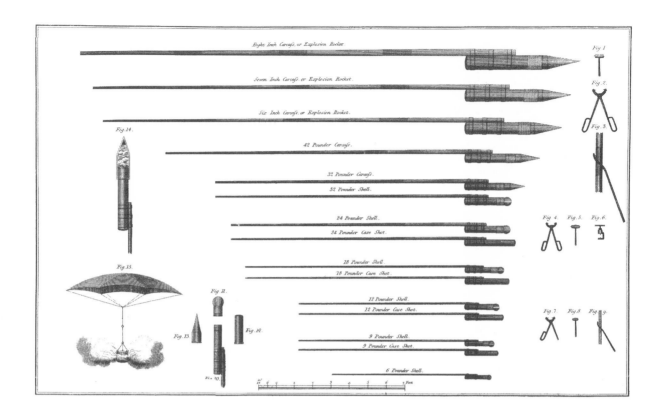

The British developed a new weapons system during the Napoleonic Wars. Congreve rockets were similar to modern skyrockets. After being tested in Europe, they were brought to America and could be fired from land or water. Although sometimes wildly inaccurate, they could frighten inexperienced troops, as they did in the Battle of Bladensburg. (William Congreve, *The Details of the Rocket System*)

THE FALL of WASHINGTON — or Maddy in full flight.

property—"models of the arts . . . useful to all mankind"—and that to burn them would be as reprehensible as the infamous Turkish decision to torch the library at Alexandria in antiquity.[29]

Captain Thomas Tingey was head of the Washington Naval Yard, which was the best-stocked naval facility in the nation. Acting on standing orders, he burned the yard as well as two ships on the stocks, the heavy frigate *Columbia* and the sloop *Argus*. Since the ships could not be moved by the British, this was perhaps premature, although the British probably would have done the job if Tingey had not. The British left intact the U.S. Marine Corp buildings, including the commandant's house, probably because they did not realize what they were.

The fires set by both sides burned all night. "The sky was brilliantly illuminated by the different conflagrations," reported a British officer.[30] People 40 miles away reported seeing the orange sky. The next day a pair of storms struck Washington. One was so violent that it blew down several buildings, killing several British soldiers in the process. The accidental explosion of a dry well filled with powder on Greenleaf Point produced an additional 50 to 75 British casualties and left a

Published in London in 1814, this engraving shows Madison fleeing the burning capital. The three gentlemen on the left, probably Quakers, suggest he is about to join "his bosom friend" Napoleon, who was then in exile on the Mediterranean island of Elba. (Library of Congress)

This portrait of George Washington hung in the White House and was saved by Dolley Madison as the British approached the city. (Based on a portrait by Gilbert Stuart. Library of Congress)

huge hole in the ground. The British departed that same day—August 25—and re-embarked at Benedict on August 30. They left their wounded behind. Commodore Barney, who had been well treated by the British and then paroled, promised to look after the wounded soldiers.

There was considerable looting during the British occupation, but most was done by locals. In spite of the destruction of his office, the editor of the Washington *National Intelligencer* credited the British with good behavior. "No houses were half as much *plundered* by the enemy," he reported, "as by the knavish wretches about the town who profited of the general distress."[31] This view was echoed by other residents, who generally found the occupation force to be respectful of their persons and property.

The Battle for Baltimore

The second major British operation in the Chesapeake in the summer of 1814 targeted Baltimore. The outcome of this assault offered a sharp contrast to the debacle in Washington. The British occupation of the capital city was probably the low watermark for Americans during the war, but it would soon be followed by one of the highlights.

The British were eager to attack Baltimore, the third largest city in the nation, because it was the base for so many American privateers and its maritime wealth offered the prospect of considerable loot. Baltimore was also known to be staunchly Republican and its residents strong supporters of the war. "I do not like to contemplate scenes of blood and destruction," said one British naval officer, "but my heart is deeply interested in the coercion of these Baltimore heroes, who are perhaps the most inveterate against us of all the Yankees."[32]

If General Ross had had cavalry, he might have marched directly overland from Washington, but without this scouting ability, he preferred to withdraw to the coast and sail north to Baltimore. This gave the city time to improve its defenses. Since 1813, Major General Samuel Smith, a U.S. senator and head of the city's militia, had been working to strengthen those defenses, and in the summer of 1814 he redoubled his efforts. After Washington fell, he had almost every available

A British view of the Washington campaign that has been compressed geographically and chronologically. In the upper right is the British army headed by Major General Robert Ross. In the lower right, Commodore Joshua Barney's flotilla is engulfed by flames, although the boats were actually torched by Americans at Pig Point. Public buildings and a ropewalk are in flames in the upper center, and the Washington Naval Yard and the federal arsenal on Greenleaf Point are burning on the left. (Engraving by C. Thompson. Library of Congress)

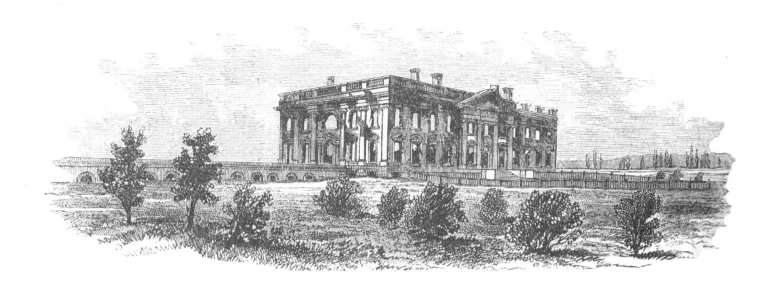

The White House after it was burned by the British in 1814. The interior was gutted, and only the shell survived. The decision to rebuild the public buildings in Washington (rather than move the capital to Philadelphia) was closely contested in Congress. The White House was not ready for occupation again until 1817. (Benson J. Lossing, *Pictorial Field-Book of the War of 1812*)

man in the city building earthworks. By the time the British made their move on Baltimore, they faced a well-fortified city.

Ross began landing his army—about 4,000 troops and upwards of 500 sailors—at North Point at 3:00 a.m. on September 12. Several hours later the British began their march to Baltimore 14 miles away. En route the lead elements of the British force ran into a detachment of militia—part of a much larger force, 3,200 strong, under the command of Brigadier General John Stricker—that blocked the road. When gunfire erupted, Ross raced ahead to scout the enemy and was mortally wounded, probably by grapeshot from American field artillery. With the loss of Ross, Colonel Arthur Brooke assumed command. After softening up the enemy militia with artillery, Brooke ordered a frontal attack that drove the Americans from the field. The Battle of North Point was a British victory but a costly one. Besides losing their beloved commander, the British had sustained 340 killed, wounded, and missing compared to 215 for the Americans. After the battle the British rested for the night.

Resuming his march to Baltimore the next day, Brooke soon realized that he faced strong defenses manned by at least 15,000 troops, mostly militia. He therefore waited for the Royal Navy to move up the Patapsco River and soften up the American lines. Admiral Cochrane had already detached bomb and rocket ships for the job. But to get close enough to hit the American lines, these ships needed first to silence the guns of Fort McHenry, a star-shaped coastal fortification that protected Baltimore's harbor. The fort and nearby batteries were manned by 1,000 troops commanded by Major George Armistead.

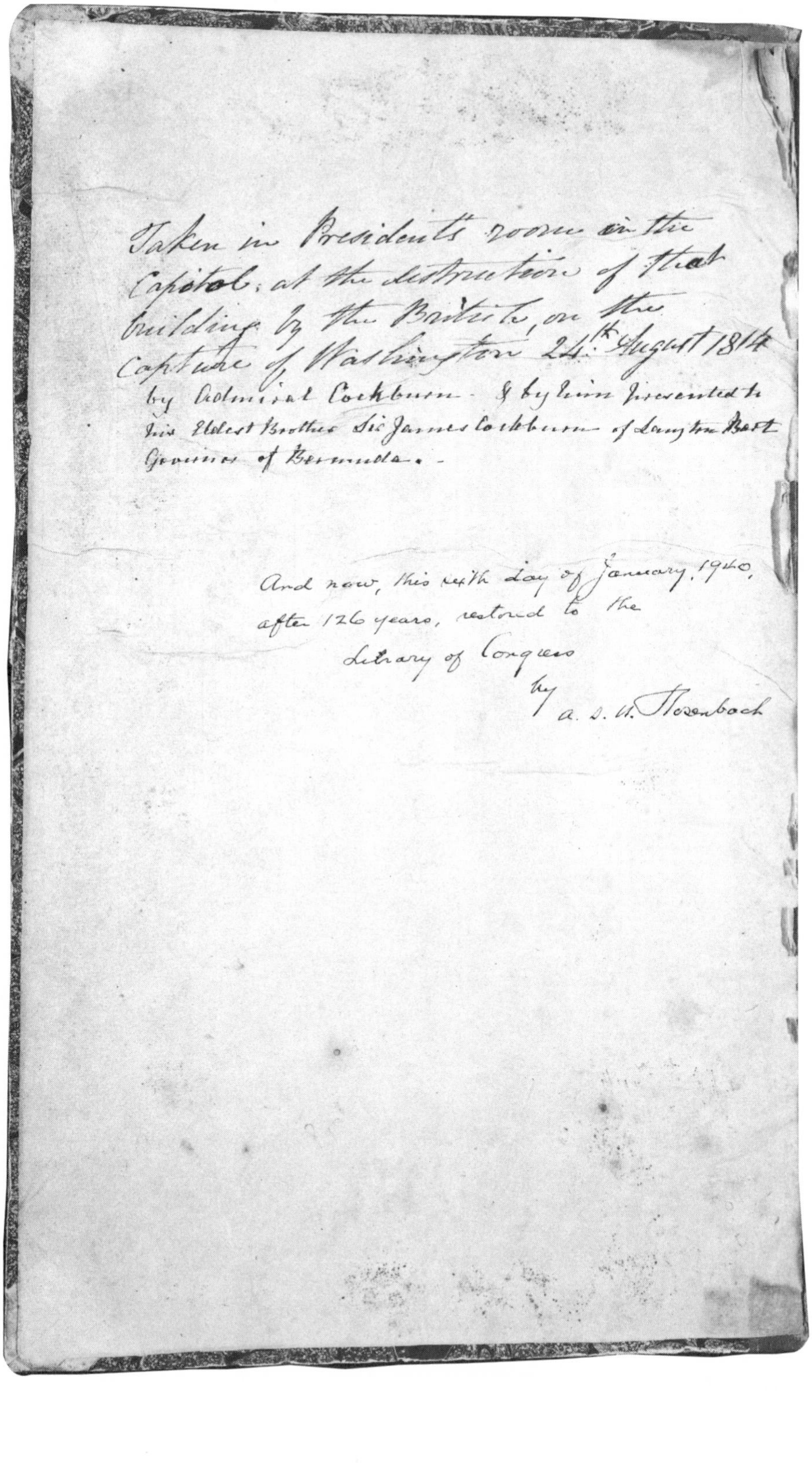

Taken in President's room in the Capitol, at the destruction of that building by the British, on the capture of Washington 24th August 1814 by Admiral Cockburn. & by him presented to his Eldest Brother Sir James Cockburn of Langton Bart Governor of Bermuda.

And now, this 24th day of January 1940, after 126 years, restored to the Library of Congress

by

A. S. W. Rosenbach

The original Library of Congress went up in flames with the Capitol Building. A book that survived the fire— *An Account of the Receipts and Expenditures of the United States for the Year 1810*—was donated to the present Library of Congress by Dr. A.S.W. Rosenbach in 1940. The inscription inside, which appears to be in Rear Admiral George Cockburn's hand, reads: "taken in the President's room in the Capitol, at the destruction of that building by the British, on the capture of Washington 24th, August 1814." (Courtesy of Library of Congress)

Samuel Smith (1752–1839), a powerful U.S. Senator, held a commission
as a major general in the Maryland
militia and headed up the defense of
Baltimore. In what was perhaps his
finest hour, Smith persuaded virtually
the entire male population to turn
out to dig earthworks and man the
defenses. The British rightly judged
the defenses too formidable to breach,
and the city was spared the fate of
Washington. (Engraving by Charles de
Saint-Mémin. Library of Congress)

A panoramic view of various militia units being
organized to meet the British in the Battle
of North Point. (Painting by Thomas Ruckle.
Courtesy of Maryland Historical Society)

On the morning of September 13 the detached squadron moved in and opened fire. The British ships remained outside the range of the fort's biggest guns, and over a 25-hour period fired 1,500 explosive shells and Congreve rockets at the fort, but only 400 found their mark, and the American casualties—four killed and 24 wounded—were light. Cochrane tried to slip 1,200 men in barges by the fort at night to attack Baltimore from the rear, but the flotilla was detected and driven back by heavy fire from the shore. With the failure of this operation, Cochrane notified Brooke that the navy could provide no supporting fire for his army. At 3:00 a.m. on September 14, exactly 48 hours after landing at North Point, Brooke ordered his army to withdraw to the safety of the fleet. This marked the end of the Battle for Baltimore.

Major General Robert Ross (1766–1814), a talented and beloved British officer, oversaw the British occupation of Washington but was killed the following month on the road to Baltimore in a skirmish at the beginning of the Battle of North Point. This idealized illustration shows Ross being helped from his horse after he was wounded. A Congreve rocket is in flight in the background. (Engraving by G. M. Brighty. Library of Congress)

"The Star-Spangled Banner"

One witness to the bombardment of Fort McHenry was Francis Scott Key, a 35-year-old Federalist lawyer from Georgetown. Key had taken a truce ship to the main British fleet at the mouth of the Patapsco to secure the release of a civilian prisoner, Dr. William Beanes, whom the British had seized earlier in the campaign. Key achieved his mission, but the British would not allow the Americans to depart until the next day. Hence, Key spent the night of September 13-14 on the deck of his truce ship watching the bombardment of Fort McHenry some nine miles away. The next morning, he could see the British squadron withdrawing down the river, and (probably with the aid of a spyglass), he saw the fort run up its huge flag, which measured 30 by 42 feet. With this, Key knew that the British bombardment had failed.

Key was so moved that he jotted down the words to a song that he called "The Defence of Fort McHenry." After returning to the mainland, Key refined the song, and it was published as a broadside. The broadside explained how the song had come to be written and suggested that it might be sung to the tune of "Anacreon in Heaven," a well-known British drinking song. The new song was printed in newspapers up and down the coast. Renamed "The Star-Spangled Banner," it became a popular air that was often sung on patriotic occasions. In the twentieth century, this song became the official national anthem. Since the Armistead family

In this illustration from 1816, the British squadron is raining down explosive shells on Fort McHenry. The British ships were actually much further away. Their mortars and rockets could reach the fort, but the fort's garrison guns did not have the range to respond. (Drawing by John Bower. Library of Congress)

Mary Pickersgill (1776–1857) was a Baltimore seamstress who sewed many flags in the early republic. Major George Armistead paid her $406 to make the huge flag that flew over Fort McHenry and that is now on display at the Smithsonian. (Library of Congress)

Francis Scott Key (1780–1843), a Federalist lawyer, was so moved by the sight of the huge American flag that was run up over Fort McHenry after the failure of the British bombardment that he wrote "The Star-Spangled Banner." (Library of Congress)

DEFENCE OF FORT M'HENRY.

The annexed song was composed under the following circumstances—A gentleman had left Baltimore, in a flag of truce for the purpose of getting released from the British fleet, a friend of his who had been captured at Marlborough.—He went as far as the mouth of the Patuxent, and was not permitted to return lest the intended attack on Baltimore should be disclosed. He was therefore brought up the Bay to the mouth of the Patapsco, where the flag vessel was kept under the guns of a frigate, and he was compelled to witness the bombardment of Fort M'Henry, which the Admiral had boasted that he would carry in a few hours, and that the city must fall. He watched the flag at the Fort through the whole day with an anxiety that can be better felt than described, until the night prevented him from seeing it. In the night he watched the Bomb Shells, and at early dawn his eye was again greeted by the proudly waving flag of his country.

Tune—ANACREON IN HEAVEN.

O ! say can you see by the dawn's early light,
  What so proudly we hailed at the twilight's last gleaming,
Whose broad stripes and bright stars through the perilous fight,
  O'er the ramparts we watch'd, were so gallantly streaming?
And the Rockets' red glare, the Bombs bursting in air,
Gave proof through the night that our Flag was still there;
    O ! say does that star-spangled Banner yet wave,
    O'er the Land of the free, and the home of the brave?

On the shore dimly seen through the mists of the deep,
  Where the foe's haughty host in dread silence reposes,
What is that which the breeze, o'er the towering steep,
  As it fitfully blows, half conceals, half discloses?
Now it catches the gleam of the morning's first beam,
In full glory reflected new shines in the stream,
    'Tis the star spangled banner, O ! long may it wave
    O'er the land of the free and the home of the brave.

And where is that band who so vauntingly swore
  That the havoc of war and the battle's confusion,
A home and a country, shall leave us no more ?
  Their blood has washed out their foul footsteps pollution
No refuge could save the hireling and slave,
From the terror of flight or the gloom of the grave,
    And the star-spangled banner in triumph doth wave,
    O'er the Land of the Free, and the Home of the Brave.

O ! thus be it ever when freemen shall stand,
  Between their lov'd home, and the war's desolation,
Blest with vict'ry and peace, may the Heav'n rescued land,
  Praise the Power that hath made and preserv'd us a nation !
Then conquer we must, when our cause it is just,
And this be our motto—" In God is our Trust ;"
    And the star-spangled Banner in triumph shall wave,
    O'er the Land of the Free, and the Home of the Brave.

This broadside printed "The Star-Spangled Banner" for the first time, although initially under the title "Defence of Fort M'Henry." The introductory paragraph explains how the song came to be written, and the broadside suggests that the song be sung to the tune of "Anacreon in Heaven." Although few people know more than the first stanza, there are actually four. (Oscar Sonneck, *The Star-Spangled Banner*)

A contemporary cartoon that shows the local militia driving the British from Baltimore. In the background, a rifleman picks off Major General Ross, although in reality Ross was probably killed by artillery fire. (Etching by William Charles. Library of Congress)

preserved the huge garrison flag, the Battle for Baltimore was not only a success but it gave the fledgling republic two powerful symbols of its nationhood, a song and a flag.

The Battle of Caulk's Field

Although the main focus of their operations was on the west side of the Chesapeake Bay, the British were not idle on the Eastern Shore. To prevent militia located in these counties from coming to the aid of Baltimore, Admiral Cochrane had dispatched a 29-year-old naval officer, Captain Sir Peter Parker, on a diversionary mission. Scion of a distinguished naval family and cousin to Lord Byron, Parker was one of the rising stars in the Royal Navy. Learning from a runaway slave of a militia encampment near present-day Georgetown, Parker decided to attack. On the night of August 31, he landed 250 seamen and marines from his frigate and marched to the American camp.

In command of the militia camp was Lieutenant Colonel Philip Reed, a Revolutionary War veteran and former U.S. senator. Learning of the British approach, Reed broke camp and prepared his men for battle. Reed headed a party of riflemen who harassed the British right flank from a grove of trees before falling back to the main American line, which was anchored by several field pieces. The militia, perhaps 200 strong, fought surprisingly well and suffered only three casualties, while the British, who advanced across open ground and were silhouetted by a full moon, lost about 40 men. Among the British casualties was Captain Parker, who bled to death from a thigh wound before he could be carried back to his ship for medical attention. Although the Americans had expended their ammunition and were on the verge of retreat, the British broke off the attack when Parker went down.

The Battle of Caulk's Field was of no great significance strategically, but it was a rare occasion in which American militia, unaided by regulars, had prevailed against a larger British force. The battle boosted American morale and cost the Royal Navy one of its most promising young officers.

The War on British Commerce

With the expanded British presence in American waters in 1814, it was not easy for U.S. warships to get to sea. Nevertheless, three sloops built for speed—the *Hornet* (20 guns), *Peacock* (22 guns), and *Wasp* (22 guns)—enjoyed successful cruises, although the *Wasp* went down at sea with all hands for unknown reasons. American warships and privateers continued to take a heavy toll on British trade. "The depredations committed on our commerce by Americans ships of war and privateers," complained the *Naval Chronicle*, have "attained an extent beyond all former precedent."[33] "Each daily book at Lloyd's," added an underwriter, "presents a *tremendous* list for our contemplation."[34]

Privateers were especially active in the waters around the British Isles because merchant ships trading from port to port were not required to sail in convoy. "In the chops of the Channel . . . in our own seas," said a member of Parliament, "American privateers had come and carried off our vessels."[35] The American threat in British waters drove up insurance rates to unprecedented levels and prompted merchants to flood the British government with complaints. In the interest of economy, the Admiralty had taken many warships out of service after Napoleon's defeat. Unfortunately for British merchants, this included many smaller warships that had the best chance of running down privateers. Much to the dismay of the

Samuel Chester Reid (1783–1861) commanded the *General Armstrong* when it was attacked by the British in the Azores. Andrew Jackson later claimed that this slowed the British approach to the Gulf Coast. After the war, Reid helped design the 1818 flag, which set the modern pattern for adding a star for each new state but restored the 13 original stripes. (Edward S. Ellis, *The History of Our Country*)

merchants, the Admiralty continued to insist that the force it had deployed was "adequate to the purpose of protecting the trade, both in St. George's Channel and the Northern Sea."[36]

Several privateers enjoyed spectacular cruises in 1814. The *Prince-de-Neufchatel* (17 guns) seized or destroyed $1 million in British property in a single cruise. The *Governor Tompkins* (14 guns) plundered and burned 14 prizes in the English Channel, and the *Harpy* (14 guns) returned from a three-week cruise with booty valued at $400,000. Captain Thomas Boyle added insult to injury by sailing the *Chasseur* (16 guns)—known as "the Pride of Baltimore"—into a British port and posting a proclamation that mocked British naval blockades. Boyle proclaimed a blockade of "all the ports, harbours, bays, creeks, rivers, inlets, outlets, islands, and sea coast of the United Kingdom of G. Britain and Ireland."[37]Although privateers usually fled from British warships, some that were cornered made a good showing. The *General Armstrong* (14 guns) inflicted some 200 casualties when attacked by boats from a squadron of Royal warships in the Azores. Although the privateer had to be abandoned, it lost only nine men. Similarly, the *Prince-de-Neufchatel,* which found itself becalmed within sight of Nantucket, beat off an attack from the boats of the British frigate *Endymion* (47 guns), inflicting at least 65 casualties on the British while losing only 30 of its men. The American privateer made it safely to port with $200,000 in prize goods on board.

Conclusion

All things considered, the campaign of 1814 did not go badly for the United States. Although the offensive on the Niagara was fruitless, and Maine had been occupied and Washington burned, it could have been far worse. The nation retained control of the Detroit frontier, and it had blunted British offensives in upper New York and at Baltimore. And if the U.S. Navy was mostly bottled up in port, privateers continued to take a significant toll on British commerce. Another year of campaigning, however, was not likely to end as well. "We are contending with an exasperated foe," declared a Republican newspaper, "whose mighty power will soon be levelled at our liberties."[38] Americans could only hope that the peace negotiations that were under way in Europe would end the war before the spring thaw ushered in another campaigning season in 1815.

CHAPTER FIVE

A Lasting Peace 1815

By the time the campaign of 1814 had ended, it was clear that the United States faced not simply a formidable foe on the battlefield but also a host of problems that called into question its ability to wage war. The U.S. army had to contend with chronic recruitment and desertion problems, the government was short of funds and teetered on the verge of bankruptcy, trade with the enemy was unchecked and growing, domestic opposition remained intractable, and there was ominous talk of secession in New England. Everyone realized that a crisis was at hand and that the very future of the republic might be at stake.

Congress, Cabinet, and Bipartisanship

Although Congress normally met in November or December, such was the gloomy state of affairs that President Madison summoned the body to meet on September 19. With the capital city in ruins, most of the diplomatic corps had fled, the Russian minister declaring that Washington had "become still more uncomfortable and more expensive than before."[1] Only the French minister remained, and he graciously offered President Madison the use of his rented quarters, the Octagon House, which became the executive mansion for the rest of the war. Congress had to make do with the cramped quarters of the patent office, one of the few government buildings to survive the British occupation. Other government offices were moved into rented homes. Crawford's Hotel, a favorite Georgetown haunt for congressmen and capital visitors alike, was especially crowded, and living conditions in the capital city tried everyone's patience. According to William

When the White House was burned, the Octagon House became the temporary executive mansion. President Madison signed the Treaty of Ghent on the top floor. The building survives and is now owned by the American Architectural Foundation. Although open to the public, its significance as the president's temporary residence remains one of Washington's best-kept secrets. (Library of Congress)

Jones, congressmen were "in bad temper, grumbling at everything."[2]

The president wrestled with several pressing problems, not the least of which was finding suitable candidates to fill cabinet openings. John Armstrong, who was blamed for the capture of Washington, was forced to resign. Relieved to have a potential rival for the presidency discredited and out of the cabinet, Monroe agreed to take over the War Department, but Madison could find no one to replace him at State. Hence, Monroe continued overseeing the nation's foreign affairs as acting secretary of state. William Jones had been an effective secretary of the navy, but he resigned to deal with mounting personal debts. To succeed him, Madison chose Jacob Crowninshield, a Massachusetts merchant who accepted the job only reluctantly and did not actually assume office until the war was nearly over.

Since George W. Campbell was in poor health and had never mastered his duties at the Treasury Department, he, too, resigned. For this crucial post, Madison nominated Alexander J. Dallas, a talented Jamaican-born and British-educated lawyer who lived in Philadelphia. Dallas agreed to take the job even though he considered the Treasury Department "the forlorn hope of executive enterprize."[3] Pennsylvania Republicans had little love for the aristocratic Dallas, who had a bearing of social and intellectual superiority, but deferred to the president's judgment. "Tell *Doctor* Madison," Senator Abner Lacock reportedly said, "that we are now willing to submit to his Philadelphia lawyer for head of the treasury. The public patient is so very sick that we must swallow anything the doctor prescribes, however, nauseous."[4]

In his opening address to Congress, the president emphasized the successes of the recent campaign, but he had to concede that the nation faced an enemy who was "powerful in men and money" and that "the situation of our country called for its greatest efforts."[5] Such was the dire state of affairs that some Federalists in the middle and southern states considered supporting the war, and although there was talk in both parties of sharing power, nothing came of it. According to one Federalist, Madison thought that it would be "a passport to the Presidency" if he appointed any member of the opposition to the cabinet, and Republicans in Congress were equally unyielding.[6]

Monroe further alienated Federalists when he publicly announced in October that he favored invading Canada again, this time with a large army raised by conscription. "The great object to be attained," he later told Major General Jacob Brown, "is to carry the war into Canada and to break the British power there."[7] This suggested, as one Federalist put it, that the "character of the war [had] not changed" and that the administration was still "eager for conquest and aggrandizement."[8] Raising troops by conscription, which smacked of French practices, went down hard as well. Annoyed by Republican political exclusiveness and strategic intransigence, Federalists dropped all talk of supporting the war. "The delusion [of bipartisanship] has vanished," concluded a Federalist newspaper. "The call to union means nothing."[9]

Moving the Capital

In spite of the persistence of partisanship, the first issue that Congress faced was not a party matter at all, but one that divided members along regional lines. This was the issue of moving the capital. Many northerners had never reconciled themselves to Washington, which was little more than a village and had few amenities, and the destruction of the public buildings only added to their discontent. Philadelphia, a more cultured and cosmopolitan city with an abundance of services, beckoned. Eager to regain the capital that they had lost in 1800, city officials in Philadelphia tried to woo the government with a promise of suitable accommodations. In spite of southern opposition, Congress appeared ready to accept this offer, but it was voted down when the administration launched a determined lobbying effort to keep the capital where it was. With the defeat of removal, Congress voted to rebuild Washington. It also adopted a companion measure to purchase Thomas Jefferson's personal library to replace the original Library of Congress, which had gone up in flames when the British burned the Capitol. Jefferson's collection was the largest private library in America, and, as always, the former president was in need of money to support his costly lifestyle and to service the huge debt load that he carried. The government paid Jefferson $24,000.

Alexander J. Dallas (1759–1817), a haughty and aristocratic Pennsylvania Republican, had a good command of public finance and served as Madison's last wartime secretary of the treasury. (Portrait by Freeman Thorp after an original by Gilbert Stuart. Wikimedia Commons)

Raising Men

Congress next turned its attention to the problem of raising troops. Although there were some 40,000 men in the army, the reporting procedures were so unreliable that the War Department thought it had only 30,000, which was less than half of the 62,500 authorized. With British troop strength in America growing and another campaign in the offing, Congress needed to raise more men. Monroe proposed raising 40,000 volunteers for local defense and 30,000 regulars by conscription for offensive operations in Canada. Monroe's conscription proposal got nowhere, and a compromise bill that went through several forms—conscripting 80,000 militia for one or two years for either local defense or for offensive operations—raised such a storm of opposition that it, too, went down to defeat.

With the defeat of conscription, Congress sought to boost enlistments in the regular army by doubling the land bounty so that recruits now received $124 in cash and 320 acres of land. This was a princely sum. Based on wage levels, it was probably the equivalent of $30,000 today. Congress also authorized the enlistment of minors without the consent of parent or guardian, a law that Federalists bitterly opposed and that Massachusetts and Connecticut openly obstructed. To boost troop strength still further, Congress authorized the War Department to recruit 40,000 volunteers for two years' service and to take another 40,000 men serving in state armies into federal service.

Securing Money

The financial problems that the administration faced were even more vexing. The government had been funding the war with public loans and treasury notes, which were short-term interest-bearing certificates. Borrowing money had become increasingly difficult until the summer of 1814, when a loan offered to the public went mostly unfilled. Unable to borrow money, the Treasury Department defaulted on the national debt as well as on some treasury notes that came due. (Ironically, bondholders abroad got paid because the London-based House of Baring, the U.S. government's banker abroad, advanced the necessary funds.)

Nor was this the only problem the Treasury faced. British raids in the Chesapeake in the summer of 1814 had caused a run on the banks there, and eventually all the banks outside of New England had suspended specie payments, refusing to redeem their notes in gold or silver. Although the banks in New England remained solvent, they contracted their operations to protect their specie position. With the suspension of specie payments, bank paper fell in value, and banks no longer honored one another's notes. This meant that the Treasury had to accept depreciated bank paper in the payment of taxes or the fulfillment of loan contracts and that it could no longer move money from bank to bank to get cash where it was most needed.

In effect, the whole system of war finance had collapsed. Public credit was nearly extinct. U.S. bonds fell to 75 percent of their nominal value and were quoted as low as 60 percent in Boston. Treasury notes depreciated as well, and there were now so many in circulation that most banks and contractors would no longer accept them. With so little money available, government departments had trouble meeting even their most pressing obligations. For many soldiers, army pay was six to 12 months in arrears even though by law the limit was supposed to be two months. In many military districts, army and navy recruiting slowed or came to a standstill, and the U.S. arsenal at Springfield was idled. "Something must be done and done speedily," warned William Jones, "or we shall have an opportunity of trying the experiment of . . . carrying on a vigorous war without money."[10]

Many southerners, including Jefferson and Monroe, favored using paper money. As Nathaniel Macon of North Carolina was fond of saying, "*paper money never was beat.*"[11] But Madison was skeptical, and Dallas positively disdainful. Dallas preferred to rely on conventional loans supplemented by treasury notes and supported by new taxes and a national bank. But the sums needed were staggering. Even with new taxes, Dallas anticipated a revenue shortfall of $12 million for 1814 and $41 million for 1815—over $50 million in all. This figure stunned congressmen on both sides of the aisle. Congress sought to shore up American finances by adopting a new round of excise taxes, which gave the nation the largest system of internal taxes adopted before the Civil War—certainly far more extensive than the system that had spelled doom for the Federalists in 1800.

Congress next turned its attention to a national bank. This was a contentious issue. Many Federalists were hostile to any bank that would simply be an engine for financing the war, and some Republicans were opposed to any bank at all. Dallas wanted a large bank subject to government control that would have to lend the Treasury $30 million, but the bill that Congress finally passed provided for a small, autonomous bank that would be under no obligation to lend the government anything. Dallas was furious. "I asked for bread," he complained, "and they gave me a stone."[12] Madison vetoed the bill and sent it back to Congress for reconsideration.

Chastened, Republicans in Congress now appeared ready to give the administration the bank it wanted. But before they could act, news of a peace treaty arrived, and the bill was postponed. Even if the administration had gotten the bank it wanted, it would have been difficult to avoid flooding the nation with more treasury notes. This would have fueled inflation and contributed to the growing financial chaos.

Trade with the Enemy

No less vexing to the administration was the growing trade with the enemy. The embargo adopted the previous year had done little to stem the flow of American food to the British army and navy, and as more British troops poured into Canada in 1814, the trade only increased. Before the British blockaded New England, much of the trade was carried on legally in neutral vessels sailing from port to port along the Atlantic coast. There were even neutral vessels flying Swedish and Spanish colors operating on Lake Champlain. The trade overland was more extensive, and though clearly illegal, there was little the administration could do to stem it. "From the St. Lawrence [River] to the [Atlantic] Ocean," reported Major General George Izard in July 1814, "an open Disregard prevails for the Laws prohibiting Intercourse with the Enemy."[13] As a result, British commissary agents had little trouble buying all the provisions they needed to feed the King's troops. "Two-thirds of the army in Canada," boasted Governor George Prevost in August, "are at this moment eating beef provided by American contractors."[14]

In November Dallas sent a report to Congress asking for additional powers to stamp out the trade. Over the protests of Federalists, Republicans rammed through a new enemy trade act that gave customs officials sweeping powers to conduct searches, seize goods, and raise posses. The bill also rendered government agents virtually immune to damage suits. Madison signed the bill into law, but the measure was never given a fair test because it expired shortly thereafter with the end of the war. Whether it would have worked is doubtful. Smugglers showed remarkable ingenuity in keeping open profitable avenues of trade, and they usually had the support of the local populace, including city and county officials. In the ongoing contest between smugglers and customs officials, most of the advantages still lay with the former, and there was little that Congress could do to tip the balance in favor of the latter.

Federalist Opposition

In October 1814, William Wirt, a Virginia lawyer and writer who later served as the nation's attorney general, visited the president in Washington. Madison was "miserably shattered and woe-begone," he reported. "His mind seems full of the

New England revolt."[15] The following month, the president confided to a friend that he considered the conduct of New England "the source of our greatest difficulties in carrying on the war."[16] Madison's concern was understandable because although Federalists everywhere opposed the war, those in New England had been the most obstreperous, and in the fall of 1814 they ratcheted up their opposition and threatened disunion.

Although some Federalists in the middle and southern states were tempted to drop their opposition in 1812 and in 1814, Republicans never offered them enough concessions to lure them into the fold. Hence, Federalists presented a united front against the conflict. In Congress, they supported bills to expand the navy and build coastal fortifications (which they considered sound long-term investments), but they opposed all bills to raise men or money or to encourage privateering. In fact, their cohesion on war measures in both houses was exceptional. In the House, over 94 percent of Federalists voted together on war-related measures; in the Senate over 92 percent. Through most of American history, a party cohesion of 70 percent has been considered good. The unity of purpose shown by Federalists during the War of 1812 was remarkable.

Even though Federalists everywhere opposed the war, in New England they went the furthest. They wrote, spoke, and preached against the war; they discouraged enlistments in the army and subscriptions to the war loans; and they used the machinery of local and state government to obstruct the war effort. In Hartford, they adopted city ordinances to curtail army recruiting, and in New Bedford they quarantined returning privateers (ostensibly on medical grounds). The New England states also feuded with the national government over the control, disposition, and pay of the militia. By the fall of 1814, these states had to pay for their own defense measures because the administration could not (because of a shortage of funds) or would not (because of a dispute over command). Growing defense costs led to the Hartford Convention, a regional conference summoned to deal with war-related matters and to air New England's long-term grievances against the Republican administration in Washington.

The Hartford Convention

Twenty-six delegates attended the Hartford Convention, which met in secret from December 15, 1814, to January 5, 1815. The delegates represented Massachusetts, Connecticut, and Rhode Island as well as several counties in New Hampshire and Vermont. Despite secessionist talk in New England, there was no serious secessionist movement, and moderates remained firmly in control at Hartford.

The Hartford Convention or *LEAP NO LEAP*.

A parody of the Hartford Convention depicts the King of England inviting Harrison Gray Otis to bring the New England states into the British Empire. The three delegates considering the "leap" represent Massachusetts, Connecticut, and Rhode Island. Governor Caleb Strong below prays for a successful leap so that he can join the British aristocracy as Lord Essex. New England would be abandoning the many heroes of the war whose names are inscribed on the left. (Etching by William Charles. Library of Congress)

Josiah Quincy of Massachusetts best captured the spirit of the meeting. When asked what the result would be, he replied "A GREAT PAMPHLET!"[17] Although willing to sanction nullification, the delegates at Hartford were careful to avoid any other action that suggested disunion. Instead, they used the convention to blow off steam and recommend remedies for New England's grievances.

The report of the Hartford Convention was made public on January 6. To deal with unconstitutional laws (like the one authorizing minor enlistments), the report recommended state nullification. To secure money needed for defense, the report proposed that the states be permitted to preempt federal tax money collected within their borders. And to secure New England's long-term interests in the Union, the report recommended a series of constitutional amendments.

The proposed amendments called for: (1) requiring a two-thirds vote in Congress to declare war, interdict foreign trade, or admit new states to the Union; (2) limiting embargoes to 60 days; (3) ending the three-fifths rule for counting slaves in apportioning Congress; (4) barring naturalized citizens from federal office; (5) limiting presidents to a single term; and (6) prohibiting the election of a president from the same state twice in succession. These amendments represented a catalogue of New England's grievances over the previous decade. They were designed to preserve the region's place in the Union and prevent a recurrence of those policies that Federalists considered most injurious to section and nation. Nothing came of any of the recommendations of the Hartford Convention because the war ended soon after the report was published.

The British on the Gulf Coast

Just as the report of the Hartford Convention was making the rounds in the East, Andrew Jackson, who was now a major general in the regular army and in command of the Gulf Coast, was preparing for a major battle at New Orleans. As early as November 1812, Admiral Sir John Borlase Warren had suggested that the British target the Gulf Coast in the hope of drawing off American troops from Canada, but by the time the campaign got under way the main objective was to occupy American territory that could be used as a bargaining chip in the peace negotiations.

Although the British hoped to capitalize on friendly Indians in Florida, particularly Creeks and Seminoles, and Spanish residents in Louisiana, most of whom had never reconciled themselves to American rule, the serious fighting would be done by battle-hardened British veterans fresh from the Peninsular War, who would be ferried to America via Jamaica by the Royal Navy. Although the expedition was supposed to be secret, it was reported in newspapers on both sides of the Atlantic.

Major General Robert Ross was chosen to command the expedition, but after he was killed outside of Baltimore, the assignment went to Major General Sir Edward Pakenham, an experienced and respected officer who was the Duke of Wellington's brother-in-law. The expedition also included Lieutenant Colonel Alexander Dickson, who was considered the ablest artillery officer in the British army, and Lieutenant Colonel John Fox Burgoyne, an experienced engineer and the illegitimate son of Major General John Burgoyne, who had surrendered at Saratoga in the American Revolution.

With the blessing of local Spanish officials, 100 British troops under the command of Major Edward Nicolls occupied the forts at Pensacola in August of 1814, but they were driven off by Jackson in November. Having neutralized the British

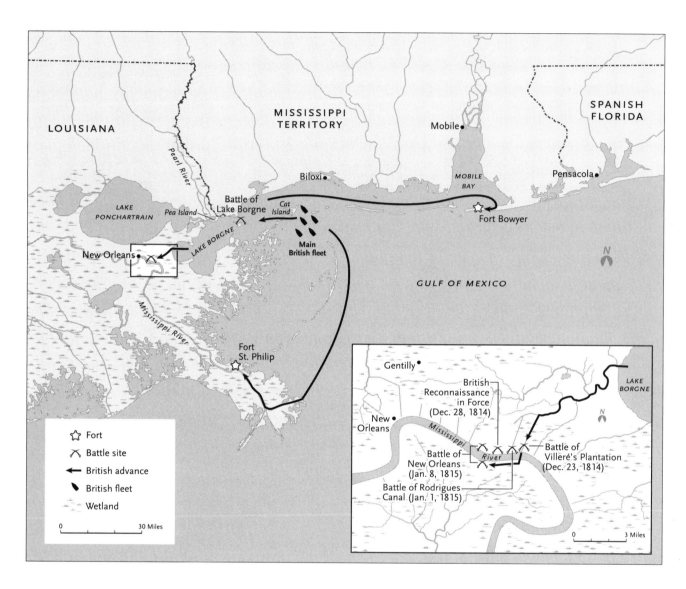

LOUISIANA

MISSISSIPPI
TERRITORY

SPANISH
FLORIDA

Mobile

Pearl River

Biloxi

Pensacola

LAKE
PONCHARTRAIN

Pea Island

Battle of
Lake Borgne

Cat
Island

MOBILE
BAY

Fort Bowyer

New Orleans

LAKE BORGNE

Main
British fleet

N

GULF OF MEXICO

Mississippi River

Fort
St. Philip

Fort

☆ Fort

⤬ Battle site

← British advance

◣ British fleet

︴ Wetland

0 ⸺ 30 Miles

Gentilly

British
Reconnaissance
in Force
(Dec. 28, 1814)

LAKE
BORGNE

New
Orleans

Mississippi

River

N

Battle of
New Orleans
(Jan. 8, 1815)

Battle of
Villeré's Plantation
(Dec. 23, 1814)

Battle of Rodrigues
Canal (Jan. 1, 1815)

0 ⸺ 3 Miles

The New Orleans Campaign, 1814–1815

at Pensacola, Jackson headed for Mobile, which initially he thought would be the main British target, but then, almost belatedly, he headed for New Orleans, arriving in the Crescent City on December 1.

Jackson quickly realized that the city was riddled with disloyalty and sapped by defeatism. According to a transplanted New Englander, "The war of the U.S. is very unpopular with us." The French and Spanish residents (who constituted a majority of the population) were called up for militia duty in early 1814 but "absolutely refused to be marched" and "declared themselves liege [loyal] subjects of Spain or France."[18] By the late fall, business was at a standstill, and cash was so scarce that government officials had no funds for defense. There was every likelihood that New Orleans would simply capitulate if a British force appeared at its gates.

Jackson's arrival transformed the city. "All classes of society were now animated with the most ardent zeal," wrote a contemporary. "General Jackson had electrified all hearts."[19] After personally reconnoitering the surrounding area, Jackson ordered the water

approaches to the city blocked, established batteries at key points, organized an intelligence network, and set about augmenting his regular force, which consisted of only 1,000 men. Over the protests of the governor and other white residents, he accepted into service a corps of free blacks made up of refugees from Santo Domingo. He also accepted the services of other volunteer units as well as the Baratarian pirates (headed by Jean and Pierre Laffite), who agreed to help if smuggling charges against them were dropped. Militia from the countryside— some from as far away as Tennessee—poured into the city. Some Cherokee and Choctaw sharpshooters also joined Jackson's force.

At the end of November, a large British force departed from Jamaica in a squadron commanded by Vice Admiral Sir Alexander Cochrane. The British arrived at Pea Island—about 30 miles from New Orleans—on December 13 and established a base there. Because they lacked enough small boats to operate further north, they decided to approach New Orleans via Lake Borgne. Blocking the way was a squadron of five U.S. gunboats and two other vessels manned by 200 seamen and commanded by Captain Thomas ap Catesby Jones. To seize

Major General Sir Edward Pakenham (1778–1815), the Duke of Wellington's brother-in-law, was given command of the Gulf Coast campaign after Major General Robert Ross was killed in the Battle for Baltimore. Pakenham was one of two British major generals who perished from the deadly American fire in the frontal assault on Andrew Jackson's line at New Orleans. (Painting by T. Heaphy. Fortier, *History of Louisiana*)

control of the lake, the British dispatched 45 boats and 1,200 sailors and marines under the command of Captain Nicholas Lockyer of the Royal Navy. Lockyer had no trouble defeating and capturing the American flotilla after it was becalmed, although the battle delayed the British advance and gave Jackson more time to prepare his defenses.

From Lake Borgne the British advanced along several bayous and a canal to the Mississippi River eight miles below New Orleans. There on December 23 an advance force of 1,600 men under the command of Colonel William Thornton occupied the plantation home of Major General Jacques Villeré, commander of the Louisiana militia. The British high command used this building as its headquarters for the rest of the campaign. Although the British captured some 30 militia at the plantation, Villeré's son escaped to warn Jackson of the enemy's approach.

The Battle of New Orleans

Determined to meet the British outside of New Orleans and before they were at full strength, Jackson quickly rounded up 1,800 men and led them to within a mile of Villeré's plantation. On the night of December 23, Jackson fought the first of three preliminary battles against the British. After his two river ships, the *Louisiana* (22 guns) and the *Carolina* (14 guns), had softened up the British, Jackson attacked. In the confused night fighting that ensued, there were many bayonet wounds from the hand-to-hand combat, and both sides suffered casualties from friendly fire. By the time the Battle of Villeré's Plantation (also known as the Night Engagement at New Orleans) had ended, the British had sustained 275 casualties to Jackson's 215.

After withdrawing, Jackson constructed a defensive line from the river to a cypress swamp in the east. In the days that followed, Jackson worked to extend and strengthen this line into a formidable defensive work. In the meantime, the American ships bombarded British positions, and sharpshooters and skirmishers took a toll on British pickets.

British reinforcements continued to pour in, and Pakenham himself arrived on Christmas Day. Two days later hot shot from a furnace that Pakenham had ordered built destroyed the *Carolina,* although Jackson's men managed to tow the *Louisiana* to safety before it, too, fell victim. The next day, December 28, Pakenham launched an assault on Jackson's position but took such heavy fire from the *Louisiana,* which expended 800 rounds, that he called off the attack. In this battle, known as the British Reconnaissance in Force, casualties on both sides were light, perhaps 35 for the Americans and 55 for the British.

On January 1, 1815, Pakenham ordered several large naval guns that had been laboriously hauled in from the fleet to open fire on Jackson's line. The fire, however, was ineffective, with the rounds either overshooting their mark or pounding harmlessly into earthworks. Jackson's counterfire took a heavier toll, and when the British ran out of ammunition, they had to withdraw. In the Battle of Rodrigues Canal (also called the Artillery Duel at New Orleans), the British sustained about 75 casualties, the Americans about half that number.

By this time, Pakenham had concluded that he had no choice but to launch a frontal assault against Jackson's line, and this set the stage for the climactic final engagement on January 8. This was *the* Battle of New Orleans. By this time, Pakenham and Jackson each had about 5,000 men. Pakenham's plan was to dispatch one brigade under Colonel Thornton across the river to overrun the militia positions and then turn the American guns there against Jackson's main army on the east bank. Meanwhile, three other brigades would attack Jackson's line. Although the British succeeded on the west bank, they were so far behind schedule that by the time they had driven off the militia, the battle on the east bank was over.

Pakenham's main assault was initially covered by fog, but when the fog lifted, his army was exposed. The big naval guns that anchored the eight batteries in Jackson's line did most of the damage, belching forth grapeshot and cannister that cut large swaths into the advancing British lines. As the British got closer they sustained additional casualties, first from rifle fire and then from muskets. One British officer, a veteran of the Napoleonic Wars, later characterized the fire from all arms as "the most murderous I ever beheld before or since."[20] Only one British column along the river bank got to the American line, but it was quickly repulsed.

The fighting was over in less than an hour, and British casualties were little short of astonishing. Some 2,000 Redcoats were killed, wounded, or missing. Among the dead were two British major generals, Pakenham and Samuel Gibbs. Jackson's own losses, by contrast, were very light: only 13 on the east bank and another 57 on the west bank.

An engraving of Andrew Jackson done in 1817 based on a portrait painted in 1816. It is thus nearly contemporaneous with the Battle of New Orleans. (Engraving by David Edwin, after a painting by Nathan W. Wheeler. John Reid and John Henry Eaton, *The Life of Andrew Jackson*)

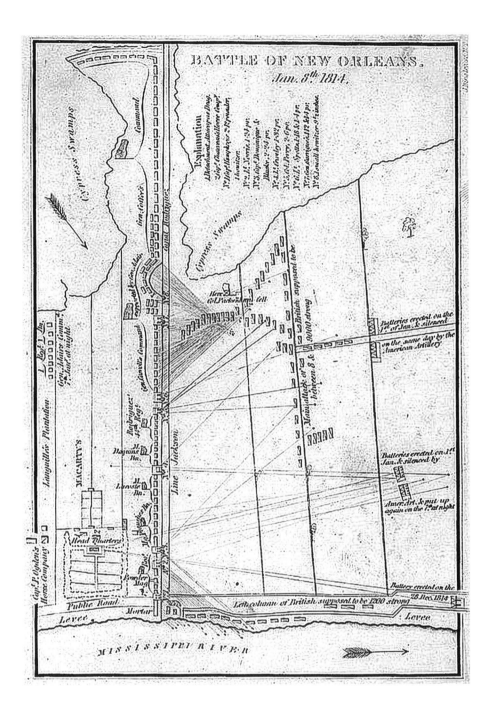

A map of the Battle of New Orleans created between 1820 and 1840. (Library of Congress)

This drawing of the Battle of New Orleans is based on a sketch prepared by Major Arsène Lacarrière Latour, Jackson's chief engineer. (Benson J. Lossing, *Pictorial Field-Book of the War of 1812*)

A romanticized depiction of the death of Major General Edward Pakenham, the ranking British army officer on the Gulf Coast, who was one of the many British victims at New Orleans. (Engraving by Felix Octavius Carr Darley. Library of Congress)

Assault on Fort St. Philip and Capture of Fort Bowyer

Although the British withdrew to lick their wounds, they were not yet done on the Gulf Coast. Cochrane sent a squadron of ships up the Mississippi River to pound Fort St. Philip, located about 65 miles south of New Orleans. Over a ten-day period (January 9–18), the British fired 70 tons of ordnance. The fort suffered considerable damage but refused to submit. Next the British turned their attention to Mobile, which was defended by Fort Bowyer. In a siege that stretched over four days (February 8–11), the Royal navy menaced the fort on three sides, while 5,000 British troops were landed on the shore. Overwhelmed by this show of power, the fort surrendered. This ended the campaign on the Gulf Coast because news arrived shortly thereafter that a peace treaty had been signed.

Martial Law and Militia Executions

Jackson emerged from the war on the Gulf Coast as a great hero, but two things sullied his reputation. Jackson had declared martial law on December 16 to prevent spies from moving freely into and out of New Orleans, but he was reluctant to rescind the decree after the fighting was over. Although news that a peace treaty had been signed arrived on February 19, Jackson waited until official news of peace reached him in mid-March before relenting. In the meantime, when a member of the Louisiana legislature protested, Jackson had him arrested. When a federal judge, Dominick A. Hall, ordered the man released, Jackson jailed Hall. Later Hall hauled Jackson into court and fined him $1,000 for contempt. "The only question," the judge said, "was whether the Law should bend to the General or the General to the Law."[21] Although Jackson paid his fine, 30 years later it was refunded (with interest) by Congress after the aging general and former president had come upon hard times.

Even more draconian was Jackson's punishment of the leaders of several militia units that had left his camp in September 1814 because they thought their tour of duty was up. Jackson disagreed, and when the militia returned, he ordered six leaders tried by military court for mutiny and desertion. Convicted, the men were executed by firing squad on February 21, 1815, after unofficial news of peace had arrived and the danger to the Gulf Coast had receded. Jackson's enemies were eager to remind the public of Old Hickory's severe brand of military justice when he later sought the presidency. During the election of 1828, they circulated handbills that featured six coffins and told the story of the unfortunate militia leaders.

Despatch   Majestic   Endymion   Tenedos   President   Pomone

The Last Naval Battles

Even though the British tightened their grip on the Atlantic Coast in the last year of the war, their naval blockade remained porous. The coast was simply too extensive for the number of ships the economy-minded Admiralty was willing to deploy, and British warships were often blown off station during winter storms. This meant that it was still possible for some American warships to get to sea. Two of the nation's heavy frigates, the *President* (53 guns) and the *Constitution* (52 guns) managed to slip out to sea and engage British warships in 1815, although the results of their battles were very different.

The *President,* now under the command of Captain Stephen Decatur, put to sea from New York during a severe snowstorm on January 14. Shortly thereafter, the heavy frigate ran aground. Although Decatur managed to free his ship, the hammering she took while aground evidently deprived her of some of her speed and sailing qualities. Decatur's aim was to sail to the Straits of Malacca to pounce on the East India Company's rich China fleet, but barely had he freed his ship when he was pursued by a British squadron that included the *Endymion* (47 guns), the fastest frigate in the Royal Navy, commanded by Captain Henry Hope. Although overmatched, *Endymion* was superbly handled and managed to cripple

Near the end of the war, a British squadron headed by the frigate *Endymion* pounded the U.S. Frigate *President* into submission and compelled it to surrender. This was the only heavy frigate defeated by the British during the war. (John H. Spears, *The History of Our Navy*)

The U.S. Frigate *Constitution's* finest hour may have come in early 1815, when the brilliant seamanship of Captain Charles Stewart (1778–1869) enabled "Old Ironsides" to capture two British warships, the *Cyane* and *Levant*. Shown here is the American frigate towing the *Cyane*. The British ship was actually put under the control of a prize crew instead of being towed. (Painting by Edward Mueller. Library of Congress)

the *President* by repeatedly pounding her starboard quarter at close range. With other British frigates in pursuit, Decatur could not bring his own ship around to take advantage of his superior firepower, nor could he escape from the rest of the enemy squadron when the *Endymion* disengaged. Hence, he surrendered. The defeat of the *President* was a significant victory for the British, the only time they captured a "super-frigate" during the war.

The *Constitution*, by contrast, continued her remarkable run of good luck by adding another successful cruise to her record. Now under the command of Captain Charles Stewart, the large frigate slipped out of Boston in December 1814. On February 20 she was near the Madeira Islands off the coast of North Africa when she encountered two British warships, the *Cyane* (33 guns), commanded by Captain Gordon Falcon, and the *Levant* (21 guns), under Captain George Douglas.

The two Royal Navy commanders were so confident of their seamanship and fighting ability that instead of fleeing the larger American ship, they engaged her but without success. In a superb display of sailing and gunnery, Captain Stewart pounded the British ships from a distance and then raked them at close range. With their masts and rigging shot away, both British ships surrendered. The *Constitution* had to abandon the *Levant* when chased by a British squadron, but "Old Ironsides" made it safely back to port with her reputation much enhanced. The *Cyane,* manned by a prize crew, also arrived safely in the United States. By then, however, the war was over.

Peace Negotiations

Within a week of the declaration of war in June 1812, the Madison administration sent out peace feelers through various channels. Republican leaders were convinced that the British had not taken their protests on the maritime issues seriously and hoped that the declaration of war by itself would elicit concessions that might make any fighting unnecessary. The American price for peace: an end to the Orders-in-Council and impressment.

British officials were puzzled by this initiative. In Europe, talk of peace usually came at the end of, rather than the beginning of, hostilities. The United States had won no battles, nor had it done anything else to suggest that it was in any position to impose terms. As it happened, the British had repealed the Orders-in-Council on June 23, five days after the declaration of war, but this news did not reach Washington until nearly two months later. Having made one major concession, the British were in no mood to make another, especially on an issue as vital as impressment. Thus, even though neither side really wanted war, the peace negotiations in the summer of 1812 went nowhere. The conflict continued for another two and one half years, although impressment was now the only major issue at stake.

In March 1813, Russia offered to mediate an end to the war. Although President Madison eagerly accepted this offer, the British declined. They had no wish to conduct negotiations under the auspices of an inland power (even an ally) that was likely to favor a broad definition of neutral rights. To demonstrate their own peaceful intentions, however, the British countered by proposing direct negotiations with the United States, although they insisted that they would make no concessions that were inconsistent "with the Maritime Rights of the British Empire."[22] With the war in Europe now going well for the British, this was a thinly veiled threat to stand firm on impressment.

To represent the United States in the negotiations, Madison picked a strong delegation that included outspoken War Hawk and onetime speaker of the house Henry Clay, former secretary of the treasury Albert Gallatin, and future presi-

The Treaty of Ghent was signed on Christmas Eve in 1814. The two delegation heads, Lord Gambier (1756–1833) on the left and John Quincy Adams (1767–1848) on the right, are pictured here shaking hands surrounded by members of their respective delegations. On the far left is Anthony St. John Baker, secretary to the British delegation. He brought the British instrument of ratification to the United States and exchanged ratifications with Secretary of State James Monroe on February 17, 1815, the day after hostilities were formally suspended. (Lithograph of painting by A. Forestier. Library and Archives of Canada)

dent John Quincy Adams, who was already in Europe as the nation's minister to Russia. Because Britain's top diplomats were busy with European affairs, the British government relied on second-tier bureaucrats for the American negotiations. Heading the British team was Lord Gambier, a rear admiral in the Royal Navy, although Henry Goulburn, an ambitious 30-year-old undersecretary in the Colonial Office who later held several important cabinet positions, actually took charge.

The Treaty of Ghent

Although the American delegates gathered in Europe in the spring of 1814, the British were now in the driver's seat in the war and thus in no hurry to start negotiations. The peace conference, which took place in Ghent in modern-day Belgium, did not get under way until August. The talks generated little interest on the Continent, where all eyes were on the Congress of Vienna, which was forging a general European peace. The "Great Congress at Vienna," conceded one of the American envoys, overshadowed "the little congress at Ghent."[23]

By the time the talks got under way, the administration had authorized the American delegation to drop the impressment issue, but the British laid down their own terms. Few thought this would be the last conflict between the two English-speaking nations, and the British were determined to provide better security for their North American provinces and Indian allies. Hence, they demanded territorial concessions in northern Minnesota and Maine, the creation of an Indian barrier state in the Old Northwest, the American demilitarization of the Great Lakes, and an end to American fishing privileges in Canadian waters.

The American envoys were stunned by these terms. "A Treaty concluded upon such terms," they insisted, "would be but an armistice. It cannot be supposed that America would long submit to conditions so injurious and degrading."[24] In the wake of the British proposal, the mood of the American delegation turned gloomy, for it now looked like the talks would end without peace. Only Henry Clay thought that a deal might still be possible. A lifelong gambler, Clay suspected that the British were bluffing, that they might be willing to settle for far less than they had demanded. Clay was soon proven right.

When the Americans stood firm against the proffered terms, the British retreated to a more modest demand: *uti possidetis,* which meant that each side would keep any territory held when the war ended. If this were agreed to, the British would retain part of Maine as well as Fort Mackinac and Fort Niagara (and perhaps Cumberland Island), while the United States would retain Fort Amherstburg and (if the treaty were signed before it was evacuated) Fort Erie. An exchange of forts and other territory would probably leave the British with little more than a strip of territory in northern Maine.

When the Americans resisted this offer, the British retreated further, dropping all their demands. By this time, the British had learned of their defeat on Lake Champlain and their rebuff at Baltimore. Public enthusiasm for the war was waning, and the government was looking for a way out. The Duke of Wellington provided the necessary cover when he told Lord Liverpool, the prime minister, that without control of the northern lakes, the British had little hope of success. Under the existing circumstances, the Iron Duke concluded, "you have no right ... to demand any concession of territory from America."[25] Emboldened by this assessment, Liverpool authorized the British delegation to agree to peace on the basis of the *status quo ante bellum*—the state that existed before the war.

The two sides worked out the details, and on December 24, 1814, signed the Treaty of Ghent, also known as the Peace of Christmas Eve. Besides ending hostilities and restoring all conquered territory, the treaty set up a series of commissions to resolve several boundary disputes. Each side also agreed to make peace with the Indians and to grant them "all the possessions, rights, and privileges" they had enjoyed in 1811 (before the Northwest Indian War had erupted at Tippecanoe).[26]

The End of the War

Conventional wisdom holds that the signing of the treaty brought the War of 1812 to an end two weeks before the Battle of New Orleans, but this is incorrect. Article I of the treaty provided for the war to end only when both sides had ratified the agreement. The British ratified on December 27, but it took six weeks for the treaty to reach the United States. On February 11 the truce ship carrying the document docked at New York because there was bad weather in the Chesapeake. From New York, the treaty was rushed to Washington, and on February 16 the Senate unanimously approved it. When the president signed off on it later that day, the war formally ended, and both sides sent out orders to suspend hostilities. After two years and eight months of inconclusive fighting, the War of 1812 was over.

* *

EPILOGUE

* *

Legacies

The arrival of the Treaty of Ghent in America touched off celebrations in cities and towns across the nation. Everyone, regardless of party, was happy that the war was over. Once the treaty was published, Federalists thought they had an additional cause for satisfaction because the terms appeared to vindicate their view that the nation would win no meaningful concessions from the British. Some Federalists predicted that, once the excitement died down, Americans would take a careful look at the treaty, would see the futility of the war, and would then turn against Republicans. But this never happened. Though the contest was far from conclusive and the United States never achieved its war aims, Americans chose to remember the conflict differently.

President Madison proclaimed the war a success, and most Americans were eager to follow his lead. They quickly forgot the causes of the war and the defeats on land and sea. They lost sight of how close the fragmented and fragile republic had come to military defeat and financial collapse. Instead, they chose to remember only the heroic deeds and the victories: at the Thames in the West; at Chippawa, Lundy's Lane, and Fort Erie on the Niagara; at Baltimore in the Chesapeake; and on the high seas and the northern lakes. Most of all, they remembered the great victory at New Orleans, where a tough and determined Tennessean leading a motley band of regulars, volunteers, militia, and Indians had defeated the conquerors of the conquerors of Europe. For nearly a half century thereafter, cities across the nation treated January 8 as a holiday, celebrating Jackson's one-sided triumph over the British.

Rendered around 1820, this treatment of the
restoration of peace is loaded with classical
symbols designed to celebrate American
heroes and victories and to promote the
myth of American victory. (Engraving by
Chataigner. Library of Congress)

Although the War of 1812 was dwarfed in size and significance by other wars before or since, the legacy it left was considerable. For the United States, it was never a second war of independence because American independence was never truly at risk, but the war did confirm the republic's nationhood. It promoted self-confidence and nationalism and enhanced the reputation of the young republic in Europe. It also contributed to the robust defense spending (especially on the navy) and the bombastic patriotism and ardent expansionism that characterized the postwar years.

The symbols and sayings of the war also did much to define the new nation. "Don't give up the ship" and "We have met the enemy and they are ours" entered the American lexicon. The Fort McHenry flag, which has survived (in the Smithsonian) as our most venerable relic and visible reminder of the war, helped generate a new reverence for the Stars and Stripes. The song honoring that flag—"The Star-Spangled Banner"—became a popular air that eventually took on special significance as the national anthem. The *Constitution* (which survived through the years and was re-commissioned in 1940) was an impressive reminder of American naval prowess against the Mistress of the Seas, and the Navy kept the captured *Macedonian* in service until 1871 to drive home the point. The Pennsylvania rifle emerged with an enhanced (if overrated) reputation for being a war-winner. Even Uncle Sam made his first appearance during the war as a symbol for the U.S. government.

Many of those who fought in the war or served in other ways were able to trade on their service in later years. To a large extent, postwar America was dominated by men who had played a conspicuous role in the War of 1812. No one capitalized on his wartime experience more than Andrew Jackson, the Hero of New Orleans, who became a symbol for the rising democracy of the postwar era and was ultimately catapulted into the presidency. But Jackson was far from unique. Veterans from other battles and campaigns invariably had a leg up on the competition in any contest for public office. The Battle of the Thames alone produced a president and vice president (William Henry Harrison and Richard M. Johnson), six governors and lieutenant governors, and 24 senators and congressmen.

The war also left a legacy of anglophobia in the United States. The hatred against Great Britain unleashed by the horrors of the Revolution was only reinforced by the War of 1812. The Indian outrages in the West and the British depredations in the Chesapeake were not soon forgotten, and those who had suffered in unhealthy British prisons or prison ships long remembered the experience. This was especially true of those who witnessed the so-called Dartmoor Massacre on April 6, 1815. Some 5,000 Americans were housed in this cold and damp prison

As "The Star-Spangled Banner" took on iconic status in the years after the War of 1812, it became embedded in popular culture. Here it has been imprinted on satin. The song is ringed by letters that say "BOMBARDMENT OF FORT M'HENRY." (Library of Congress)

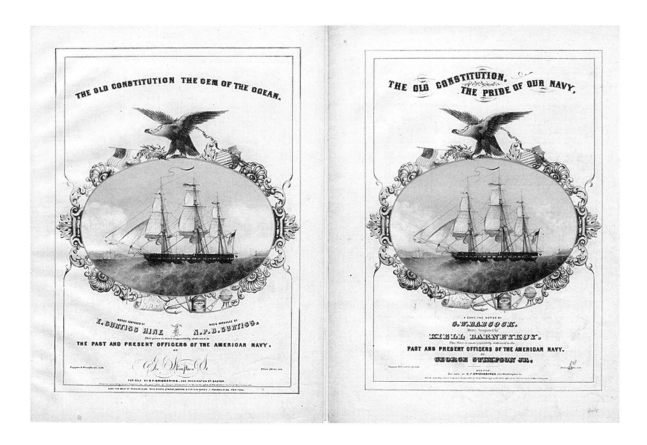

in southwestern England. Nearly two months after peace had been proclaimed, guards at Dartmoor fired on unruly inmates who were angry over a delay in their repatriation home. When the smoke cleared, six Americans lay dead and another 60 were wounded.

In Canada, the war was also fraught with significance. For people living in British North America, it was a true war of independence because defeat would probably have meant an end to Canada as a distinct entity. Britain's North American provinces probably would have been swallowed by the American Union, forever depriving Canadians of any chance of establishing a separate nation. Because French Canadians had done their part, especially in the Battle of Châteauguay, the war also fostered a sense of Anglo-French dualism that continues to characterize Canada today. The war brought home to Canadians the potent dangers they faced from south of the border. With good reason this fear did not soon abate. As late as the 1930s, the Canadian army had an operational plan on the shelf to fight a war against the United States.

The war also gave Canadians some of the symbols that would later serve in

"Old Ironsides," celebrated in this 1850 song as "The Gem of the Ocean" and "The Pride of Our Navy," emerged from the war as the most famous ship in the U.S. Navy. It was withdrawn from active service in 1855 and thereafter served mainly as a training ship. In 1940, President Franklin Roosevelt ordered the venerable ship re-commissioned. It has since been restored to its 1812 appearance and is now on display at the Charlestown Navy Yard north of Boston. (Library of Congress)

This portrait, which was used in Andrew Jackson's successful presidential campaign in 1828, showed the Tennessee general as "PROTECTOR & DEFENDER OF BEAUTY AND BOOTY." This was a reference to the American claim that the sign and countersign for the British on the eve of the Battle of New Orleans were "beauty" and "booty," suggesting that the city would be sacked if the British won. This is highly unlikely because British officers almost always kept a tight leash on their men whenever they occupied an enemy city. (Engraving by C. G. Childs based on a painting by Joseph Wood. Library of Congress)

Winfield Scott was one of many army and navy officers whose careers were launched by the War of 1812. The hero of three wars, he also served in the Mexican War and the Civil War. This daguerreotype from later in his career celebrates his participation in the Battle of Lundy's Lane, which was sometimes called the Battle of Niagara. (Robert Tomes, *Battles of America by Land and Sea*)

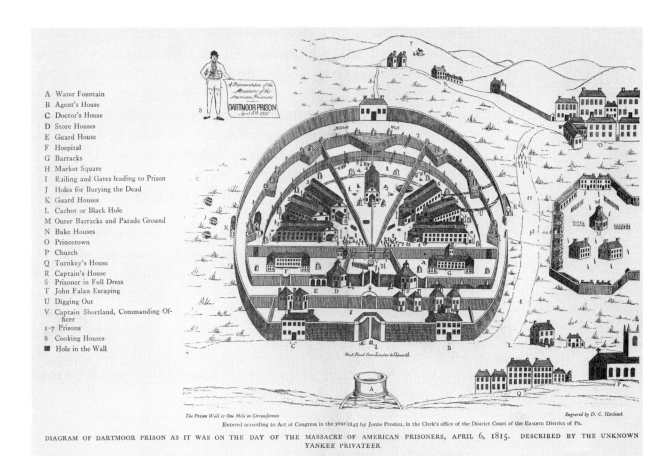

A Water Fountain
B Agent's House
C Doctor's House
D Store Houses
E Guard House
F Hospital
G Barracks
H Market Square
I Railing and Gates leading to Prison
J Holes for Burying the Dead
K Guard Houses
L Cachot or Black Hole
M Outer Barracks and Parade Ground
N Bake Houses
O Princetown
P Church
Q Turnkey's House
R Captain's House
S Prisoner in Full Dress
T John Falan Escaping
U Digging Out
V Captain Shortland, Commanding Officer
1–7 Prisons
8 Cooking Houses
■ Hole in the Wall

The Prison Wall is One Mile in Circumference

Entered according to Act of Congress in the year 1845 by Jonas Preston, in the Clerk's office of the District Court of the Eastern District of Pa.

Engraved by D. C. Hitchcock

DIAGRAM OF DARTMOOR PRISON AS IT WAS ON THE DAY OF THE MASSACRE OF AMERICAN PRISONERS, APRIL 6, 1815. DESCRIBED BY THE UNKNOWN YANKEE PRIVATEER

T. THOMAS   J. SMALL   L. CLOVER   R. CONKLIN
B. MARSHAL   J. DEAGLE
B. HOWARD   Mrs. SMALL   J. SWAIN   G. SAUNDERS
DARTMOOR, PRISONERS OF 1812.

A sketch of the layout of Dartmoor prison and a daguerreotype taken years later of a group of the surviving prisoners. The banner they hold appears to proclaim "Sailors Rights" and perhaps "No Impressment." It is not clear why a woman is in the group portrait. She may have been a prisoner or the wife of one of the survivors. (Nathaniel Hawthorne, *The Yarn of a Yankee Privateer;* John H. Spears, *The History of Our Navy*)

crafting their own national identity. Among those from the War of 1812 who became part of the Canadian pantheon were Major General Isaac Brock, the victor at Detroit who perished at Queenston Heights; Tecumseh and John Norton, the great native leaders who fought on Britain's side; Laura Secord, whose warning helped set up the victory at Beaver Dams; John Strachan, the rector of York, who played a significant role in promoting resistance to the American invaders and standing up to the occupation force in York; and Lieutenant Colonel Charles de Salaberry, the French Canadian responsible for the victory at Châteauguay. It is a measure of the significance of this war to Canadians that in an opinion poll taken in 2000 it ranked third in importance behind the establishment of the Confederation (1867) and the completion of the Canadian Pacific Railway (1885).

In Great Britain, the war, which was never more than a footnote to the Napoleonic Wars, was quickly forgotten by the public, but not by the Royal Navy. William James published the first serious naval history of the war in 1817 to uphold the reputation of Britain's sea service. The *Shannon,* which had dispatched the *Chesapeake* so quickly in battle, remained a tourist attraction in England for many years, and a replica of the captured *President* was kept in commission until 1903 as a public statement that even America's powerful heavy frigates could not withstand the might of the Royal Navy.

The British government could not afford to forget the war either. In the years that followed the conflict, British officials had to find a way to defend Canada at a time when the rapid growth of the United States was tipping the balance of power in North America against them. Although the British shed their Indian allies, they poured considerable money into the defense of Canada even though report after report showed that the amount needed to do the job right was staggering, and Canadians themselves were reluctant to pick up even part of the cost.

Increasingly, the British government saw that its best chance of saving Canada was by accommodating America. Maintaining good relations with the United States became one of the cornerstones of British foreign policy in the nineteenth century. Occasionally the British sacrificed the interests of Canadians or other people in the Empire, but ultimately this policy paid off. Although many people on both sides of the Atlantic feared that the Treaty of Ghent would be little more than a truce, the two English-speaking nations had so much in common—a commitment to democracy, the rule of law, and free markets—that by the end of the nineteenth century their uneasy relationship had turned into a mutually beneficial accord. This, in turn, paved the way for the Pax Britannia of the nineteenth century to give way seamlessly to the Pax Americana of the twentieth.

And what about the native people? Sadly, they were the only real losers in the

HISTORY

OF THE

AMERICAN WAR,

OF EIGHTEEN HUNDRED AND TWELVE.

FROM THE COMMENCEMENT UNTIL THE FINAL TERMINATION
THEREOF,

ON THE MEMORABLE EIGHTH OF JANUARY 1815.
AT NEW ORLEANS:

EMBELLISHED WITH A STRIKING LIKENESS OF GENERAL PIKE.
AND SIX OTHER ENGRAVINGS.

PHILADELPHIA:

PUBLISHED BY WM. M'CARTY.

PRINTED BY M'CARTY & DAVIS, S. W. CORNER OF FIFTH AND
CHERRY-STREETS.

1816.

William McCarty used the phrase "War of Eighteen Hundred and Twelve" and "War of 1812" as early as 1816 in the first editions of a book he published, but most Americans called the conflict "the late war" or "the late war with Great Britain." Only after the Mexican War erupted in the late 1840s did the term "War of 1812" come into general usage to distinguish it from later conflicts.

Featured here are the medals that the British government later awarded to those who had taken part in three of the battles in the war—the capture of Detroit in 1812 and the victories at Châteauguay and Crysler's Farm in 1813. (Alexander C. Casselman, *Richardson's War of 1812*)

War of 1812. This was the last war in which they played a role in shaping the future of the continent, the last time they could count on European allies to make up for their declining numbers. Tecumseh's confederacy was shattered on the Thames battlefield, Creek resistance was broken at Horseshoe Bend, and the native tribes in the Old West never recovered. Article 9 of the Treaty of Ghent was supposed to guarantee that Indians would be restored to their status as of 1811, but this was a dead letter. The United States ignored the clause, and the British showed no interest in trying to force Americans to honor it. With the Treaty of Ghent, the British effectively abandoned their Indian allies, which left those inside the American boundary with little choice but to come to terms with an unyielding foe. Even in Canada, the Indians lost their leverage and saw their lands shrink and their traditional way of life wither. Time was never on the Indians' side because the demographic clock was ticking against them, but the War of 1812 quickened the march of history.

For all the belligerents, then, the War of 1812 left a lasting imprint on the future. It may have been a small and inconclusive war, but it helped shape the future of North America and the larger transatlantic community. Even today the legacy of the War of 1812 is still visible to those who know where to look for it.

The dates for all events mentioned in the text are listed in this chronology. The more important military and diplomatic events are in **bold** type. Current U.S. states and Canadian provinces where events took place are identified by their two-letter postal codes.

Abbreviations

BG	Brigadier general
Cap	Captain
FR	France
GB	Great Britain
HM	His Majesty's
LC	Lower Canada
MG	Major general
(n)	Number of guns an armed ship carried
PM	Provincial Marine
RU	Russia
UC	Upper Canada
US	United States

1789

April 30   George Washington inaugurated as president of US in New York City (NY)

July 14   Mob storms Bastille in Paris (French Revolution begins) (FR)

1792

April 20   FR declares war on Austria (French Revolutionary Wars begin)

September 22   French revolutionaries in Paris proclaim a republic (FR)

1793

January 21   French revolutionaries execute Louis XVI in Paris (FR)

February 1   FR declares war on GB

1793–94   Reign of Terror (FR)

1794

November 19   US and GB sign Jay Treaty in London (GB)

1795

October 27   Directory assumes power (French Revolution ends) (FR)

1797

March 4   John Adams inaugurated as president of US in Philadelphia (PA)

1798–1801   US and FR in Quasi-War

1799

| November 9–10 | Coup of Brumaire ends rule of Directory (FR) |
| December 25 | Napoleon becomes First Consul of FR |

1801

| March 4 | Thomas Jefferson inaugurated as president of US in Washington (DC) |
| October 1 | GB and FR sign preliminary Treaty of Amiens (French Revolutionary Wars end) (FR) |

1802

| March 25 | GB and FR sign final Treaty of Amiens (FR) |

1803

| May 17 | GB issues letters of marque and reprisal against FR (Napoleonic Wars begin) |
| October 1 | Commercial clauses in Jay Treaty expire |

1804

| May 18 | Napoleon becomes Emperor of FR |

1805

| October 21 | Battle of Trafalgar off coast of Spain in Atlantic |
| December 2 | Battle of Austerlitz (Czech Republic) |

1806

| April 18 | US adopts (but suspends) partial non-importation law against GB |
| December 31 | US and GB sign Monroe-Pinkney Treaty in London (GB) |

1806–07	FR issues Continental Decrees

1807

March 3	US rejects Monroe-Pinkney Treaty
June 22	*Chesapeake* affair (HM Ship *Leopard* [52] fires on US Frigate *Chesapeake* [40] off coast of Virginia in Atlantic)
December 14	US activates partial non-importation law of 1806
December 22	US adopts embargo prohibiting US ships and goods from leaving port

1807–09	GB issues Orders-in-Council

1809

March 1	US adopts non-intercourse law against GB and FR
March 4	James Madison inaugurated as president of US in Washington (DC)
September 3	US and Delawares, Miamis, Potawatomis, and Eel River sign Treaty of Fort Wayne (IN)

1810

May 1	US adopts law that reopens trade with GB and FR
August 5	FR sends Cadore letter to US, offering to rescind Continental System

1811

March 2	US adopts non-importation law against GB
May 16	*Little Belt* affair (clash of US Frigate *President* [53] and HM Sloop *Little Belt* [20] off coast of Virginia in Atlantic)

October 21	George Prevost appointed captain-general and governor-in-chief of Canada
November 4	War Congress convenes in Washington (DC)
November 7	Battle of Tippecanoe (IN)
November 8	US burns Prophet's Town (IN)
November 12	US and GB settle *Chesapeake* affair in Washington (DC)
December 24–April 10	US enacts war preparations

....

1812

March 9	Madison exposes John Henry spy mission to New England
May 18?	Duck River Massacre (TN)
May 22	Dispatches from US Sloop *Hornet* (20) reach Washington (DC)
June 1	Madison sends war message to US Congress
June 4	US House of Representatives adopts war bill
June 8	Earl of Liverpool becomes prime minister of GB
June 16	GB offers to suspend Orders-in-Council
June 17	US Senate adopts war bill
June 18	**President Madison signs war bill into law (War of 1812 begins)**
June 18–26	US sends out peace feelers
June 19	President Madison issues proclamation announcing that state of war exists and urging all Americans to support war effort
June 22–August 4	Baltimore Riots (MD)
June 23	FR invades RU
June 23	US Frigate *President* (53) clashes with HM Ship *Belvidera* (42) in North Atlantic
June 23	**GB repeals Orders-in-Council**
June 25	News of war reaches Quebec (QC)
June 27	News of war reaches Halifax (NS)

July 1	US doubles customs duties
July 2	GB captures *Cuyahoga* in Detroit River
July 6	US adopts first enemy trade law
July 11	In Boston Harbor GB restores deserters taken in *Chesapeake* affair (MA)
July 12	US invades Canada across Detroit River (MI/ON)
July 12	BG William Hull issues proclamation at Sandwich promising to liberate Canada (ON)
July 16	British squadron captures US Brig *Nautilus* (14) in North Atlantic
July 16	Skirmish at Canard River (ON)
July 16–19	US Frigate *Constitution* (55) outruns British squadron in eastern Atlantic
July 17	**GB captures Fort Mackinac (MI)**
July 30	News of war reaches London (GB)
August 5	Battle of Brownstown (MI)
August 7	US withdraws from Canada across Detroit River (ON/MI)
August 9	Battle of Maguaga (MI)
August 13	News of repeal of Orders-in-Council reaches Washington (DC)
August 13	US Frigate *Essex* (46) captures HM Sloop *Alert* (18?) in North Atlantic
August 15	Fort Dearborn Massacre (IL)
August 16	**GB captures Detroit (MI)**
August 19	US Frigate *Constitution* (55) defeats HM Ship *Guerrière* (49) in North Atlantic
September 19–November 29	State elections ensure Pres. Madison's re-election
October–November	GB establishes a blockade from Charleston (SC) to St. Marys (GA)
October 8–9	US captures PM Brig *Detroit* (6) and PM Brig *Caledonia* (3) in Niagara River

October 13	**Battle of Queenston Heights**; MG Isaac Brock killed (ON)
October 13	**GB authorizes general reprisals against US**
October 18	US Sloop *Wasp* (18) defeats HM Sloop *Frolic* (22) in North Atlantic
October 18	HM Ship *Poictiers* (80) captures US Sloop *Wasp* (18) in North Atlantic
October 19–December 14	FR retreats from RU
October 25	US Frigate *United States* (56) captures HM Ship *Macedonian* (49) in North Atlantic
November 19	US invades LC (NY/QC)
November 20	Battle of Lacolle Mill (QC)
November 22	HM Ship *Southampton* (41) captures US Schooner *Vixen* (14) in North Atlantic
November 23	US withdraws from LC (QC/NY)
December 17–18	Battle of the Mississinewa River (IN)
December 29	US Frigate *Constitution* (54) defeats HM Ship *Java* (49) off coast of Brazil in Atlantic

1813

January 22	**Battle of Frenchtown (MI)**
January 23	**River Raisin Massacre (MI)**
February 6	**GB proclaims blockade of Delaware and Chesapeake bays**
February 24	US Sloop *Hornet* (20) defeats HM Sloop *Peacock* (20) off coast of Guiana in Atlantic
March 8	RU offers to mediate end to War of 1812
March 11	US accepts RU's mediation offer
March 19	Sir James Yeo appointed commander of British naval forces on northern lakes
April 27	**US captures York (ON)**
April 29	GB raids Frenchtown (MD)
April 29	Battle of Fort Defiance (MD)

May 1–9	**First Siege of Fort Meigs (OH)**
May 3	GB burns Havre de Grace (MD)
May 3	GB destroys Principio Ironworks (MD)
May 5	Battle of Fort Meigs (OH)
May 5	Massacre of US POWs at Fort Miami (OH)
May 6	GB burns Fredericktown and Georgetown (MD)
May 26	**GB proclaims blockade of major ports in middle and southern states**
May 27	**US captures Fort George (ON)**
May 28	GB evacuates all posts along Niagara River (ON)
May 29	**Battle of Sackets Harbor (NY)**
June 1	HM Ship *Shannon* (52) defeats US Frigate *Chesapeake* (50) off coast of Massachusetts in Atlantic
June 3	GB captures US Sloop *Eagle* (11) and US Sloop *Growler* (11) in Richelieu River (QC)
June 5–6	**Battle of Stoney Creek (ON)**
June 22	**Battle of Craney Island (VA)**
June 22–23	**Laura Secord's trek (ON)**
June 24	**Battle of Beaver Dams (ON)**
June 25	GB attacks Hampton (VA)
July 5	GB rejects RU's mediation offer
July 21–28	**Second siege of Fort Meigs (OH)**
July 24–August 2	US adopts internal taxes
July 27	Battle of Burnt Corn (AL)
August 1–2	**Battle of Fort Stephenson (OH)**
August 2	US adopts law barring use of enemy licenses
August 13	Battle of Queenstown (MD)
August 26	GB raids St. Michaels (MD)
August 30	**Fort Mims Massacre (AL)**
September 10	**Battle of Lake Erie**
September 18	GB evacuates Fort Detroit (MI)

September 27	US re-occupies Fort Detroit (MI) and occupies Fort Amherstburg (ON)
September 28	"Burlington Races" on Lake Ontario
October 5	**Battle of the Thames/Moraviantown**; Tecumseh killed (ON)
October 16–19	Battle of Leipzig (Germany)
October 26	**Battle of Châteauguay (QC)**
November 3	Battle of Tallushatchee (AL)
November 4	GB offers US direct peace negotiations
November 9	Battle of Talladega (AL)
November 11	**Battle of Crysler's Farm (ON)**
November 16	GB proclaims blockade of Long Island Sound and remaining ports in middle and southern states
December 10	US evacuates Fort George and burns Newark (ON)
December 12	GB re-occupies Fort George (ON)
December 17	US adopts embargo barring all US ships and goods from leaving port
December 19	**GB captures Fort Niagara (NY)**
December 19–21	GB burns Lewiston, Youngstown, and Manchester (NY)
December 30	GB burns Buffalo and Black Rock (NY)

1814

January 22	Battle of Emuckfau Creek (AL)
January 24	Battle of Enitachopco Creek (AL)
March 26	US military court in Albany finds BG William Hull guilty of cowardice and neglect of duty (NY)
March 27–28	**Battle of Horseshoe Bend (AL)**
March 28	HM Ship *Phoebe* (46 or 53) and HM Sloop *Cherub* (26) defeat US Frigate *Essex* (46) off coast of Chile in Pacific
March 31	European allies enter Paris (FR)

April 2	GB issues proclamation urging slaves in Chesapeake to join British forces
April 6	Napoleon abdicates throne (FR)
April 7–8	GB raids Pettipaug Point (CT)
April 14	US repeals embargo and non-importation law
April 25	**GB proclaims blockade of New England**
April 28	Napoleon exiled to Elba in Mediterranean
May 5–6	GB captures Oswego (NY)
May 14–15	US raids Dover (ON)
May 30	Battle of Sandy Creek (NY)
May 30	European allies and FR sign First Treaty of Paris (Napoleonic Wars suspended) (FR)
June 9–10	Militia carry great rope from Sandy Creek to Sackets Harbor (NY)
June 27	**US drops impressment demand**
July 3	US captures Fort Erie (ON)
July 5	**Battle of Chippawa (ON)**
July 11	GB captures Eastport (ME)
July 18	US burns St. Davids (ON)
July 22	US and Miamis, Potawatomis, Ottawas, Shawnees, Kickapoos sign peace treaty at Greenville (OH)
July 25	**Battle of Lundy's Lane (ON)**
August	US public credit collapses
August	US banks suspend specie payments
August 3	Battle of Conjocta Creek (NY)
August 4	US attacks Fort Mackinac (MI)
August 7–14	GB bombards Fort Erie (ON)
August 8	**Peace negotiations begin in Ghent (Belgium)**
August 9	US and Creeks sign peace treaty at Fort Jackson (AL)
August 9–11	Battle of Stonington (CT)
August 12	GB captures US Schooner *Somers* (2) and US Schooner *Ohio* (1) in Niagara River

August 14	GB occupies Pensacola (FL)
August 14	Battle of Nottawasaga River (ON)
August 15	**Battle of Fort Erie (ON)**
August 19–20	GB lands at Benedict en route to Washington (MD)
August 19–September 17	GB bombards Fort Erie (ON)
August 20–September 16	Skirmishing at Fort Erie (ON)
August 22	US blows up its Chesapeake flotilla at Pig Point (MD)
August 24	**Battle of Bladensburg (MD)**
August 24	US burns Washington Naval Yard, US Frigate *Columbia*, and US Sloop *Argus* (DC)
August 24–25	**GB occupies Washington (DC)**
August 27	Cap Thomas Boyle of US privateer *Chasseur* (16) proclaims mock blockade of GB and Ireland
August 28	Nantucket declares neutrality (MA)
August 29	GB captures Alexandria (VA)
August 31	Battle of Caulk's Field (MD)
August 31	GB invades New York
September 1–11	**GB occupies 100 miles of US coast from Eastport to Castine (ME)**
September 3	GB captures US Schooner *Tigress* (1) on Lake Huron
September 6	GB captures US Schooner *Scorpion* (2) on Lake Huron
September 11	Battle of Plattsburgh (NY)
September 11	**Battle of Lake Champlain**; Cap George Downie killed
September 12	**Battle of North Point;** MG Robert Ross killed
September 13–14	**GB bombards Fort McHenry (MD)**
September 14	Francis Scott Key writes "The Star-Spangled Banner" (MD)
September 14	GB withdraws from Baltimore (MD)

September 15–June 9	Congress of Vienna (AU)
September 17	**US sortie from Fort Erie (ON)**
September 26–27	British squadron defeats US privateer *General Armstrong* (14) in Azores
October 11	US privateer *Prince-de-Neufchatel* (17) defeats flotilla of boats from HM Ship *Endymion* (47) near Nantucket
October 15	US House of Representatives defeats bill to move capital
October 19	Battle of Cook's Mills / Lyon's Creek (ON)
October 21	Congress adopts resolution to purchase Thomas Jefferson's library
October 22–November 17	**BG Duncan McArthur's Raid (ON)**
November 5	US evacuates Fort Erie (ON)
November 6	Battle of Malcolm's Mills (ON)
December 14	**Battle of Lake Borgne (LA)**
December 15–January 5	Hartford Convention meets (CT)
December 15–February 27	US adopts internal taxes
December 16	MG Andrew Jackson proclaims martial law in New Orleans (LA)
December 23	Battle of Villeré's Plantation / Night Engagement at New Orleans (LA)
December 24	**US and GB sign Treaty of Ghent (Belgium)**
December 27	British artillery destroys US Schooner *Carolina* (13) (LA)
December 27	**GB ratifies Treaty of Ghent**
December 28	British Reconnaissance in Force at New Orleans (LA)
December 28	US Congress rejects conscription

....

1815

January 1	Battle of Rodriquez Canal / Artillery Duel at New Orleans (LA)

January 2	HM Sloop *Favourite* (26?) departs from Portsmouth with Treaty of Ghent (UK)
January 8	**Battle of New Orleans**; MG Edward Pakenham and MG Samuel Gibbs killed (LA)
January 9–18	GB Bombards Fort St. Philip (LA)
January 10	GB occupies Cumberland Island (GA)
January 13	GB attacks Point Peter on Cumberland Island (GA)
January 15	British squadron captures US Frigate *President* (53)
January 28	British military court in Montreal finds MG Henry Procter guilty of mismanaging Thames campaign (QC)
February 4	US adopts second enemy trade law
February 11	HM Sloop *Favourite* (26?) reaches New York City with Treaty of Ghent (NY)
February 8–11	Siege of Fort Bowyer (AL)
February 14	Treaty of Ghent reaches Washington (DC)
February 16	US Senate unanimously approves Treaty of Ghent
February 16	**Madison ratifies Treaty of Ghent (War of 1812 officially ends)**
February 17	US Congress rejects national bank
February 17	US and GB exchange ratifications of Treaty of Ghent (treaty becomes binding)
February 20	US Frigate *Constitution* (52) defeats HM Ship *Cyane* (33) and HM Ship *Levant* (21) off coast of North Africa in Atlantic
February 21	US executes 6 militiamen in Mobile (AL)
March 1	News of peace reaches Quebec (QC)
March 11	British squadron recaptures HM Ship *Levant* (21) in North Atlantic
March 13	Official news of peace reaches New Orleans (LA)
March 13	MG Andrew Jackson lifts martial law in New Orleans (LA)

March 28	News of peace reaches London (GB)
March 31	MG Andrew Jackson convicted of contempt and fined $1,000 (LA)
April 6	Dartmoor Massacre (GB)

....

1815–16 | US and western Indian tribes sign peace treaties

....

Prologue. The Suspense Was Hell

1. Irving to H. Brevoort, Jan. 13, 1811, in Pierre M. Irving, ed., *The Life and Letters of Washington Irving,* 4 vols. (New York, 1862–64), 1: 263; and Francis Jeffrey (later Lord Jeffrey), quoted in Winslow Marston Watson, comp., *In Memoriam: Benjamin Ogle Tayloe* (Washington, 1872), 118.

2. Madison to Congress, Nov. 5, 1812, in U.S. Congress, *Annals of Congress: Debates and Proceedings in the Congress of the United States, 1789–1824,* 42 vols. (Washington, DC, 1834–56), 12th Congress, 1st session, 13 (hereafter cited as *AC,* 12-1, and similarly for other sessions).

3. Madison to Congress, June 1, 1812, in *AC,* 12-1, 1629.

4. Roberts to Matthew Roberts, June 17, 1812, in Roberts Papers, Historical Society of Pennsylvania, Philadelphia, PA.

Chapter 1. Endless War in the Atlantic World (1793–1812)

1. See table in Curtis P. Nettels, *The Emergence of a National Economy, 1775–1815* (New York, 1962), 396.

2. Speech of Harrison Gray Otis, May 26, 1798, in U.S. Congress, *Annals of Congress: Debates and Proceedings in the Congress of the United States, 1789–1824,* 42 vols. (Washington, DC, 1834–56), 5th Congress, 2nd Session, 1819 (hereafter cited as *AC,* 5-2, and similarly for other sessions); Report of House Naval Committee, Jan. 17, 1799, in *AC,* 5-3, 2684; Robert G. Albion and Jennie B. Pope, *Sea Lanes in Wartime: The American Experience,* 2nd ed. ([Hamden, CT], 1968), 83. British naval operations and a more conciliatory French policy probably also contributed to the decline. See speech of Albert Gallatin, Feb. 7, 1799, in *AC,* 5-3, 2826.

3. See tables in Nettels, *Emergence of a National Economy,* 385, 396.

4. Speech of Nathaniel Macon, Apr. 16, 1810, in *AC,* 11-2, 1863.

5. Randolph to Joseph H. Nicholson, June 25, 1807, in Nicholson Papers, Library of Congress, Washington, DC.

6. Speech of Robert Wright, Mar. 2, 1812, in *AC,* 12-1, 1123; John A. Harper to William Plumer, Feb. 17, 1812, in Plumer Papers, Library of Congress, Washington, DC, microfilm edition, reel 3.

7. Speech of Josiah Quincy, Jan. 19, 1809, in *AC*, 10-2, 1112.

8. Jefferson to William Duane, Aug. 4, 1812, in Jefferson Papers, Library of Congress, Washington, DC, microfilm edition, reel 46; speech of Henry Clay, Feb. 22, 1810, in *AC*, 11-2, 580.

Chapter 2. Canada, Canada, Canada (1812)

1. Speech of John Randolph, Dec. 16, 1811, in U.S. Congress, *Annals of Congress: Debates and Proceedings in the Congress of the United States, 1789–1824*, 42 vols. (Washington, DC, 1834–56), 12th Congress, 1st session, 533 (hereafter cited as *AC*, 12-1, and similarly for other sessions).

2. Henry Clay to Thomas Bodley, Dec. 18, 1813, in James F. Hopkins and Mary W.M. Hargreaves, eds., *The Papers of Henry Clay*, 11 vols. (Lexington, KY, 1959–92), 1:842.

3. Harrison to secretary of war, Aug. 7, 1811 in Logan Esarey, ed., *Messages and Letters of William Henry Harrison*, 2 vols. (Indianapolis, 1922), 1: 549.

4. Harrison to secretary of war, Nov. 8, 1811, ibid., 1: 614.

5. Elliott to Isaac Brock, Jan. 12, 1812, in William Wood, ed., *Select British Documents of the Canadian War of 1812*, 3 vols. (Toronto, 1920–28), 1: 282.

6. Lexington *Reporter*, Nov. 23, 1811, and Mar. 14, 1812.

7. William H. Crawford to James Monroe, Sept. 9, 1812, in Monroe Papers, Library of Congress, Washington, DC, microfilm edition, reel 5.

8. Jonathan Roberts to Matthew Roberts, Mar. 27, 1812, in Roberts Papers, Pennsylvania Historical Society, Philadelphia, PA.

9. Nathaniel Macon to Joseph H. Nicholson, in Nicholson Papers, Library of Congress, Washington, DC.

10. Prevost to Lord Liverpool, May 18, 1812, in J. Mackay Hitsman, *The Incredible War of 1812: A Military History* (1965; updated by Donald E. Graves, Toronto, 1999), 286.

11. Proclamation of William Hull, July 13, 1812, in Ernest A. Cruikshank, ed., *Documents Relating to the Invasion of Canada and the Surrender of Detroit, 1812* (Ottawa, 1912), 59.

12. Hull to secretary of war, Aug. 26, 1812, in U.S. Department of War, *Letters Received by the Secretary of War, Registered Series, 1801–1870*, National Archives, Washington, DC, microfilm series M221, reel 45.

13. Brock to Hull, Aug. 15, 1812, in John Brannan, ed., *Official Letters of the Military and Naval Officers of the United States, during the War with Great Britain in the Years 1812, 13, 14, & 15* (Washington, 1823), 41.

14. Van Rensselaer to [Henry Dearborn], Oct. 14, 1812, in U.S. Department of War, *Letters Received . . . Registered Series*, microfilm series M221, reel 45.

15. Charles J. Ingersoll, *History of the Second War between the United States of America and Great Britain,* 2 vols. (Philadelphia, 1853) 1: 102.

16. Ships in Sea Pay, Admiralty Office, July 1, 1812, in William S. Dudley, Michael J. Crawford, *et al.,* eds., *The Naval War of 1812: A Documentary History,* 4 vols. (Washington, DC, 1985–), 1: 180–82.

17. Letter from British naval officer at Halifax, Oct. 15, 1812, in *Naval Chronicle* 28 (July-Dec. 1812), 426.

18. Quoted in Oliver H. Perry to secretary of the navy, July 26, 1812, in Dudley and Crawford, *Naval War of 1812,* 1: 200.

19. Quoted in George Coggeshall, *History of the American Privateers, and Letters-of-Marque, during Our War with England in the Years, 1812, '13 and '14* (New York, 1856), 27.

20. Moses Smith, *Naval Scenes in the Last War* (Boston, 1846), 33.

21. Thomas Jesup to James Taylor, Dec. 28, 1812, in Jesup Papers, Library of Congress, Washington, DC.

22. Speech of Lemuel Sawyer, Dec. 16, 1812, in U.S. Congress, *Annals of Congress: Debates and Proceedings in the Congress of the United States, 1789–1824,* 42 vols. (Washington, DC, 1834–56), 12th Congress, 2nd Session, 405.

23. The Earl of Harrowby, quoted in Bradford Perkins, *Castlereagh and Adams: England and the United States, 1812–1823* (Berkeley, CA, 1964), 18.

24. Admiralty to Station Commanders, July 10, 1813, in Dudley and Crawford, *Naval War of 1812,* 2: 183.

25. Thomas Law to Phineas Bond, July 18, 1812, in Gen. Thomas Cadwalader Papers, Historical Society of Pennsylvania, Philadelphia, PA.

26. Coggeshall, *History of American Privateers,* 3.

27. Joseph Marx to [Wilson Cary Nicholas], Sept. 9, 1812, in Nicholas Papers, University of Virginia, Charlottesville, VA.

28. Salem *Essex Register,* Dec. 16, 1812.

29. Letter from Guadeloupe, Aug. 15, 1812, in London *Morning Chronicle,* Sept. 18, 1812.

Chapter 3. Don't Give Up the Ship (1813)

1. Speech of Henry Clay, Dec. 7, 1812, in U.S. Congress, *Annals of Congress: Debates and Proceedings in the Congress of the United States, 1789–1824,* 42 vols. (Washington, DC, 1834–56), 12th Congress, 2nd Session, 299–300 (hereafter cited as *AC,* 12-2, and similarly for other sessions).

2. James Breckinridge to Dr. Campbell, June 29, 1812, in Breckinridge Papers, University of Virginia, Charlottesville, VA.

3. Hartford *Connecticut Courant,* Aug. 25, 1812.

4. Memorandum of [Harrison Gray Otis], [1812], in Alexander Washburn Collection, Massachusetts Historical Society, Boston, MA.

5. The play, *Election Scene*, is reprinted from the Worcester (MA) *National Aegis* in the Philadelphia *Aurora,* Oct. 13, 1812.

6. Rush to Charles J. Ingersoll, Nov. 14, 1812, in Ingersoll Papers, Historical Society of Pennsylvania, Philadelphia, PA.

7. Adam Seybert to Albert Gallatin, Oct. 3, 1812, in Albert Gallatin Papers, Scholarly Resources microfilm edition, reel 25.

8. Speech of John Randolph, Jan. 9, 1813, in *AC,* 12-2, 678.

9. Calhoun to James Macbride, June 23, 1813, in Robert L. Meriwether et al., *The Papers of John C. Calhoun,* 28 vols. (Columbia, SC, 1959–2003), 1: 177.

10. John Lovett to Joseph Alexander, June 17, 1813, and to Solomon Van Rensselaer, July 16, 1813, in Catharina V.R. Bonney, *A Legacy of Historical Gleanings,* 2 vols., 2nd ed. (Albany, 1875), 1: 300, 302.

11. William Jones to Isaac Chauncey, Jan. 27, 1813, in U.S. Department of the Navy, *Letters Sent by the Secretary of the Navy to Officers, 1798–1868,* National Archives, Washington, DC, microfilm series M149, reel 10.

12. See Alton Ketchum, *Uncle Sam: The Man and the Legend* (New York, 1959), 40–41.

13. Troy (New York) *Post,* Sept. 7, 1813.

14. Croghan to Harrison, [July 30, 1813], in [Robert B. McAfee], *History of the Late War in the Western Country* (Lexington, KY, 1816), 323.

15. Procter to Sir George Prevost, Aug. 9, 1813, in William Wood, ed., *Select British Documents of the Canadian War of 1812,* 3 vols. (Toronto, 1920–28), 2: 46.

16. Estimates of the broadsides of the two squadrons vary because the exact number and arrangement of their guns are unknown. We have used the figures provided by David Curtis Skaggs and Gerard T. Altoff, *A Signal Victory: The Lake Erie Campaign, 1812–1813* (Annapolis, MD, 1997), 109.

17. David Bunnell, *The Travels and Adventures of David C. Bunnell, during Twenty-Three Years of a Sea-Faring Life* (Palmyra, NY, 1831), 115.

18. Perry to Harrison, Sept. 10, 1813, in Benson J. Lossing, *The Pictorial Field-Book of the War of 1812* (New York, 1868), 530. Perry actually took two ships, *two* schooners, *one* brig, and a sloop.

19. Procter to Francis de Rottenburg, Sept. 12, 1813, in Wood, *Select British Documents,* 2: 273.

20. Speech of Tecumseh, Sept. 18, 1813, in *Niles' Register* 5 (Nov. 6, 1813), 175.

21. Quoted in Thomas D. Clark, "Kentucky in the Northwest Campaign," in Philip P. Mason, ed., *After Tippecanoe: Some Aspects of the War of 1812* (East Lansing, MI, 1963), 94.

22. FitzGibbon to William J. Kerr, Mar. 30, 1818, in Ernest A. Cruikshank, ed., *The Documentary History of the Campaign on the Niagara Frontier,* 9 vols. (Welland, ON, [1896]-1908), 6: 120–21.

23. Quoted in Notes by Capt. W. Hamilton Merritt, n.d., ibid., 6: 123.

24. Letter to Albany *Argus,* Dec. 26, 1813, ibid., 9: 55.

25. Tompkins to John Armstrong, Jan. 2, 1814, in Hugh Hastings, ed., *Public Papers of Daniel D. Tompkins, Governor of New York, 1807–1817,* 3 vols. (New York, 1898–1902), 3: 408.

26. Wilkinson to secretary of war, Sept. 16, 1813, in Cruikshank, *Niagara Frontier,* 7: 133; Ellery Harrison, ed., *The Memoirs of Gen. Joseph Gardner Swift* (Worcester, MA, 1890), 116.

27. Wilkinson to secretary of war, Oct. 19, 1813, in U.S. Department of War, *Letters Received by the Secretary of War, Unregistered Series, 1789–1861,* National Archives, Washington, DC, microfilm series M222, reel 9.

28. Dr. Lovell, quoted in James Mann, *Medical Sketches of the Campaigns of 1812, 13, 14* (Dedham, MA, 1816), 119.

29. James Parton, *Life of Andrew Jackson,* 3 vols. (New York, 1860), 1: 428.

30. Jackson to William Lewis, Feb. 21, 1814, in Andrew Jackson Papers, Scholarly Resources, supplement to microfilm edition, reel 3.

31. John Reid and John Eaton, *The Life of Andrew Jackson* (Philadelphia, 1817), 143.

32. Jackson to Rachel Jackson, Apr. 1, 1814, in Andrew Jackson Papers, Library of Congress, Washington, DC, microfilm edition, reel 9.

33. Address of Andrew Jackson, Apr. 2, 1814, ibid., reel 10.

34. See Nathaniel Macon to Joseph H. Nicholson, Mar. 1, 1813, in Nicholson Papers, Library of Congress, Washington, DC; and John Lovett to Joseph Alexander, May 18, 1813, in Bonney, *Legacy of Historical Gleanings,* 1: 297.

35. Journal of Charles Napier, Aug. 12, 1813, in William F. P. Napier, *The Life and Opinions of General Sir Charles James Napier,* 4 vols. (London, 1857), 1: 221.

36. *Niles' Register,* 4 (May 15, 1813), 182; 5 (Jan. 8, 1814), 312; and 6 (June 25, 1814), 279.

37. Broke to captain of the *Chesapeake,* June [1], 1813, in U.S. Department of the Navy, *Letters Received by the Secretary of the Navy: Captains' Letters, 1805–1885,* National Archives, Washington, DC, microfilm series M125, reel 29.

38. *Naval Chronicle* 30 (July-Dec. 1813), 41; Edgar Stanton Maclay, *A History of the United States Navy from 1775 to 1902,* rev. ed., 3 vols. (New York, 1902), 1: 461.

39. Quoted in Alfred Thayer Mahan, *Sea Power and Its Relations to the War of 1812,* 2 vols. (Boston, 1905), 2: 20.

40. Quoted in Edgar S. Maclay, *A History of American Privateers* (New York, 1899), 275.

Chapter 4. Don't Give Up the Soil (1814)

1. Speech of William H. Murfree, Jan. 10, 1814, in U.S. Congress, *Annals of Congress: Debates and Proceedings in the Congress of the United States, 1789–1824*, 42 vols. (Washington, DC, 1834–56), 13th Congress, 2nd Session, 856 (hereafter cited as *AC*, 13-2, and similarly for other sessions).

2. William Hunter to James A. Bayard, Jan. 29, 1814, in Elizabeth Donnan, ed., *Papers of James A. Bayard, 1796–1815* (Washington, DC, 1915), 266.

3. Madison to Congress, Dec. 7, 1813, in *AC*, 13-2, 542, 544.

4. Jonathan Roberts to Alexander Dallas, Dec. 12, 1813, in Dallas Papers, Historical Society of Pennsylvania, Philadelphia, PA.

5. Speech of James Fisk, Jan. 13, 1814, and Speech of Felix Grundy, Jan. 15, 1814, in *AC*, 13-2, 934, 993.

6. Worcester (MA) *National Aegis*, Jan. 5, 1814.

7. Salem (MA) *Essex Register*, Apr. 16, 1814; Circular Letter of William Gaston, Apr. 19, 1814, in Noble E. Cunningham, Jr., ed., *Circular Letters of Congressmen to Their Constituents, 1789–1829*, 3 vols. (Chapel Hill, NC), 2: 896.

8. Jefferson to Samuel Brown, Apr. 28, 1814, in Jefferson Papers, Library of Congress, Washington, DC, microfilm edition, reel 47.

9. London *Times*, June 2, 1814.

10. Nicholson to William Jones, May 20, 1814, in Jones Papers, Historical Society of Pennsylvania, Philadelphia, PA.

11. John B. Campbell to John B. Walbach, May 18, 1814, in U. S. Department of War, *Letters Received by the Secretary of War, Registered Series, 1801–1870*, National Archives, Washington, DC, microfilm series M221, reel 51.

12. Narrative of Alexander McMullen, in Ernest A. Cruikshank, ed., *The Documentary History of the Campaign on the Niagara Frontier*, 9 vols. (Welland, ON, [1896]-1908), 2: 370.

13. Duncan McArthur to secretary of war, Nov. 18, 1814, in Cruikshank, *Niagara Frontier*, 1: 311.

14. Quoted in Donald E. Graves, *Where Right and Glory Lead! The Battle of Lundy's Lane, 1814*, rev. ed. (Toronto, 1997), 45.

15. Quoted in Winfield Scott, *Memoirs of Lieut.-General Scott*, 2 vols. (New York, 1864), 1: 129. Where Scott got this quote is unknown.

16. Letter of James Miller, July 28, 1814, in Cruikshank, *Niagara Frontier*, 1: 105.

17. Gaines to secretary of war, Aug. 23, 1814, in, U.S. Department of War, *Letters Received . . . Registered Series*, microfilm series M221, reel 61.

18. General Orders of Sept. 5, 1814, in Plattsburgh *Republican*, Sept. 24, 1814.

19. Macomb to secretary of war, Sept. 15, 1814, in U.S. Department of War, *Letters Received . . . Registered Series*, microfilm series M221, reel 64.

20. Robertson to Daniel Pring, Sept. 12, 1814, in William Wood, ed., *Select British Documents of the Canadian War of 1812*, 3 vols.. (Toronto, 1920–28), 3: 374.

21. London *Morning Chronicle,* Nov. 18, 1814.

22. Quoted in Henry Adams, *History of the United States [during the Administrations of Jefferson and Madison],* 9 vols. (New York, 1889–91): 8: 125.

23. Cochrane to station commanders, July 18, 1814, in William S. Dudley, Michael J. Crawford, *et al.*, eds., *The Naval War of 1812: A Documentary History,* 4 vols. (Washington, DC, 1985–), 3: 140.

24. Proclamation of Alexander Cochrane, Apr. 2, 1814, ibid., 3: 60.

25. James Scott, *Recollections of a Naval Life,* 3 vols. (London, 1834), 3:314–15.

26. Quoted in Barry J. Lohnes, "A New Look at the Invasion of Eastern Maine, 1814," *Maine Historical Society Quarterly,* 15 (Summer 1975): 9.

27. [George R. Gleig], *A Subaltern in America, Comprising His Narrative of the Campaigns of the British Army . . . during the Late War* (Philadelphia, 1833), 67.

28. G.C. Moore Smith, ed., *The Autobiography of Lieutenant-General Sir Harry Smith,* 2 vols. (London, 1908), 1: 200.

29. William Thornton to the Public, Aug. 30, 1814, in Washington *National Intelligencer,* Sept. 7, 1814.

30. [George R. Gleig], *A Narrative of the Campaigns of the British Army at Washington, Baltimore, and New Orleans* (Philadelphia, 1821), 132.

31. Washington *National Intelligencer,* Aug. 31, 1814.

32. Edward Codrington to wife, Sept. 10, 1814, in Lady Jane Bourchier, *Memoir of the Life of Admiral Sir Edward Codrington,* 2 vols. (London, 1873), 1: 320.

33. *Naval Chronicle* 32 (July-Dec. 1814), 244.

34. Letter to London *Statesman,* Sept. 29, 1814, reprinted in Lexington *Reporter,* Dec. 31, 1814.

35. Speech of Alexander Baring, Dec. 1, 1814, in T.C. Hansard, ed., *The Parliamentary Debates from the Year 1803 to the Present Time,* [First Series], 41 vols. (London, 1803–20), 29: 651.

36. John W. Croker to London Assurance Corporation, Aug. 19, 1814, in *Niles' Register* 7 (Nov. 19, 1814), 174–75.

37. Proclamation of Thomas Boyle, [Aug. 27, 1814], in *Niles' Register* 7 (Jan. 7, 1815), 290–91.

38. Hartford *American Mercury,* Oct. 15, 1814.

Chapter 5. A Lasting Peace (1815)

1. Andrei Dashkov to Nikolai P. Rumiantsev, Nov. 14, 1814, in Nina K. Bashkina *et al.*, eds., *The United States and Russia: The Beginning of Relations, 1765–1815* [Washington, DC, 1980], 1097.

2. Jones to Alexander J. Dallas, Sept. 25, 1814, in Dallas Papers, Historical Society of Pennsylvania, Philadelphia, PA.

3. Dallas to William Jones, Oct. 2, 1814, in Jones Papers, Historical Society of Pennsylvania, Philadelphia, PA.

4. Lacock, quoted in Charles J. Ingersoll, *Historical Sketch of the Second War Between the United States of America, and Great Britain*, 2 vols. (Philadelphia, 1845–49), 2: 253.

5. Madison to Congress, Sept. 20, 1814, in U.S. Congress, *Annals of Congress: Debates and Proceedings in the Congress of the United States, 1789–1824*, 42 vols. (Washington, DC, 1834–56), 13th Congress, 3rd Session, 14 (hereafter cited as *AC*, 13-3, and similarly for other sessions).

6. Alexander Contee Hanson to Robert Goodloe Harper, Oct. 9, 1814, in Harper Papers, Maryland Historical Society, Baltimore, MD, microfilm edition, reel 2.

7. Monroe to Brown, Feb. 10, 1815, in U.S. Department of War, *Confidential and Unofficial Letters Sent by the Secretary of War, 1814–1847*, National Archives, Washington, DC, microfilm series M7, reel 1.

8. Speech of Lyman Law, Dec. 17, 1814, in *AC*, 13-3, 944.

9. Georgetown *Federal Republican*, Nov. 26, 1814.

10. Jones to Alexander J. Dallas, Sept. 15, 1814, in Dallas Papers, Historical Society of Pennsylvania, Philadelphia, PA.

11. Quoted in Ingersoll, *Historical Sketch*, 2: 254.

12. Dallas to William Jones, Jan. 29, 1815, in Jones Papers, Historical Society of Pennsylvania, Philadelphia, PA.

13. Izard to secretary of war, July 31, 1814, in U. S. Department of War, *Letters Received by the Secretary of War, Registered Series, 1801–1870*, microfilm series M221, reel 62.

14. Prevost to Earl Bathurst, Aug. 27, 1814, in Ernest A. Cruikshank, ed., *The Documentary History of the Campaign on the Niagara Frontier*, 9 vols. (Welland, ON, [1896]-1908), 1: 180.

15. Wirt to Elizabeth Wirt, Oct. 25, 1814, in Wirt Papers, Maryland Historical Society, Baltimore, MD, microfilm edition, reel 2.

16. Madison to Wilson Cary Nicholas, Nov. 25, 1814, in Madison Papers, Library of Congress, Washington, DC, microfilm edition, reel 16.

17. Quoted in Edmund Quincy, *Life of Josiah Quincy of Massachusetts*, 4th ed. (Boston, 1868), 358.

18. [John Windship] to William Plumer, Jr., Mar. 20, 1814, in Plumer Papers, New Hampshire Historical Society, Concord, NH, microfilm edition, reel 2.

19. Arsène Lacarrière Latour, *Historical Memoir of the War in West Florida and Louisiana in 1814–15* (1816; edited and expanded by Gene A. Smith, Gainesville, FL, 1999), 59.

20. G.C. Moore Smith, ed., *The Autobiography of Lieutenant-General Sir Harry Smith,* 2 vols. (London, 1908), 1:247.

21. Report of Court, [Mar. 21, 1815], in Andrew Jackson Papers, Library of Congress, Washington, DC, microfilm edition, reel 17.

22. Lord Castlereagh to secretary of state, Nov. 4, 1813, in U.S. Department of State, *Records of Negotiations Connected with the Treaty of Ghent, 1813–1815,* National Archives, Washington, DC, microfilm series M36, reel 1.

23. Jonathan Russell to John L. Lawrence, Oct. 7, 1814, in Russell Papers, Brown University, Providence, RI.

24. American commissioners to British commissioners, Aug. 24, 1814, in Henry Goulburn Papers, University of Michigan, Ann Arbor, MI, microfilm edition, reel 1.

25. Wellington to Liverpool, Nov. 9, 1814, in Duke of Wellington [son of Iron Duke], ed., *Dispatches, Correspondence, and Memoranda of Field Marshall Arthur, Duke of Wellington, K.G.,* 15 vols. (London, 1858–72), 9: 425–26.

26. Article 9, Treaty of Ghent, Dec. 24, 1814, in David S. Heidler and Jeanne T. Heidler, eds., *Encyclopedia of the War of 1812* (Santa Barbara, 1997), 586.

SUGGESTIONS FOR FURTHER READING

Even though the War of 1812 is sometimes portrayed as an obscure and forgotten conflict, it has generated a vast literature in the United States and Canada. For the American side of the war, the interested reader may consult Donald R. Hickey, *The War of 1812: A Forgotten Conflict* (Urbana, IL, 1989), or J.C.A. Stagg, *Mr. Madison's War: Politics, Diplomacy, and Warfare in the Early American Republic, 1783–1830* (Princeton, NJ, 1983). For the Canadian side, the best work is J. Mackay Hitsman, *The Incredible War of 1812: A Military History* (1965; updated by Donald E. Graves, Toronto, 1999). There is no good work presenting the British side of the war, although Reginald Horsman, *The War of 1812* (New York, 1969), does a pretty good job of presenting all sides in a compact volume. The most readable short accounts of the war are probably Harry L. Coles, *The War of 1812* (Chicago, 1965); Donald R. Hickey, *The War of 1812: A Short History* (Urbana, IL, 1995); and Carl Benn, *The War of 1812* (Oxford, UK, 2002).

For the military history of the war, the best works are John K. Mahon, *The War of 1812* (Gainesville, FL, 1972); Robert S. Quimby, *The U.S. Army in the War of 1812: An Operational and Command Study*, 2 vols. (East Lansing, MI, 1997); and George F.G. Stanley, *The War of 1812: Land Operations* ([Toronto], 1983). For the naval history of the war, the best work is still Theodore Roosevelt's classic *The Naval War of 1812*, 3rd ed. (New York, 1883), which is readily available in several modern editions.

Those interested in the role of Indians should consult Robert S. Allen, *His Majesty's Indian Allies: British Indian Policy in the Defence of Canada, 1774–1815* (Toronto, 1992); Carl Benn, *Iroquois in the War of 1812* (Toronto, 1998); Frank L. Owsley, Jr., *Struggle for the Gulf Borderlands: The Creek War and the Battle of New Orleans, 1812–1815* (Gainesville, 1981), and George F.G. Stanley, "The Indians in the War of 1812," *Canadian Historical Review* 31 (June 1950), 145–65. R. David Edmunds has written two fine biographies of the Shawnee leaders allied to the British: *Tecumseh and the Quest for Indian Leadership*, 2nd ed. (New York, 2006), and *The Shawnee Prophet* (Lincoln, NE, 1983).

Most of these works have detailed notes and bibliographies that will guide readers to more specialized accounts of the many dimensions of the war.

Bold page numbers indicate the subject is in an illustration.

Site locations are shown with two-letter abbreviations of modern US states and Canadian provinces.

Military rank is highest achieved during the war.

Adm	Admiral
BG	Brigadier General
Cap	Captain
Col	Colonel
Com	Commodore
Lt	Lieutenant
Maj	Major
MC	Master Commandant
MG	Major General
PM	Provincial Marine

Abenaki (Indians), 103

Adams, John, 11

Adams, John Quincy, 119, **182**, 182

Adams, US Corvette, 145

after-action report, 82, **85**

Albany (NY), 53

Alert, HM Brig, **54**, 60

Alexandria (Egypt), 151

Alexandria (VA), 111, 144

America, US privateer, **65**

American Architectural Foundation, 164

American Revolution, 11, 34, 51, 71, 75, 86, 109, 144, 171

Amiens, Peace of, 13

"Anacreon in Heaven," 157, 159

Anglo-French dualism, 189

Annapolis (MD), 84

Appalachian Mountains, 71

Appling, Maj Daniel, 136

Argus, US Sloop, **54**, 151

Armistead, Maj George, 154, 158; family of, 157

Armstrong, John, 20, **72**; appointed secretary of war, 71; and campaign of 1813, 73–74; alienates William Henry Harrison, 90; and campaign against Montreal, 101–3; and invasion of New York, 137; and defense of Washington, DC, 146; resigns from cabinet, 164

Army, British: troop levels, 35, 72, 124. *See also individual battles*

Army, US: troop levels, 23, 72, 124, 166;

Army, US (*cont.*)
enlistment bounty, 23, 72, 120–21, 166; pay, 23; quality of, 23, 129, 135; and Uncle Sam, 75; and American Revolution, 71. *See also individual battles*
arsenal, US, 148, 153, 167
Artillery Duel at New Orleans, 175
Atlantic Coast, **33**, 111, 125, 143–44, 168, 179
Atlantic Ocean, 9, 11, 13, **54**, 57, 66, 75, 111, 118, 171, 192
Atrocities: Indian, 43, 79, 107; British, 113
Austerlitz, Battle of, 15
Austin, Cap Loring, 134
Austria, 15, 118
Azores, 162

Backus, Lt Col Electus, 96–97
Bainbridge, Com William, 60
Baker, Anthony St. John, **182**
Baltic, ports in, 20
Baltimore (MD), 19, 64, 98, 146; site of prowar riots, 68; Battle for, 152–60, 162, 171, 173, 183, 185
Bangor (ME), 145
Baratarian pirates, 173–74
Barbados, 60
Barclay, Acting Commander Robert H., 75, 82–84, 86, 91
Baring, House of, 166
Barney, Com Joshua, 64, **144**, 144, 148–49, 152–53
Barron, Cap James, 16
Bastille (French), 10
Bathurst, Lord, 9, 145
Baynes, Col Edward, 95, 97
Beanes, Dr. William, 157
Beasley, Maj Daniel, 107
Beaver Dams (ON), Battle of, 98–99, 192
Beckwith, Col Thomas Sidney, 112
Belgium, 182
Bell, William, 82
Belvidera, HM Frigate, 56–57, **57**

Benedict (MD), 148, 152
Berlin decree, 18
Bermuda, 56
"Big Bugs," 23
bilious fever, 82
Bingham, Cap Arthur, 16
Bissell, BG Daniel, 135
Black Rock (NY), 81–82, 100, 132
blacks, free, 173
Black Swamp, 36
Bladensburg (MD), Battle of, 144, 148–50
Bladensburg races, 149
Block Island (RI), 142
Bloomfield, BG Joseph, 53
Boerstler, Lt Col Charles, 98
Bonaparte. *See* Napoleon
Boston (MA), 3, 51, 53, 58, 111, 114, 167, 180, 189
Boxer, HMS, **54**
Boyd, BG John P., 105–6
Boyle, Cap Thomas, 162
Brazil, 60
Breese, John Malbone, 17
Bristol (RI), 64
British Guiana, 60
British Reconnaissance in Force, 174
Brock, MG Isaac, 40, **40**, 41, 43, 47, **49**, 50, 192
Broke, Cap Philip, 57, **114**, 114, 116
Brooke, Col Arthur, 148, 154, 157
Brother Jonathan, 116
Brown, MG Jacob, **97**, 124; and Battle of Sackets Harbor, 96–97; and Battle of Hoople's Creek, 104; at French Mills, 106; and campaign on Niagara in 1814, 128–34; and campaign of 1815, 165
Brown, Noah, 81–82
Brownstown (MI), Battle of, 39
Buck, Maj Thomas, 128
buck and ball, **37**
Buffalo (NY), 43, 45, 81, 99–101, 127–29, 132
Burgoyne, MG John, 75, 137, 171

Burgoyne, Lt Col John Fox, 171
Burlington Heights (ON), 95, 97, 99
Burnt Corn (AL), Battle of, 107
Byron, Lord, 160
Byron, Cap Richard, 56–57

cable, carrying of, **136**, 137
Caledonia, PM Brig, 81–82
Calhoun, John C., **73**, 73, 120
camels (floats), 82
campaign, military: of 1812, 8, 36–67; of
    1813, 73–106, 111–18; of 1814, 123–64; of
    1815, 162, 166, 171–81
Campbell, George W., 120, 149, 164
Campbell, Col John B., 127, 143
Canada: defenses of, 35–36; conquest of,
    26, 31, 33–35, 72–74, 118, 124, 165–66; US
    trade with, 111, 121, 168; privateering of,
    66; and causes of war, 27–28; and news
    of war, **7**, **8**; and legacy of war, 189, 192.
    See also campaign, military
Canadian Pacific Railway, 192
Canadian Voltigeurs, 103–4
Canadian Volunteers, 126–29, 133
Canard River, 5, 37
Canary Islands, 60
Cape Breton Island (NS), 31
Cape Horn, 116
Capitol, US, 149, 155, 165
Carden, Cap John S., 60
Carolina, US Schooner, 174
carronades, **55**, 56, 116, 138
Cass, Col Lewis, 37, 40, 41
Cassin, Cap John, 112
Castine (ME), 145–46
Castlereagh, Lord, 9, 28
Caulk's Field (MD), Battle of, 160–61
Cecil County (MD), 112
certificates of citizenship, 15, **17**
Chandler, BG John, 97
Charleston (SC), 3, 111
Chasseur, US privateer, **54**, 162

Chateaugay (NY), 103–4
Châteauguay (QC), Battle of, 102–4, 189,
    192–93
Châteauguay River, **37**, 103
Chauncey, Com Isaac, **74**; given command
    of lakes, 74; and Lake Erie, 81–82;
    and Sackets Harbor, 90, 95, 97; and
    attack on York, 91; and capture of Fort
    George, 93, 95; and campaign against
    Montreal, 104; and Niagara campaign
    in 1814, 130
Cherokee (Indians), 47, 173
Cherub, HM Sloop, **54**, 116–17, **117**
Chesapeake, US Frigate, **17**, **54**, 113–15, 192
Chesapeake affair, 16, 25
Chesapeake Bay, 112–13, 127, 143, **147**, 161,
    166, 184–85, 187
Cheves, Langdon, 120
Chicago (IL), 41
Chinn, Julia, 90
Chippawa (ON), Battle of, 128–29, **130**,
    185
Chippawa River, 128–29, 130, 134
Chippewa (Indians), 29, 91
Choctaw (Indians), 173
Chub, HM Sloop, 138
Civil War, US, 106, 127, 167, 190
Clarke, Col Allen, 137
Clay, Green, 77–79
Clay, Henry, **4**, 4, 26, 28, 67, 73, 119–20, 181,
    183
Clayton (NY), 104
Clinton, De Witt, 68–71, **69**
Cochrane, Vice Adm Sir Alexander, **143**;
    and retaliatory warfare, 143; and eman-
    cipation of slaves, 143; and conquest of
    Passamaquoddy islands, 145; and attack
    on Washington, DC, 148; and attack
    on Fort McHenry, 154, 157; and Battle
    of Caulk's Field, 160; and Gulf Coast
    campaign, 173, 178
Cockburn, Rear Adm Sir George, 112–13,

Cockburn, Rear Adm Sir George (*cont.*)
 113, 148–49, 155
Coffee, BG John, 108, **109**
Cognawaga (Caughnawaga Indians), 98
Colonial Marines, British Corps of,
 143–44
Columbia, US Frigate, 151
commerce. *See* trade
Confederation, Canadian, 192
Confiance, HM Frigate, 138, 140–41
Congress, Twelfth, 3–5, 27–28, 67–68,
 71–72; adopts prewar restrictive system,
 20–21; enacts war preparations,
 23–24; declares war, 4–5, 25
Congress, Thirteenth, 72–73, 119–23, 163–68
Congreve rockets, 136, 149, **150**, 157, **157**
Conjocta Creek (NY), Battle of, 132
Connecticut River, 143
conscription, US, 165–66
Constellation, US Frigate, **12**, 112
Constitution, US, 4, 27, 47, 59, 170
Constitution, US Frigate, **54**, 56, 58–60,
 58–61, 179–80, **180**, 187, **189**
Continental System, 18, 20
contraband, definition of, 16
Cook's Mills (ON), Battle of, 134–35
Coosa River, 108
Cornwall (ON), 104, 106
Covington, BG Leonard, 106
Craig, Sir James, 24, 35
Craney Island (VA), Battle of, 112–13
Crawford's Hotel, 163
Creek (Indians), 86, 106–7, 109–10, 171–72,
 180
Creek War, 106–10, 171–72
Crillon, Count Edward de, 25
Crockett, Davy, 108
Croghan, Maj George, 80, 125
Crowninshield, Jacob, 164
Crutchfield, Maj Stapleton, 113
Crysler's Farm (ON), Battle of, **105**, 105–6,
 193

Cumberland Head (NY), 102, 138
Cumberland Island (GA), 144, 183
Cuyahoga, 36
Cyane, HM Corvette, **54**, 180–81
Czech Republic, 15

Dacres, Cap James R., 59
Dallas, Alexander J., 164, **165**, 167–68
Dartmoor Massacre, 187, 189
Dartmoor prison, **191**
Daveiss, Maj Joseph H., **32**
Dearborn, MG Henry, 23, **53**, 102, 124;
 career, 51; appointed MG, 51, 53;
 and campaign of 1812, 53; and attack
 on York, 91, 93; and capture of Fort
 George, 93; and Battle of Stoney
 Creek, 97; removed from combat
 command, 98–99
Decatur, Cap Stephen, 56, 60, 62, 179–80
"Defence of Fort McHenry, The." *See*
 "Star-Spangled Banner, The"
Detroit (MI), 8, 36–41, 43, 86–87, 90, 125,
 127–28, 192–93
Detroit, HM Sloop, 82–84
Detroit, PM Brig, 81
Detroit River/front/frontier, **38**, 45, 82–83;
 and news of war, 8; and campaign of
 1812, 8, 35–41, 43, 51, 90; and campaign
 of 1813, 74, 86–90; and campaign of
 1814, 124, 126–28, 162
Dickson, Lt Col Alexander, 171
Directory, French, 10, 13
Dobbins, Daniel, 81–82
Dobbs, Cap Alexander, 132
"Don't Give Up the Ship," **83**, 83, 114, 116,
 124, 187
"Don't Give Up the Soil," 124
Douglas, Cap George, 180
Dover (ON), 127, 143
Downie, Cap George, 138–41
Doyle, Fanny, **51**
Dru, Pierre le, 86

Drummond, Lt General Gordon, 99, 128, 130, 132–35
Drummond, Lt Col William, 133
Duck River Massacre (TN), 107
dysentery, 73, 82, 102

Eagle, US Brig, 138
Eagle, US/HM Sloop, 138
Eastern Shore (MD), 160
East India Company, 179
Eastport (ME), 145
Eckford, Henry, 91
economic sanctions. *See* restrictive system
economy, US, **22**; in 1790s, 11; in prewar years, 21; during war, 111, 142
Elba (Italy), 123, 151
election: of 1800, 24; of 1812, 67–71, **70**; of 1828, 178; and Hartford convention, 171
Elkton (MD), 112
Elliott, Lt Jesse D., 74, 81, 83–84
Elliott, Matthew, 31
embargo, 170; of 1807, **21**, 14, 20–21, 119; of 1813, 121, 123, 168
Emuckfau (AL), Battle of, 108–9
Endymion, HM Frigate, **54**, 162, **179**, 179–80
Enemy Trade Act, 121, 168
England. *See* Great Britain
Enitachopco Creek (AL), Battle of, 108
Enterprise, USS, **54**
Erie (PA), 81
Essex (CT), 143
Essex, Lord, 170
Essex, US Frigate, **54**, 60, 116–17, **117**
Eustis, William, 34, 71–72
executive mansion. *See* White House

Falcon, Cap Gordon, 180
Fallen Timbers (OH), Battle of, 43
Federalists, in 1790s, 11–13; in prewar years, 18; and war preparations, 24; and Henry affair, 25; and declaration of war,

4–5, 21; and election of 1812, 69–71; and opposition to war, 68, 72–73, 111, 120, 146, 164–65, 167–68; and wartime trade restrictions, 123; in New England, 34, 67, 168–71; and peace terms, 124, 185
Federal Republican, Baltimore, 68
finances, US public, 12, 21, 24, 72–73, 166–68
Finch, HM Sloop, 138
First Lady. *See* Madison, Dolley
Fischer, Lt Col Victor, 133, 135
Fisk, James, 120
FitzGibbon, Lt James, 98–99
Florida, Spanish, 108, 111, 171
Forsyth, Maj John, 91
Fort Amherstburg (ON), 36–37, 40, 43, 82, 86, 183
Fort Bowyer (AL), 178
Fort Covington (NY), 106
Fort Dearborn Massacre (IL), 41, **42**
Fort Detroit (MI), 36
Fort Erie (ON), 45, 81, 95, 128, 132–35, 183; Battle of, 132–33, 185
Fort George (ON), 45–46, 50–51, 82, 93–95, **94**, 97–101, 129–30
Fort Harrison (IN), 30, 42
Fort Jackson (AL), Treaty of, 110
Fort Mackinac (MI), 8, 37, **39**, 125–26, 183
Fort McHenry (MD): bombardment of, 154, 157, **158**; flag of, 157–58, 160, 187
Fort Meigs (OH), 76–79, **78**
Fort Miami (OH), 79
Fort Mims Massacre (AL) 107
Fort Niagara (NY), 46, **51**, 93; artillery duel with Fort George, 50–51; and capture of Fort George, 93–94; captured by British, 99–100; and campaign of 1814, 124; retained by British until end of war, 141, 146, 183
Fort Schlosser (NY), 45
Fort Stephenson (OH), 79–80, **80–81**, 125
Fort St. Philip (LA), 178

Fort Strother (AL), 108

Fort Sullivan (ME), 145

Fort Tompkins (NY), 96

Fort Wayne (IN), 42; treaty of, 29

Four Corners (NY), 103

France, 10, 173; and Second Hundred
Years War, 9–11, 13; and Quasi-War,
12–13; and Napoleonic Wars, 15, 25, 35,
61, 123; and neutral rights, 1, 4, 18, 20;
and restrictive system, 1, 20–21; and US
declaration of war, 5

Fredericksburg (VA), 111

Fredericktown (MD), 112

"free trade and sailors' rights," 28, 114–16,
124, 192

Fremont (OH), 80

French Creek (NY), 104

French Mills (NY), 106

French Revolution, 10

French Revolutionary Wars, 10–11, 13

Frenchtown (MD), 112

Frenchtown (MI), 5; Battle of, 41–43,
44–45, 77

Frolic, HM Sloop, **54**, 60

Gaines, BG Edmund P., 132–33

Gallatin, Albert, **24**, 24, 71, 119–20, 181

Gambier, Lord, **182**, 182

General Armstrong, US privateer, **54**, 162

General Pike, US Sloop, 96

Georgetown (DC), 157, 163

Georgetown (MD), 112, 160

Georgian Bay, 125

Gerry, Elbridge, 68, 73

Ghent, Treaty of, 164, **182**, 182–83, 185, 192,
194

Gibbs, MG Samuel, 175

Gibraltar (MI), 39

Glengarry Light Infantry, 135

"Good Bess," 80

Gosport Navy Yard (VA), 112

Goulburn, Henry, 182

Governor Tompkins, US privateer, 162

Grand River, 127

Granger, Gideon, 73, 120

Great Britain: and Second Hundred Years
War, 9–10; and Napoleonic Wars, 10,
15, 55, 122, 150, 192; and prewar maritime
practices, 15–20, 28–29; and declaration
of war, 66; wartime strategy of, 35–36,
73–75, 124–25; and restoration of peace,
181–84; and legacy of war, 192

Great Lakes, 31, 74, 183

Greenleaf Point (DC), 149, 151, 153

Grenadier Island (NY), 104

Griffith, Rear Adm Edward, 145

Growler, US Sloop, 138

Grundy, Felix, 120

Guadeloupe, 66

Guerrière, HM Frigate, **54**, **58**, 58–59, **60**

Gulf Coast, 106, 109, 125, 162, 171, 173,
177–78

Gulf of St. Lawrence, 31, 64

Halifax (NS), 55–58, 64, 66, 113–14, 122, 145

Hall, Dominick A., 178

Hamilton (ON), 95

Hamilton, Alexander, 24

Hamilton, Paul, 34, 71–72

Hampden (ME), 145

Hampton (VA), 113

Hampton, MG Wade, 102–4, 106, 124

Hanks, Lt Porter, 37

Harper's Weekly, 76

Harpy, US privateer, 162

Harrison, MG William Henry, **30**, 105;
and Indian treaties, 29; and Tecumseh,
30; and Battle of Tippecanoe, 30–32;
takes command in Old Northwest,
41–44; and Siege of Fort Meigs, 76–77;
and defense of Fort Stephenson, 80;
and Battle of Thames, 84–87, 90, 187;
resigns command, 90

Hartford (CT), 169

Hartford Convention, 169–71, **170**
Harvey, Lt Col John, 98
Havre de Grace (MD), 112
Heald, Cap Nathan, 41
Henry, John, 24–25
Henry affair, 24–25
Hillyar, Cap James, 116–17
Hoople's Creek (ON), Battle of, 104
Hope, Cap Henry, 179
Hornet, US Sloop, 4, **54**, 60, 114, 161
Horse Island (NY), 96
Horseshoe Bend (AL), Battle of, 109–10,
    110, 194
hot shot, **51**
Houston, Sam, 108–9
Hudson River, 135
Hull, Cap Isaac, **58**, 58–59
Hull, BG William, 23, 36–41, **37**, 124
Humphreys, Cap Salusbury Pryce, 16

impressment, 15, **16**, 18, 28–29, 181, 183, 191
Independent Company of Foreigners, 112
India, 105
Indians: as British allies, 29, 75; and
    resistance to US expansion, 29–30;
    and Battle of Tippecanoe, 29–31; and
    Battle of Thames, 86–90; atrocities of,
    43, 79, 100, 107; and Treaty of Ghent,
    183–84; and legacy of war, 192, 194. *See
    also* Creek War; *individual tribes; other
    battles*
Indian war, 29–31. *See also* Creek War
Ingersoll, Charles J., 53
Ingersoll, Jared, 69
international law, 16, 18, 20
International Rapids, 104
"Ironsides." *See Constitution,* US Frigate
Iroquois (Grand River Indians), 43, 47, 128
Irving, Washington, 1
Izard, MG George, 103, 134, 168

Jackson, Andrew, 88, **108**, 124, 162, **175**, **190**;

and Creek War, 108–10; and Treaty
    of Fort Jackson, 110; and Gulf Coast
    campaign, 171–78; and legacy of war,
    185, 187
Jacobins, 10
Jamaica, 56–57, 164, 171, 173
James, William, 192
Java, HM Frigate, **54**, 60, **61**
Jay Treaty, 11, 13, 18
Jefferson, Thomas, 1, 3, **14**, 19, 24, 27–28, 51;
    and retrenchment, 13; and Monroe-
    Pinkney Treaty, 18; and conquest of
    Canada, 26; and fall of Napoleon,
    123–24; and Library of Congress, 165;
    and paper money, 167
John Bull, 76, 116
Johnson, Lt Col James, 87
Johnson, Col Richard M., 86–87, **88–89**,
    187
Jones, Cap Thomas ap Catesby, 173
Jones, William, 71, **72**, 163–64, 167

Kansas City (KS), 31
kedging, 58
Key, Francis Scott, 157, **158**
Kickapoo (Indians), 30
Kingston (ON), 74, 91, 95, 124, 135

Lacassinier, 174
Lacock, Abner, 164
Lacolle Mill (QC), Battle of, 53
Lacolle River, 53
Laffite, Jean, 173, **174**
Laffite, Pierre, 173
Lake Borgne (LA), Battle of, 173–74
Lake Champlain, 35, 51, **52**, 53, 102, 138, 141,
    168; Battle of, 137–41, **139**, 183
Lake Erie, 35–36, 40, 43, 45, 74–76, 90, 100,
    124–27; Battle of, 81–85, **84**, 91, 93, 116
Lake Huron, 5, 37, 39, 125–26
Lake Michigan, 5, 37, 39
Lake Ontario, 45, 74–75, 90–91, 96–97, 100,

Lake Ontario (*cont.*)
  124, 135
Lake Superior, 5
Lambert, Cap Henry, 60
Langdon, John, 68
Latour, Maj Arsène Lacarrière, 177
laudanum, 102
law of retaliation, 20
Lawrence, Cap James, 83, **114–15**, 114–16
Lawrence, US Brig, 83, **84**
Lee, MG Light-Horse Harry, 68
Lee, Robert E., 68
Leipzig (Germany), Battle of, 118, 123
Leonard, Cap Nathaniel, 100
Leopard, HM Frigate, 16
letters-of-marque, 63–64
Levant, HM Sloop, **54,** 180–81
Lewis, MG Morgan, 93
Lewiston (NY), 100
Library of Congress, 149, 155, 165
licenses (British), 18, 20, 28–29, 121–23
Lingan, BG James M., 68
Linnet, HM Brig, 138
L'Insurgente, French Frigate, **12**
Little Belt affair, 16, 59
Liverpool (NS), 66
Liverpool, Lord, 9, **10,** 183
Liverpool Packet, British privateer, 66
Lloyd's (of London), 161
Lockyer, Cap Nicholas, 174
logistics, 34–36, 39–40, 50, 75, 83, 91, 130, 148
London (Great Britain), 5, 45, 56, 166
long guns, **55,** 56, 138
Long Point (ON), 40, 127, 143
Long Sault, 104
"Long Tom," 64, **65**
Lossing, Benson J., 85–86
Louisiana, US Sloop, 174
Lundy's Lane (ON), Battle of, 130–33, **131,** 185, 190

Lyon's Creek (ON), Battle of, 134–35

Macdonell, Lt Col John, 47
Macdonough, MC Thomas, **138,** 138–39, 141
Macedonian, HM/US Frigate, **54,** 60, **62,** 187
Machias (ME), 145
Mackinac Island (MI), 5, 37, **39,** 124–25, 141, 146
Macomb, BG Alexander, 137–38, 141
Macon, Nathaniel, 23, 167
Madeira Islands, 180
Madison, Dolley, **3,** 3, 149, 152
Madison, James, **2,** 13, 27, 51, **151;** and declaration of war, 1, 3–5, 23; as a war leader, 1, 23, 34, 73; and war cabinet, 19, 71, 120, 164–65; and restrictive system, 1, 20, 121, 123, 168; and repeal of Orders-in-Council, 29; and court martial of William Hull, 41; and election of 1812, 68–71; illness of, 119; and British attack on Washington, DC, 146, 148–49, 163; and public finances, 167; and bi-partisanship, 164; and New England's opposition, 168–69; and peace negotiations, 119, 181, 184; and outcome of war, 185
Maguaga (MI), Battle of, 39–40
Malcolm's Mills (ON), Battle of, 127–28
Malden (ON), 82–83
Maritime Provinces, 66
Markle, Abraham, 127
martial law, 178
Martin, Daniel, **17**
Maumee Rapids, 42
Maumee River, 36, 77
McArthur, BG Duncan, 40–41, **127,** 127–28
McCarty, William, 193
McClure, BG George, 99

McDouall, Lt Col Robert, 125

medals (British), **193**

Meigs, Return J., 77, 120

Melville, Viscount, 9

Mexican War, 190, 193

Miami (Indians), 41–42

Milan decree, 18

military court, 16, 41, 90, 178

militia, British/Canadian, 35. *See also individual battles*

militia, US, 24, 26; refusal to serve outside US, 34–35, 47, 53; executed, 109, 178; and carrying of cable, 137; and victory at Caulk's Field, 160–61; and conscription, 166; and New England, 169; and legacy of war, 185. *See also individual battles*

Miller, Col James, 39–40, 130, **131**, 132–33

Mississauga (Indians), 91, 95

Mississinewa River, 42

Mississippi River, 5, 31, 174, 178

Mitchell, Lt Col George E., 135

Mobile (AL), 107, 173, 178

Mohawk (Indians), 47, 95, 98, 105, 128

Mohawk River, 135

Monroe (MI), 42

Monroe, James, 18, **19**, 34, 71, 148–49, 164–67, 182

Monroe-Pinkney Treaty, 14, 18, 23

Montreal (QC), 53; importance of, 35; and campaign of 1812, 35, 51; and campaign of 1813, 74, 99, 101–6; and invasion of New York, 124, 137

Moody, John, 122

Moose Island (ME), 145

Moraviantown (ON), Battle of. *See* Thames, Battle of

Morgan, Maj Lodowick, 132

Morris, Cap Charles, 145

Morrison, Lt Col Joseph W., 105

Morrisville (NY), 104

Muir, Cap Adam, 40

Mulcaster, Cap William H., 104

Murray, Col John, 99

musket, Springfield, **37**

Muskogee (Indians). *See* Creek (Indians)

Nancy, HM Schooner, 125, **126**

Nantucket (MA), 142, 162

Napoleon (Bonaparte), 10; and Napoleonic Wars, 9, 15, 55, 66, 118, 123; and Continental System, 18, 20; and War of 1812, 75, 142, 151, 161

Napoleonic Wars, 10–11, 15, 55, 122, 150, 175, 192

Nashville (TN), 107

Nast, Thomas, 76

national anthem, 157–60, 187, **188**

national bank, 71, 167

Nations, Battle of the, 118, 123

Native Americans. *See* Indians *and individual tribes*

Naudee, John, **89**

Nautilus, US Brig, **54**, 60

Naval Academy, US, 84

naval blockades (American), 162

naval blockades (British), 16, 35, 55, 189; of middle and southern states, 111, 113; of New England, 142, 168. *See also* Orders-in-Council

Naval Yard, Washington (DC), 151, 153

Navy, Royal (British): and Napoleonic Wars, 15, 55–56; and British maritime practices, 15–20; and defense of Canada, 35; and campaign of 1812, 55–63; and campaign of 1813, 74–75, 82–84, 95–97, 111–18; and campaign of 1814, 142–62; and Gulf Coast campaign, 171–78; and campaign of 1815, 179–81; and legacy of war, 192

Navy, US: and Quasi-War, **12**, 13; and war at sea, **54**; and campaign of 1812, 55–63; and campaign of 1813, 74–75, 81–85,

Navy, US (*cont.*)
  90–95, 113–17; and campaign of 1814,
    125–26, 136, 138–41, 161; and campaign
    of 1815, 173–74, 179–81; and legacy of
    war, 187
Navy Department, US, 16, 71–72, 81, 149
Navy Yard, Charlestown (MA), 189
Navy Yard, Portsmouth (NH), 58
Nelson, Adm Lord Horatio, 15, 75
neutral rights, 1, 11, 15–16, 18, 27–28, 181
neutral trade, 18, 20
Newark (ON), 99–101
New Bedford (MA), 169
Newburgh Letters, 71
New England: and Henry affair, 24–25;
    and war, 34, 67, 168–69; and British
    blockade, 111, 113, 142; and license trade,
    121; and wartime prosperity, 142; and
    secession, 163; and banking crisis, 166;
    and trade with enemy, 168; and Hart-
    ford Convention, 169–71
New Orleans (LA), 5, 23, 101, 109, 171, **172**,
    173–74, **176–77**, 178, 187; Night Engage-
    ment at, 174; Battle of, 173–77, 184–85
Newport (RI), 17, 74
news of war, 5–8, **8**, 56–57, 65
New York City (NY), 3–4, 58, 179, 184; and
    logistics, 75, 135; and wartime economy,
    111; and James Lawrence's funeral, 116
Niagara (ON), 99–101
Niagara, US Brig, 83, **84**
Niagara Escarpment, 45
Niagara Falls, 45, 130
Niagara front/frontier, **48**; and campaign
    of 1812, 8, 43–51; and campaign of 1813,
    93–95, 97–101, and campaign of 1814,
    97, 124, 128–35, 137, 162, 185; and John
    Norton, 45
Niagara Peninsula, 124, 130, 135
Niagara River, 35, 43, 45–46, 74, 81, 93–95,
    97, 100, 128
Nicholson, Joseph H., 124

Nicolls, Maj Edward, 171
Nipissing (Indians), 103
"Nitchies," 29
non-importation act: of 1806, 20; of 1811,
    20, 28, 67, 121, 123
non-intercourse act, 20
Norfolk (VA), 112
Norristown (PA), 68
North Point (MD), 154, 157; Battle of, 154,
    156, 157
Norton, John, 43, 45, **47**, 47, 98, 128, 192
Nottawasaga River, 125–26

Oakland (ON), 127
oath of allegiance (British), 145
Octagon House, 163, **164**
Odelltown (QC), 102
Ogdensburg (NY), 104
Ohio, US Schooner, 132
Ojibwa (Indians), 91
"Old Hickory." *See* Jackson, Andrew
"Old Ironsides." *See Constitution*, US
    Frigate
Oneida (Indians), 136
Orders-in-Council (British), 18, 28, 181
Oshawahnah, **89**
Oswego (NY), 95, 97, 124, 136; Battle of,
    135
Oswego Falls, 136
Oswego River, 136
Otis, Harrison Gray, **170**

Pacific Ocean, **54**, 116–17
Pakenham, MG Sir Edward, 171, **173**,
    174–75, **177**
Paris (France), 10, 20, 118, 123
Paris, Treaty of (1783), 145
Parker, Cap Sir Peter, 160–61
Parliament, British, 10, 28, 116
Passamaquoddy Bay, 145
Patapsco River, 154, 157
patent office, US, 149, 163

Patuxent River, 144, 148

Pax Americana, 192

Pax Britannia, 192

peace, restoration of, **186**

peace commission: US, 4, 120, 181–82;
British, 182

Peace of Christmas Eve. *See* Ghent,
Treaty of

Peacock, HM Sloop, **54**, 60, 114

Peacock, US Sloop, 161

Pea Island (LA), 173

Pearson, Lt Col Thomas, 128

Pechell, Cap Samuel J., 112

Pelican, HMS, **54**

Peninsula War, 9, 121, 123, 137, 148, 171

Pennsylvania rifle, 187

Penobscot Bay, 145–46

Penobscot River, 145

Pensacola (FL), 107, 171, 173

Perceval, Spencer, 10

Perry, MC Oliver H., 74, **82, 84,** 82–84, 86,
90, 93, 116

Perrysburg (OH), 77

Pettipaug (CT), 143

Philadelphia (PA), 3, 71, 75, 111, 154, 164–65

Phoebe, HM Frigate, **54,** 116–17, **117**

Pickersgill, Mary, 158

Pig Point (MD), 144, 153

Pike, BG Zebulon, 53, 91, 93

Pilkington, Lt Col Andrew, 145

Pinkney, William, 18, **19,** 120

Pittsburgh (PA), 75

Plattsburgh (NY), 51, 53, 101–3, 106, 134,
137–38; Battle of, 137–38, **140,** 141

Point Peter (GA), 144

Poitiers, HMS, **54**

Popham, Cap Stephen, 136

Portage River, 86

Port Clinton (OH), 86

Port Dover (ON), 127

Porter, Cap David, **116,** 116–17

Porter, BG Peter B., 50, 128–29, 133

Potawatomi (Indians), 30, 41, 127

Potomac River, 4, 144

Preble, US Sloop, 138

Prescott (ON), 104

President, US Frigate, 16, 56–57, **57, 179,** 179

Presque Isle (PA), 81–82

Prevost, Sir George, **36**; career of, 35, 141,
145; and defense of Canada, 35–36; and
attack on Sackets Harbor, 95–97; and
Battle of Plattsburgh, 137–41; and retali-
atory warfare, 101, 128, 143; and US
smuggling, 168

Prince-de-Neufchatel, US privateer, **54,** 162

Principio Creek, 112

prisoners of war, 43–44, 79, 87, 112, 187, 189,
191

privateering commission, **64**

privateers: US, 5, 58, 63–66, 117–18, 142, 152,
161–62, 169; British, 66, 117; French, 13,
16

Proctor, MG Henry, 42–44, **45,** 77, 79–80,
86–87, 90

projectiles (ammunition), **55**

Prophet, the, 29–31, **31,** 34, 86

Prophet's Town, 30

"protections," 15, **17**

Provincial Marine, 74

Prussia, 118

Purdy, Col Robert, 103–4

Put-in-Bay (OH), 82

Putnam, Maj Perley, 145

Quasi-War, 12, 13

Quebec (QC), 5, 8, 34–35, 145

Queen Charlotte, HM Sloop, 83–84

Queenston (ON), 98

Queenston Heights (ON), Battle of, 8, 40,
43–50, **49,** 192

Queenstown (MD), 112

Quincy, Josiah, 25, **26,** 170

Randolph, John (of Roanoke), 23, 27–28,

Randolph, John (of Roanoke) (*cont.*)
28, 72
Rattlesnake, US privateer, 118
Red Jacket, 128–29
Red Sticks, 107–10
Reed, Lt Col Philip, 161
Reid, Samuel Chester, **162**
Reign of Terror (French), 10
"Remember the Raisin," 43, 87
Republicans, Jeffersonian, 13; and European war, 11, 123–24; and factionalism, 4, 27–28, 73; and restrictive system, 3, 61, 121, 123, 168; and war preparations, 24; and Henry affair, 24–25; and declaration of war, 5, 21, 25–26, 181; and election of 1812, 68–71; and public finance, 24, 67, 72, 167; and bipartisanship, 164–65, 169; and Federalist opposition, 120; and course of war, 67, 72, 119, 162; and outcome of war, 185
Republicans, Old, 27–28
restrictive system, 1, 20–21, 67–68, 120–23
Rhea, Cap James, 42
Riall, MG Phineas, 128–30, 132
Richelieu River, 35, 51, **52**, 53
Richmond (VA), 64, 111
riots, pro-war, 68
River Raisin, 40, 42, 77; massacre at, 43, 107. *See also* Frenchtown, Battle of
Roberts, Cap Charles, 37
Roberts, Jonathan, 5
Robertson, Lt James, 140
Rodgers, Com John, 16, 56–58, 75
Rodrigues Canal (LA), Battle of, 175
Roosevelt, Franklin, 189
Rosenbach, Dr. A.S.W., 155
Ross, MG Robert, 148, 153, **157**, 160, 171, 173
Rossie, US privateer, 64
Rottenburg, MG Francis de, 53
Roundhead, **45**
Rule of 1756, 18
Rush, Richard, 69, 120, 149

Russia, 15, 66, 118–19, 181–82
Russian mediation proposal, 119, 181

Sackets Harbor (NY), 5, **96**, 99, 124, 130, 135; as US naval base, 90–91, 135; and attack on Fort George, 93; Battle of, 95–97; and attack on Montreal, 101, 104; and carrying of cable, 136–37
Salaberry, Lt Col Charles de, 53, **103**, 103–4, 192
Salem (MA), 65
Sandusky River, 80
Sandwich (ON), 37, 39
Sandy Creek (NY), 136–37; Battle of, 136
Santo Domingo, 173
Saranac River, 137, 140–41
Saratoga (NY), Battle of, 75, 90, 171
Saratoga, US Sloop, 138, 140, **141**
Sault Ste. Marie (ON), 125
Savannah (GA), 68, 111
Sawyer, Vice Adm Herbert, 57
Scorpion, US Schooner, 125–26
Scott, Col Hercules, 133
Scott, Col William, 148
Scott, BG Winfield, **94**, 124, **190**; and Battle of Queenston Heights, 47, 50; and capture of Fort George, 93–95; and Battle of Hoople's Creek, 104; and campaign on Niagara in 1814, 128–32
Scourge, US privateer, 118
secessionist movement, 169–70
Second Hundred Years War, 9–11, 63
Secord, Laura, 98, **99**, 192
Seminole (Indians), 110, 171
Seneca (Indians), 128
Seven Years War, 34
Shannon, HM Frigate, **54**, 57, 113–16, 192
Shawnee (Indians), 29, 31, 86, 107
Sheaffe, MG Roger, 47, **50**, 91–93
Shelby, Isaac, 86
Sherbrooke, Sir John, 122, **145**, 145
Sinclair, Cap Arthur, 125

Sir Isaac Brock, HM Brig, 93
Sixth Coalition, 118, 123
Smith, MG Samuel, 152, **156**
Smithsonian Institution, 158, 187
smuggling, 121, 168, 173
Smyth, BG Alexander, 23, 43, 46, 50, 124
Somers, US Schooner, 132
Southampton, HMS, **54**
South Bass Island (OH), 82
Spain, 9, 11, 15, 20, 61, 107, 173
Springfield (MA), 167
"Star-Spangled Banner, The," 157–60, 187, **188**
St. Davids (ON), 129
Stewart, Cap Charles, 180–81
St. George, Lt Col Thomas B., 36
St. George's Channel, 162
St. Joseph Island (ON), 5, 37, 125
St. Lawrence, HMS, **54**
St. Lawrence River, 31, 34–35, 53, 75, 91, 101–4, 168
St. Marys River, 144
St. Michaels (MD), 112
Stone, Lt Col Isaac, 129
Stoney Creek (ON), Battle of, 97–99
Stonington (CT), 143
Strachan, John, **92**, 93, 192
Straits of Malacca, 179
Street's Creek, 129
Stricker, BG John, 154
Strong, Caleb, 146, **170**
supply lines. *See* logistics
Swift, BG John, 129

Talladega (AL), Battle of, 108
Tallapoosa River, 109
Tallushatchee (AL), Battle of, 108
taxes, US, 13, 24, 67, 72–73, 142, 167
Taylor, BG Robert B., 112
Taylor, Cap Zachary, 42
Tecumseh, **79**, **86**, **88**; and pan-Indian movement, 29–30, 124, 204; and

Creeks, 107; and fall of Detroit, 39–40, 45; and siege of Fort Meigs, 77–79; and Battle of Thames, 86–87; death of, 87–90; reputation of, 40, 192
Tenskwatawa. *See* Prophet, the
Terre aux Boeufs (LA), 23
Terre Haute (IN), 30
Thames (ON), Battle of, 30, 86–90, **87–88**, 126, 185, 187, 194
Thames River, 87, 127
Thornton, Col William, 148, 174–75
Thornton, Dr. William, 149
Thunder Bay (ON), 5
Ticonderoga, US Schooner, 138–40
Tigress, US Schooner, 125–26
Tingey, Cap Thomas, 151
Tippecanoe (IN), Battle of, 29–31, **32**, 41, 90, 105–6, 184
Tippecanoe River, 30
Tompkins, Daniel D., 101
Toronto (ON), 92–93
Towson, Cap Nathan, 129
trade, British, 18, 20–21, 55, 116, 121, 123, 146, 161–62
trade, French, 1, 20
trade, US: prewar, 11, 18, 20–21; wartime, 58, 69, 111, 142; with enemy, 121–23, 146, 168
Trafalgar, Battle of, 15, 56, 75, 83, 114
Trail of Tears, 110
treason, 24–25, 120
Treasury Department, US, 121, 149, 164, 166
Trenton (MI), 40
Trenton (NJ), 111
Troy (NY), 75–76
True-Blooded Yankee, US privateer, 118
Tucker, Lt Col John, 132

Uncle Sam, 75–76, **76–77**, 187
United States: and war preparations, 4; and declaration of war, 4–5; and

United States (*cont.*)
    wartime strategy, 34–35, 73–74, 124; and
    restoration of peace, 81–84; and legacy
    of war, 185–89
United States, US Frigate, **54**, 56, **62**
Uphold's Creek (ON), Battle of, 104
Upper Marlboro (MD), 144, 148
Urbana (OH), 36
Ussher's Creek, 129

Valparaiso, Chile, 116–17
Van Buren, Martin, 69
Van Horne, Maj Thomas, 39
Van Rensselaer, Lt Col Solomon, 43, **46**,
    46–47
Van Rensselaer, MG Stephen, 43, 45–47,
    46, 50
Vienna, Congress of, 182
Villeré, MG Jacques, 174
Villeré's Planation (LA), Battle of, 174
Vincennes (IN), 30
Vincent, BG John, 95, 97–98
Virginia Dynasty, 69
Vixen, US Brig, **54**, 60
Voltigeurs, Canadian, 103–4
Volunteers, US, 24, 34, 43, 166

Wabash River, 30–31
Wales, Prince of, 99
war at sea, **54**. *See also* Navy, Royal; Navy,
    US
War Department, US, 71, 101–2, 121, 149,
    164, 166
War Hawks, 4, 23, 28, 67, 73, 181
War of 1812: declaration of, 4–5, 25–26; end
    of, 181–84; legacy of, 187–94
war preparations, 4, 23–24, 27

Warren, Adm Sir John Borlase, 111–13,
    143, 171
Wasaga Beach (ON), 126
Washington (DC), **153**; character of, 3–4,
    73; British burning of, 101, 127, 146–52,
    162, 164; capital nearly moved from, 165
Washington, George, 11, **152**
Wasp, US Sloop, **54**, 60, 161
Waterloo (Belgium), Battle of, 9
Wellington, Duke of, 9, 123, 137, 171, 173,
    183
Wells, William, 41
West, Benjamin, 49
Westbrook, Andrew, 127
West Indies, 12–13, 35, 55, 64, 66, 118, 143
White House, 3, 149, **154**, 163–64
Wile Ranerd, US privateer, 64
Wilkinson, MG James, 23, **101**, 101–2,
    104–6, 124
Willcocks, Lt Col Joseph, 99, 127–28, 133
Wilson, Samuel, 75, 76
Winchester, BG James, 42, 44, **45**
Winder, BG William H., 97, **98**, 146, 148
Windsor (ON), 37
Winnebago (Indians), 30, 113
Wirt, William, 168
Woods, John, 109
Wool, Cap John E., 47
Woolsey, Lt Melancthon T., 90, 136
Worsley, Lt Miller, 125–26
Wyandot (Indians), **45**

Yankee, US privateer, 64
Yeo, Com Sir James, **74**, 74, 91, 95–96, 130,
    135–36, 141
York (ON), 74; Battle of, 50, 74, 91–93, **92**,
    192